HEROES
ON THE
FRONT LINE

HEROES
ON THE
FRONT LINE

TRUE STORIES OF THE DEADLIEST
MISSIONS BEHIND ENEMY LINES IN
AFGHANISTAN AND IRAQ

NIGEL CAWTHORNE

JOHN BLAKE

Published by John Blake Publishing Ltd,
3 Bramber Court, 2 Bramber Road,
London W14 9PB, England

www.johnblakepublishing.co.uk

First published in 2009 as *Special Forces*
This edition published 2011

ISBN: 978 1 84358 290 8

British Library Cataloguing-in-Publication Data:

A catalogue record for this book is available from the British Library.

Design by www.envydesign.co.uk

Printed in Great Britain by CPI Bookmarque, Croydon CRO 4TD

1 3 5 7 9 10 8 6 4 2

Papers used by John Blake Publishing are natural, recyclable products made
from wood grown in sustainable forests. The manufacturing processes
conform to the environmental regulations of the country of origin.

All images © Getty Images Ltd

CONTENTS

INTRODUCTION

In Britain and the Commonwealth we are blessed with a long military tradition. Thanks to a rigorous training programme that started essentially with the Duke of Wellington, we have some of the finest soldiers in the world. None are finer than our Special Forces. They have come into particular play after the unprovoked attacks on the twin towers of the World Trade Center in New York and on the Pentagon on 11 September 2001. Since then, the world has become unimaginably more dangerous. There have been attacks by Islamist terrorists on Madrid and London, but nowhere is safe. There have been other minor attacks – as on Glasgow airport – and numerous thwarted attempts, we are told. Our Special Forces are on a constant vigil to protect us from this threat.

On 20 September 2001, United States President George

W Bush addressed a joint session of Congress and the American people – and, indeed, the people of the world. In his speech, President Bush declared a 'War on Terror'. 'Our enemy,' he said, 'is a radical network of terrorists, and every government that supports them. Our War on Terror begins with al-Qaeda, but it does not end there. I will not end until every terrorist group of global reach has been found, stopped and defeated.'

In particular Bush picked out the Taliban regime in Afghanistan for providing a safe haven for al-Qaeda. But it was clear that the list of enemies in his War on Terror did not end there. It is known that since his election in the year 2000, Bush had wanted to topple Saddam Hussein in Iraq, finishing the job his father, President George Herbert Walker Bush, had failed to complete in the First Gulf War in 1991. He knew he had a willing partner. Britain's prime minister, Tony Blair, had made a speech in Chicago in 1999, unveiling his 'Doctrine of the International Community'. After NATO's intervention in Kosovo, Blair argued, it was no longer acceptable for the world to sit back and do nothing while tyrants and dictators wrecked their own countries and persecuted their own people. He picked out two dictators for particular censure.

'Many of our problems have been caused by two dangerous and ruthless men – Saddam Hussein and Slobodan Milosevic,' he said. 'Both have been prepared to wage vicious campaigns against sections of their own community. As a result of these destructive policies, both have brought calamity on their own peoples.' In these cases the 'principle of non-interference must be qualified.' It was right, he said, to remove regimes that had lost their legitimacy. 'As John Kennedy put it, "Freedom is indivisible and, when one man is enslaved, who is free?" '

In his State of the Union address in January 2002, George W Bush again talked of the War on Terror. This time he added a new goal in the struggle: those who sponsored terror. He called them an 'Axis of Evil', naming North Korea, Iran and Iraq. And with Afghanistan seemingly subdued, the invasion of Iraq went ahead.

In the forefront of this War on Terror would be the American armed forces, accompanied by the British, the Australians and others in the 'coalition of the willing'. Both in Afghanistan and Iraq, US Special Forces would play a key role behind the lines before the main force went in, training, arming and shaping forces that would ally themselves to the Western cause. After the occupation, they would then take on the insurgents.

The US Special Forces hold the British Special Forces in high regard. The Green Berets, Delta Force and the US Navy SEALS all draw their inspiration directly from the British Special Air Service – the SAS – founded in 1941 by Captain David Stirling. Through their campaigns in North Africa during the Second World War and later in Oman, the SAS had been particularly adept at desert warfare. Experience in these conditions would come in useful in Afghanistan and Iraq.

The roots of the US Special Forces (aka the Green Berets) lie in the Office of Strategic Services (OSS), an intelligence agency established by America in July 1942 at the suggestion of British spymaster William Stephenson. The OSS and the 1st Special Service Force – the 'Devil's Brigade' (a joint American-Canadian commando unit) duly cooperated with Britain's nascent Special Air Service and wartime Special Operations Executive. After the war, in 1952, one of the OSS, Colonel Aaron Bank, set up the 10th Special Forces Group at Fort Bragg, North Carolina. They borrowed their Green Beret from the Royal Marines, but maintained close relations with the SAS through exchange programmes, attending each other's training school, staging joint exercises and fighting common enemies.

The predecessors of the US Navy SEALs – the OSS's Operational Swimmers – had been put under the command of British Combined Operations veteran Lieutenant-Commander Wooley of the Royal Navy in June 1943. The SEALs had maintained a close relationship with the Royal Marine Commandos and their Special Forces unit, the Special Boat Service – or SBS. Men are often exchanged between the two units.

Finally, the US Army's 1st Special Forces Operational Detachment Delta – more commonly known as Delta Force – was set up 1977 in direct response to the growing number of terrorist incidents that had occurred in the 1970s. Its founder, US Army Colonel Charles 'Charging Charlie' Beckwith, had undergone a year-long tour with SAS in 1962-63 and had organised his forces along its lines. Like the SAS, it was initially organised into three operating squadrons – A, B and C Squadron – each divided into three troops: assault, sniper and reconnaissance. As with the SAS, each troop specialised in scuba, HALO (high-altitude, low-opening) parachute or other skills. These troops could be further divided into smaller units (usually four or five four- or five-man teams) to fit the requirements of a particular mission.

Delta Force had maintained especially close ties with the SAS, so it was natural the Americans would want the British Special Forces working alongside them in Iraq and Afghanistan. The Australian and New Zealand Special Forces – along with the Special Forces of certain NATO nations – were also deployed in Afghanistan. Indeed, the Americans were so impressed by the Australian SASR – Special Air Service Regiment – in Afghanistan that they were given a key role in the invasion of Iraq.

Since the speedy invasions of Afghanistan and Iraq, both countries have fallen foul of an insurgency that almost amounts to civil war, and once again the Special Forces have found themselves key players. The British even established a new Special Forces unit called the Special Reconnaissance Regiment (SRR) in 2005 to take on the insurgents. The same year, the joint Special Forces Support Group (SFSG) was also established to work alongside the SAS and SBS in counterterrorist operations. Based on the 1st Battalion of the Parachute Regiment (1 Para), the SFSG work as a cut-off or blocking force, or as a quick-reaction force if things go wrong.

British Special Forces personnel are highly trained. But they are not just trained to kill. They know that killing the 'bad guys' is not enough. You must also protect the 'good guys' to win hearts and minds. Indiscriminate killing only wins you more enemies. Controversially, however, British Special Forces in Afghanistan and Iraq have been tied in ever more closely with the American special units, who have a much more indiscriminate approach to killing. Some SAS and SBS men have also expressed qualms about arresting people and handing them over to those involved in 'special rendition', whereby prisoners are likely to be tortured.

Nevertheless, when President George W Bush wanted to make one last-ditch attempt to capture Osama bin Laden before leaving office, whom did he call on? The men, and now women, of the British Special Forces – the SAS, SBS and SRR.

Special operations are, by their very nature, secretive. The SAS, SBS and SRR do not reveal the names of serving officers, even when they are decorated. The War on Terror is still going on, so this book includes no operational details that have not received previous publication and are thus in the public domain. However, members of the US Special Forces regularly publish details of their operations and those who take part in them. British and Commonwealth Special Forces often participate in American-led missions in Iraq and Afghanistan, but due to security concerns, their parts are often overlooked. This book attempts to rectify that imbalance and to show the disproportionate contribution that British, Australian and New Zealand Special Forces make. Indeed, British Special Forces have found their skills so much in demand that they have become enmeshed in the US command structure to a worrying degree, especially in Iraq.

Since the beginning of the War on Terror, the essential nature of the British Special Forces has changed. They now rarely operate in their famous four-man teams, such as the two that broke the Iranian Embassy siege in 1980. Since the beginning of operations in Afghanistan, they have even deployed in 60-man squadron strength. The SRR has now taken over much of the SAS's small-team reconnaissance work and, when four-, eight- or 12-man SAS teams now undertake an assault, they are usually backed by the joint SFSG. This means that a higher proportion of the UK Armed Forces are now involved in Special Forces operations, while the larger deployments reflect the practices of US Special Forces.

Despite these changes, the ethos of the British Special Forces has not altered. They remain elite units. Although candidates for the SAS are recruited from other units, only ten per cent of them survive the induction course. Troopers are highly trained and well equipped. Special Forces men are allowed to pick their own individual armaments, rather than carry standard-issue weapons. They are also encouraged to use their own initiative, so that they can operate behind enemy lines and in volatile situations without the constant need for orders.

As the War on Terror continues, it seems there will be a greater reliance on Special Forces. Large conventional forces with tanks, armour and massed ranks of infantry are of little use against terrorists and suicide bombers. For that, we need specialist intelligence units and highly trained teams who can make surgical strikes against terrorist cells. The British forces criticise the Americans for their overreliance on air power. Dropping bombs has not rid the world of Osama bin Laden, though British Special Forces did have him in their sights before being thwarted. And bombs fall on the just and the unjust alike.

For the British Special Forces men, it is just as important to know when *not* to pull the trigger – or call in an airstrike – as it is to 'slot' (i.e. kill) the individual in their sights. From its early days in Malaya, the SAS learned that the best way to fight a campaign against insurgents was to bring medical attention and aid to the general populace, denying the enemy their sympathy and sustenance. In the War on Terror, it is necessary to win the hearts and minds of the people all over the world who simply want to live in peace. This, too, is a Special Forces role.

PART ONE
AFGHANISTAN

CHAPTER ONE
JOINING TASK FORCE DAGGER

On 11 September 2001 news that terrorists had flown planes into the twin towers of New York's World Trade Center sent SAS men rushing for the television at their headquarters in Stirling Lines, Herefordshire. They had already received a message from their two liaison officers with Delta Force at Fort Bragg, North Carolina. The flash informed the SAS that the entire US Special Operations Command had immediately gone on full alert. All three regiments of the SAS – the 22 SAS with the Regular Army and 21 and 23 SAS in the Territorials – then went onto a similar footing. The commanding officer called in MI6 liaison officers and gave them six hours to possible targets.

To insiders, it was already clear who was responsible for the attack on the World Trade Center. Within a few hours of the attacks, the Bush administration concluded that Osama bin Laden and his al-Qaeda organisation were to blame. The British government concurred. Bin Laden was known to be in Afghanistan, where he and his terrorist-training camps had found a safe haven with the hardline Islamist Taliban regime. The White House sent an ultimatum to the Taliban government in the Afghan capital Kabul, saying simply, 'Give us bin Laden, or share his fate.'

Before the end of 11 September, a preparatory meeting had taken place at the headquarters of the Special Operations Command (SOCOM) and Central Command (CENTCOM) in Tampa, Florida. A number of the officers there had already been planning the destruction of al-Qaeda and the Taliban and were hoping that the Kabul government would refuse to hand over bin Laden. This would give them the excuse to go in. Lieutenant Colonel Dave Miller of the SOCOM explained that, with the aid of the Northern Alliance – a group of dissident warlords in northeastern Afghanistan – the Taliban regime could be ousted from power. To pull this off, Special Forces would have to make contact with the warlords. Arms and equipment would have to be delivered behind enemy lines. Air support would be required at the behest of the Special Forces' advisers. But further, they would need the commitment of Washington, in particular Secretary of Defense Donald Rumsfeld. Unconventional warfare is never easy, and an operation like this one would depend totally on the warlords trusting that the Special Forces men on the ground were able to deliver on their promises.

To those sitting around the table at SOCOM, the alternative – a conventional war – was unthinkable. The

Afghans had soundly thrashed a Soviet Army who invaded from a neighbouring country in a war that lasted ten years. Even the British, at the height of the Empire, could not hold onto Afghanistan, though they had tried three times – 1839-42, 1878-80 and 1919. Famously, in the First Afghan War, the British Army retreating through the Khyber Pass had been massacred – only one man, Dr William Brydon, escaped to tell the tale. An attempt to use conventional forces in Afghanistan could result in a similar disaster, but Lieutenant Colonel Miller believed that by using the Afghans' own guerrilla tactics against them, the Taliban could be defeated, and he argued that the Green Berets were the force best trained to do it.

Back at Stirling Lines, at 09.25 hours on 13 September, 350 men were packed into the Main Briefing Room for a 'Scale A' (must-attend) meeting to discuss the ramifications of the attacks on 9/11. There were sixty men from each of the SAS's frontline Sabre squadrons – A, B, D and G – plus their support units, notably the 264 (SAS) Signals Squadron. Liaison officers from the Royal Air Force, the Royal Engineers, the Royal Intelligence Corps and the Royal Army Medical Corps were also there. All were in uniform except for the anti-terrorist unit, who wore T-shirts and jeans and were ready to be whisked by helicopter at a moment's notice anywhere in Britain if there was a terrorist incident.

At 09.30 hours precisely, the regiment's CO and regimental sergeant major (RSM) arrived and the meeting came to order. 'There is no distorting the seriousness of what has happened,' said the CO. 'The word from Camp David is that there will be an all-out assault, and there is even a chance that nuclear weapons will be used. After the actions of September 11, the future implications are that when the war starts it will not be short and will probably go on for generations, and will probably not only involve us and our children, but their children and probably theirs too.'

For the moment, though, daily routines would not be changed. Those who were on anti-terrorist alert would remain at the ready. The days ahead, however, would be spent in planning and preparation, and further information would be disseminated on a strictly need-to-know basis. The CO warned his men about spreading rumours. Even discussing the matter with their wives and girlfriends was forbidden. Security was a paramount concern. Anyone not living up to the highest traditions of the regiment would be RTU'd – returned to unit. SAS men are recruited from within the armed forces and being returned to their original unit effectively ends their SAS career.

Although the daily routine ostensibly remained as normal, the regiment now switched to 'operational status' – i.e. from peacetime to wartime footing. The planners then began to second-guess the political decisions, so that the regiment would be ready when the word came down. They were helped in this by regular communications from Delta Force in Fort Bragg and the intelligence briefings at Camp David, the US President's country retreat in Maryland. It soon became clear that they were to take on al-Qaeda in Afghanistan.

This would be a full-scale commitment – a 'big party' in the jargon of the SAS – requiring two full squadrons with a third in reserve. Consequently, they began building up stocks of weapons, ammunition and supplies in Oman, the likely jumping-off point for any operation in Afghanistan. A Squadron had been on exercises in Oman since July: they were already acclimatised and were told to prepare for operations in Afghanistan. The second unit told to ready themselves were G Squadron, who had missed out on the First Gulf War, even though they had completed five months of desert training in the United Arab Emirates in the build-up to the action. They were eager to see action and still boasted a veteran of the Falklands War among their number.

A Squadron's desert training in Oman was called Exercise Barren Land. It was being run alongside a combined UK training exercise called Exercise Saif Sareea II (*saif sareea* is Arabic for 'swift sword'). The operation cost £90 million and involved 22,000 troops. It was the biggest movement of British forces overseas since the Gulf War and was essentially a dry run for Gulf War II. Conveniently, it put a hundred aeroplanes and helicopters, 17 Royal Navy surface ships and two nuclear submarines within striking distance of Osama bin Laden. Britain was already prepared to go to war.

Leaving behind a few men to guard the kit, A Squadron returned briefly to Hereford. Then, after a briefing, a few beers and a little time with their families, they flew back to Oman with G Squadron. Movements were made at night under armed guard, even in the English countryside. At their stopovers at Cyprus's Western Sovereign Base, they were kept isolated from other military personnel. It seemed they had been committed to combat.

On 16 September, the men of Britain's SBS – Special Boat

Service – gathered in Poole, Dorset, for their first formal post-9/11 briefing. Their CO, Colonel Jim Saunders, addressed the meeting. 'Gentlemen,' he said, 'you all know why we are here. Our foremost ally, America, has been attacked. In a cowardly and unprovoked action, terrorists from al-Qaeda have flown passenger aircraft into the twin towers in New York and the Pentagon in Washington. Thousands of innocent people have been killed. One of the intended terror strikes has been foiled. If it were not for the brave acts of passengers on board that hijacked aircraft, the casualty figures might be even higher. That much you are aware of.

'Now, as we speak, America is preparing for her response: Operation Enduring Freedom. Make no mistake: that response will be rigorous and deadly, and aimed at taking out those responsible for planning, financing and executing these heinous acts. As our own Prime Minister has made it abundantly clear, Britain and her armed forces will stand shoulder to shoulder with America in this struggle against world terrorism.'

Saunders knew his men well. They were not interested in mere words. He needed to promise action. 'I know that you are all itching to be in on the action, to play your part in bringing justice or otherwise dealing with those responsible. You will aware that the main alleged culprit is Osama bin Laden, presently sheltered by Afghanistan's Taliban regime. Unless he is handed over to the US authorities, which is looking increasingly unlikely, then Afghanistan will be the first target of any US – and British – response. That much is abundantly clear. However, should the war kick off in Afghanistan, as I am certain it will do, I have to inform you that the SAS have been given Afghanistan as their theatre of operation. We have been given the rest of the world.'

For the men of the SBS, this was not good enough and there was an audible groan.

'Now, I know that every man among you would want to be in Afghanistan, where the war will be fought at its fiercest,' Saunders continued. 'But your role is equally, if not even more, vital. On September 11, the world changed. A group of extremist Islamist terrorists – al-Qaeda, bin Laden, call them what you will – declared war on Western interests. That war will now be fought anywhere and everywhere that they feel they can strike at us. We are fully expecting further terrorist attacks, which means that the global counter-terrorism role that you are being given is a vitally important one. The visible war will be fought in Afghanistan. But the covert, shadow war will be fought wherever these people try to hit us. And that, gentlemen, will be your responsibility – to stop those terror strikes before they can do us any harm.'

Understandably, the men of the SBS were disappointed. Once again, their sister organisation, the SAS, had been given the high-profile role. But there was no argument they could put up for greater participation – for the moment, at least. After all, Afghanistan was landlocked and the SBS's particular skill in seaborne insertion would not be called for. For the moment, they had to bide their time. Eventually, they got the word that the SBS Mountain Troop – rehearsed in cliff assaults as well as Arctic warfare – along with the Mountain Leaders' section of the Royal Marines, were to prepare for action.

These units were trained to operate in mountainous terrain, such as Afghanistan, for periods up to two weeks without resupply.

Addressing a joint session of Congress on 20 September, President Bush reiterated his threat to the Taliban. 'The United States respects the people of Afghanistan,' he said. 'After all, we are currently its largest source of humanitarian aid. But we condemn the Taliban regime. It is not only repressing its own people. It is threatening people everywhere by sponsoring and sheltering and supplying terrorists. By aiding and abetting murder, the Taliban regime is committing murder.

'And tonight, the United States of America makes the following demands on the Taliban: deliver to United States authorities all the leaders of al-Qaeda who hide in your land. Release all foreign nationals, including American citizens, you have unjustly imprisoned. Protect foreign journalists, diplomats and aid workers in your country. Close immediately and permanently every terrorist training camp in Afghanistan, and hand over every terrorist, and every person in their support structure, to appropriate authorities. Give the United States full access to terrorist training camps, so we can make sure they are no longer operating. These demands are not open to negotiation or discussion. The Taliban must act, and act immediately. They will hand over the terrorists, or they will share in their fate.'

During the weeks that followed 9/11 in the US, other branches of the service tried to muscle in on the action. The US Army wanted to make it a 'heavy metal' war, using conventional armaments – tanks, artillery and mass infantry assaults. The US Air Force wanted to put forward air controllers on the ground to direct the precision ordnance and coordinate the dropping of the food and medical supplies that would be needed after the fighting was finished.

However, in overall command of the operations was General Tommy Franks, who would go on to command the invasion of Iraq two years later. Even though his officers were urging a full-scale invasion of Afghanistan, he knew that America's conventional forces were not ready for such an operation. The war in Bosnia had left US arsenals depleted by almost 40 per cent. Franks knew that the US did not have enough ammunition, cruise missiles or smart bombs to mount an operation like the First Gulf War's Operation Desert Storm in the uplands of Afghanistan, even if such a thing were possible in the mountainous terrain. But America wanted revenge and Donald Rumsfeld wanted Osama bin Laden's head on a spike. The Taliban had refused to hand him over, point blank, and there was no way that he could tell the White House that the US military – still far and away the largest force on Earth – could not make good on President Bush's promise and invade.

The Green Berets were ready for war, Colonel Miller insisted.

'We're underfunded, underpaid, underequipped and undermanned,' said one Special Forces officer at the briefing. But they were not unready. 'Unleash one hundred of our dogs of war with no rules and no orders, and we'll bring down the whole fucking Taliban and al-Qaeda Afghan empire in just a hundred days.'

It seems that this gruff Green Beret took a phone call from the White House during the briefing, which may have spurred him on. Donald Rumsfeld was already demanding that the military stop talking and start fighting. So Franks gave Miller the go-head while the Air Force were told to prepare to give the Special Forces and their Northern Alliance allies close-air support.

Both the SAS and the SBS were quickly alerted to these developments and were unofficially invited to the fray by their American counterparts. However, official word was sent to the Ministry of Defence, requesting their assistance. Because 78 Britons had died in the World Trade Center, Britain's Special Forces and intelligence services were immediately put at the Americans' disposal.

MI6 had always had a direct line to the SAS. Now, they would organise joint operations with SAS operatives specifically trained for tasks too dangerous or too military in nature for their own men. SAS men were now to take direct action against al-Qaeda operations in foreign countries, and even assassinate its leaders if necessary. They had been given a licence to kill. SAS men, it seemed, were about to become the real James Bond.

While diplomats went to work pressuring President Musharraf of Pakistan to support what was being called the 'War on Terror', Special Forces teams visited the countries to the north – Kazakhstan, Kyrgyzstan, Tajikistan, Turkmenistan and Uzbekistan – promising military aid and money. Protracted negotiations took place in Tashkent. As a result, a Special Forces base called K2 was built in Uzbekistan just over the border from Afghanistan itself. This would be the headquarters of Task Force Dagger.

The first problem the Special Forces faced was how to airlift their teams in and out of Afghanistan, parts of which were over 14,000 feet high. At that height, helicopters' engines did not get much oxygen, cutting their power, and rotors did not produce much lift in the thin air – though once it was airborne a helicopter could maintain altitude. Consequently, the loads carried by the helicopters would have to be severely restricted. Further, to get safely in and out of the combat zone, they would have to carry over half a ton of fuel. The only way for this to be achieved was for the helicopter to take off with a bare minimum of fuel and refuel in the air. But how was that to be done two miles up in the mountains without endangering air-to-air refuelling planes? A solution was proposed by a clever pilot-mechanic. While the helicopter was on the ground, the fuel would be pumped out into a large rubber bladder. Once the helicopter was airborne, the fuel would simply be pumped back into the tanks again through a long rubber hose.

Meanwhile, in Stirling Lines, the Counter-Revolutionary Warfare (CRW) wing of the SAS, with the aid of MI6, were preparing target folders on every terrorist that might be remotely linked to Osama bin Laden and al-Qaeda. As the US Special Forces planned their first military strikes, the 22nd SAS brought into play all four of its 60-man squadrons. The two in Oman would prepare for full deployment in Afghanistan. A third would join American teams knocking down the doors of suspected terrorists worldwide, while the fourth would remain in England, ready to defend the homeland if it was attacked. The reserve, R Squadron – who were Territorials – would also be used to augment any understrength teams.

In Afghanistan, the role of the British Special Forces would be a vital adjunct to the Americans, otherwise bin Laden would have the upper hand. He and his mujahideen had been trained by the US Special Forces to fight the Soviets, so they knew how the US Special Forces worked. While the SAS had also been active in Afghanistan during the war with the Soviets, they had had little contact with bin Laden and the mujahideen, so it would be much more difficult for the enemy to predict their moves.

On 7 October, British and American submarines and ships began bombarding targets in Afghanistan with Tomahawk cruise missiles. These were followed by strike aircraft and bombers flying from carriers in the Arabian Sea, the British island of Diego Garcia in the Indian Ocean and Whiteman US Air Force base in Missouri, striking the Taliban air defences and al-Qaeda training camps. Targets included the airport and power station in Kabul, a military base in Kondoz, three al-Qaeda training camps in Jalalabad, bin Laden's base at Farmada, an oil depot at Herat, a Taliban equipment store at Mazar-i-Sharif and the Taliban headquarters in Kandahar, along with a hundred al-Qaeda housing units, the airport buildings, though not the runway, and a compound thought to be the headquarters of Taliban supreme leader Mullah Mohammed Omar.

It is thought these targets were identified by SAS and SBS men, alongside Delta Force operations and US Army Rangers, who had been on the ground in Afghanistan for the previous two or three weeks. Indeed on 24 September, British newspapers reported that the SAS had already been involved in a firefight with the Taliban outside Kabul.

Quoting military sources, the paper said that the SAS troops were fired on in a 'more symbolic than directed' fashion after the four-man team had 'spooked' the Taliban soldiers. None of the SAS men were thought to be injured. The Ministry of Defence, in normal fashion, refused to confirm or deny the report. 'We never discuss Special Forces or operational matters,' said a spokesman. 'We are currently in our planning phase to decide what help we can offer the Americans.'

It was thought that the SAS patrol had infiltrated Afghanistan via Tajikistan and, along with US Special Forces, were working alongside Jamiat-i-Islam, the military wing of the Northern Alliance, who were already mounting an offensive against the Taliban.

On the first day of the bombing campaign, transports dropped 37,500 daily rations to refugees. Winning hearts and minds was essential. However, as the bombing campaign continued, both sides knew that neither the Taliban or al-Qaeda would be dislodged without British and American boots on the ground.

The main aim of the Special Forces was to capture – or, better, kill – Osama bin Laden. President Bush had already said that he wanted the al-Qaeda leader 'dead or alive'. However, no one knew where he was. He was certainly not where he was expected to be as the Taliban quickly announced that neither bin Laden or Mullah Omar had been killed in the airstrikes. But then the West got lucky.

Just two hours after the first airstrikes, a prerecorded propaganda video by bin Laden was shown on Al Jazeera, the satellite news station based in Qatar. It threatened fresh attacks on America and urged all Muslims to rise up and fight for their religion. Bin Laden was shown sitting with his Kalashnikov in front of a rocky outcrop. American geologist Jack Shroder from the University of Nebraska immediately knew where he was. Shroder had been conducting a geological survey of Afghanistan when he was expelled in 1978, accused of spying. He identified the sedimentary rock in the background. It occurred in only two areas of eastern Afghanistan – Patika and Paktia.

On the night of 19 October, the first Special Forces unit – the US Army Airborne Rangers – staged a surprise attack on a heavily guarded airfield 60 miles southwest of Kandahar, known to the US military as Objective Rhino. Two hundred men from the Army's 75th Ranger Regiment, commanded by Colonel Joe Votel, parachuted in from four MC-130 Combat Talons. They left 40 Taliban dead at the airfield, according to Ranger estimates. The whole thing was filmed and broadcast on TV worldwide to show that the US had not taken 11 September lying down.

That same night, a Delta Force detachment calling itself Task Force 11 – after 11 September – landed by Black Hawk and Pave Low helicopter outside Kandahar and attacked a compound owned by Mullah Mohammed Omar, the Taliban leader who had refused to hand over Osama bin Laden. (The only daughter of Mullah Omar's tenth wife is married to bin Laden.) In the raid, more than 30 Taliban soldiers were killed by an AC-130 Spectre gunship supporting the raid. This fearsome piece of kit carries multi-barrelled 25mm Gatling guns that fire 1,800 rounds a minute along with mini-guns and a 105mm howitzer, which can be locked onto a target as the gunship circles above. According to *New Yorker* magazine, 16 were used on the operation. Each cost $46 million.

But Delta Force were not alone that night. The SAS were considered a vital component of the American-led operation as they spoke Pashto, the language spoken in the Kandahar region. The CRW (Counter-Revolutionary Warfare) Wing of the 22nd SAS now hit a related target, which, it was thought, contained high-ranking al-Qaeda and Taliban figures. Operating in four-man teams, 40 SAS men hit the target, killing and wounding more than 25 Taliban. They also took prisoners.

The compound turned out to be a potholed road with a brick house and two mud huts behind a low wall. It was Mullah Omar's summer home and he was not there. This was not the first attempt on Mullah Omar's life. His headquarters in Kandahar and a vehicle he was thought to be travelling in had been hit by Cruise missiles and airstrikes in the days immediately before the raid on the compound. It was thought he might have sought refuge in his summer home, possibly thinking that the Allies had no knowledge of the place. But he was either dead or had fled. He has not been since. However, although the compound was unoccupied, Delta Force did pick up important intelligence material.

But the raid was not without its problems. General Tommy Franks, not being a Special Forces commander, had insisted that the attack force be larger than necessary. Delta Force sent almost an entire squadron and the SAS, with 40 men, were not used to attacking in such large units. On the way out, the assault team were ambushed by more Taliban fighters from the surroundings awoken by the noise of such a large force in action. They opened fire with rocket-propelled grenades – RPGs – and, as one senior Special Forces officer put it, 'the shit hit the fan.'

Later, in a press conference, the chairman of the Joint Chiefs, General Richard B Myers, said that resistance was 'light'. But there had been plans to leave behind a four-man team and they were forced to pull out. Bracketed by sustained and accurate fire, the assault force withdrew to a prearranged rendezvous point, where they were picked up by helicopters. By that time, 20 or more Delta Force men were wounded. The SAS also took casualties. The US Department of Defense put the number wounded in the operation at 12, but it seems that these figures have been deliberately massaged by the DoD, who consider a man a casualty if he had a wound that needed stitching or prevented him from walking. One man was reported to have lost a foot and at least three were seriously wounded. General Myers downplayed this, saying, 'There were some other wounds from some of the activity that was ongoing, but none of it was inflicted by the enemy.'

Did the injuries come from a friendly-fire incident, then? Certainly the Taliban fire was intense. One of the Chinooks left behind part of its landing gear. The Taliban claimed, falsely, to have shot it down with an RPG, which is now the terrorists' weapon of choice. A well-aimed RPG can pierce about a foot (30cm) of conventional armour at a range of up to 546 yards (500 metres), and a recent edition of *Soldier* magazine said that an RPG could be picked up from street markets in the world's trouble spots for as little as $10. Although a helicopter was not down, one of these weapons certainly hit it, though. Whatever happened that night, the reputation of Special Forces was left in tatters. According to Pulitzer Prize-winning investigative journalist Seymour Hersh – who broke the story of the My Lai Massacre during the Vietnam War – writing in the *New Yorker* magazine, the operation was a 'total goat fuck' – US Army slang for an operation where everything went wrong.

General Franks came under considerable criticism for making the raid 'too heavy, too slow and too stupid'. Several senior Special Forces officers suggested that he needed 'adult supervision'. Another was quoted as saying, 'Franks is clueless.' The general responded by saying that it had been a mistake to send in Special Forces units. It was a job for 'heavy-metal conventional units'. But having convinced Donald Rumsfeld of the need for Special Forces boots on the ground, he was committed to the strategy.

This, however, was not good enough for the SAS. They did not want to be committed this way by a general who knew little about how Special Forces units operated. Hereford sent word that, from now on, the SAS would work independently of Central Command. They should be given a task. They would then get on with it and complete it alone.

Despite this falling-out, the United States requested an entire regiment of the SAS to be deployed. The British government were committed, but the British liaison officers with Central Command disagreed with the US tactics. They told the Americans that they should stop the bombing campaign and establish a large firebase in Afghanistan so that the Taliban would have to come to them. One officer explained, 'We should tell the Taliban, "We're now part of your grid square [on Taliban territory]. What are you going to do about it?" '

There were, however, other fallings-out in US Central Command. There was criticism that the senior officers had lost their 'ass' since the incident in the Battle of Mogadishu in 1993, in which two Black Hawk helicopters were brought down. The operation in Afghanistan, they said, was 'Special Ops 101' – a beginner's course for conventional-warfare officers who had little understanding of special operations. As a consequence, General Franks was relieved of his special-operations brief, though remained in charge of the overall operation, and command was handed over to General Charles Holland of the US Air Force.

Further down the chain of command, General Doug Brown, commander of the US Army Special Operations Command, gave Task Force Dagger's CO, Colonel John Mulholland, a free hand. As long as he succeeded in overthrowing the Taliban, destroying al-Qaeda's safe haven and putting bin Laden on the run, he could conduct the war in any way he chose. Having no other option, General Franks reluctantly agreed. Colonel Mulholland's responsibility would also encompass the SAS forces in Afghanistan. Though still independent, they were to work closely with Delta Force and Task Force 160, a commando group tasked to ride towards the sound of gunfire.

In late October, the SAS made a HALO insertion into Afghanistan, but their operations on the ground were dogged by terrible weather conditions, and in early November, after just two weeks in the country, they were withdrawn. This gave the SBS the opportunity it had been looking for. Rear Admiral Sir Michael Boyce, chief of the defence staff in Whitehall, contacted the director of Special Forces to discuss SBS tasking. A lifelong Navy man, he had been urging SBS involvement in Afghanistan for some time. The director agreed that the SBS should be sent in to secure the Bagram airbase, some 30 miles (48km) north of Kabul. Bagram would become the centre of Allied operations in northeast Afghanistan.

Barely six weeks after they'd been told they were not deploying in Afghanistan, the men of C Squadron left Poole, to the envy of M and Z Squadrons who were left behind on a fuzzy counter-terrorist remit. CT – as counter-terrorism was known – had already come to stand for 'cushy time', and M and Z Squadrons longed to get into action too.

C Squadron shipped out in three Hercules C-130 transports from RAF Brize Norton in Oxfordshire. The 16-hour flight went via Cyprus and Oman, where they refuelled. They then flew in over Afghanistan under cover of darkness. Showing no lights, the lead Hercules landed on the runway at Bagram, dodging potholes and the wrecks of abandoned Russian aircraft left behind after the Soviet-Afghan War. Once on the ground, C Squadron quickly deployed. Only 48 hours earlier, the airbase had been in the hands of what the Americans were calling AQT – al-Qaeda-Taliban – forces, but repeated air strikes and the inroads of the Northern Alliance to the west (under Special Forces guidance) had forced them to withdraw.

The SBS teams drove off the rear ramps of the Hercules in their Land Rovers while the huge planes were still moving. They were battle-ready and moved out to secure the airport perimeter. The enemy might have abandoned the airbase, but they still inhabited the surrounding hills. That night, however, the SBS met no resistance.

The airbase had been built by the Soviets in the early 1980s and they had used it as a centre for their operations in Afghanistan. Both al-Qaeda and the Taliban knew it was vital. The Americans also had their eyes on the base, as did the Northern Alliance. Neither was best pleased when they discovered that the SBS had moved in without their approval or prior knowledge and secretly claimed the base.

As the SBS spread out to take up defensive positions, they found the old airbase was full of gutted MiG fighters, Antonov transport planes and Mi-24 helicopter gunships, a poignant reminder of how superpowers can come to grief in Afghanistan. Although Bagram was in the middle of a desert, freezing winds blew in at night from the surrounding hills and the SBS men took shelter in the fuselages of the old Soviet planes, unrolling their sleeping bags and eating their first rations. The men out on sentry duty had little idea that just a few miles to the west 20,000 Northern Alliance troops were massing. Once they realised what was happening, the Northern Alliance wanted to take the airbase back. If they attacked, the SBS would find themselves outnumbered 200 to one.

While the men on the ground might be ignorant of the odds, those in command knew what was going on. Angry words were already being exchanged via satellite phone between the British, US and Northern Alliance commanders. The Northern Alliance demanded that the British quit the airbase immediately. If the SBS were not gone by dawn, they would launch a massive counterattack. It should be remembered that the British were far from welcome in Afghanistan, thanks to their previous three excursions from their base in India.

If the Americans had taken the airbase, there would have been no problem with the Northern Alliance. They had only ever come as allies to help kick the Russians out. Indeed, the Americans had supplied the Afghans with the vital ground-to-air Stinger missiles that they had used to down 315 Soviet helicopters that the Red Army had used to ferry men and materials over the high mountain passes.

During the night the Americans had presented the Northern Alliance with an ultimatum. 'The Brits are our allies,' the US commander said. 'They are part of the equation. They're here to stay.' Either they let the British stay in Bagram or the British and Americans would stop their airstrikes against their common enemy, the AQT. This would leave them without close-air support. The Northern Alliance backed down, but to sweeten the pill the Americans sent Delta Force into Bagram to make an ostentatious show of taking over the airbase.

When they woke in the morning and began the first brew of the day, the SBS men saw American C-130s coming in to land. The elite Delta Force had arrived and they were surprised to find their British counterparts camped out in the wreckage of old Soviet aircraft, making tea. 'We take it you didn't fancy a night at the airport,' was the SBS's sardonic greeting as they offered the American troops some tea. Insisting on coffee, the Delta Force men explained how close the SBS had been to having 20,000 angry Afghans coming down on them.

'The Afghans?' said one SBS man. 'They've been no trouble. It's been quiet as a grave all night long.'

The Delta Force troops were also taken aback because they had expected to find the airbase had been taken by the SAS, not the SBS. The SBS men simply told them the SAS had 'found the weather too cold for their liking – and been sent home'.

Once the buildings had been cleared, the SBS moved into a three-storey accommodation block to the side of a massive Soviet-built hangar. Later that day, an advance party of SAS arrived, along with detachments of the Royal Marines and Paras. They set up their headquarters tent inside the hangar itself, along with a quartermaster's tent housing stores and an armoury.

After 18 hours on the ground, the SBS had their first operational briefing – only to be told that they had not yet been assigned a task. Due to the hostility of the Northern Alliance they were to keep a low profile and integrate with the US forces, but as soon as possible they were to prove themselves to their Afghan allies by taking on the AQT. For the moment, they were to secure the perimeter of the airport. But they had to be careful. There were spies everywhere. All communication back to the UK was to be via secure, encrypted lines. There were to be no mobile-phone calls home and no emails.

Three days after the SBS took the Bagram airbase, two squadrons of SAS landed in C-130s and the SBS were told they were going to join the US Navy SEALs and Task Force Dagger on an assault on the Naka Valley. Meanwhile, the SAS were to head for a tactical landing zone in Northern Alliance-held territory in northwest Afghanistan. However, there was a problem. SAS Squadrons A and G and their 'Pinkies' – their trademark, long-wheelbase Land Rovers painted pink for desert camouflage – had been flown in by a fleet of American C-130s. Unfortunately, the planes arrived via Pakistan, which allowed them to land there only if they were not on offensive missions.

Consequently, they were assigned Operation Determine, a reconnaissance and bomb-damage-assessment mission. The men of the SAS were not best pleased when they were told that they could not even engage targets of opportunity. It seemed as if the SBS were going to get all the action. The SAS grumbled as they mounted their Pinkies and headed off into the hills. Their mission was indeed going to be a boring one. After just two weeks of filing intelligence reports via satellite, they were shipped back to Herefordshire, arriving on 8 November.

CHAPTER TWO
PENETRATING THE NAKA VALLEY

On the night of 12 November, SBS Team Six set off for the uncharted Naka Valley in eastern Afghanistan, where Allied intelligence had identified 'the mother of all terrorist training camps'. By this time, one of their number had been injured in an accident involving a quad bike and replaced by a US Navy SEAL who had been on secondment to the SBS for 18 months. They deployed by Chinook to a forward mounting base some 12 miles short of their first objective. From there they would infiltrate the enemy-held Naka Valley – or Knackered Valley, as the SBS would have it. Their objective was to climb one of its highest peaks and set up a covert observation post (OP). From there they would observe enemy activity and report back. Once they had identified the terrorist training camp, they would pick key targets for an American airstrike scheduled for 21

November. Equipped with laser target-designators, they would 'paint' the targets with laser light for the bombers to take out with laser-guided smart bombs.

The forward operating base (FOB) was a small Afghan fort occupied by some 60 US Special Forces troops – Delta Force and CIA – who were also with Task Force Dagger. The accommodation was far from luxurious. They had camp beds out in the open or lined up under canvas sheeting. Fortunately, the old fort was surrounded by a 30ft (nine-metre) wall, topped off with battlements. This provided some protection from the AQT, who regularly took potshots at the emplacement. No one knew how many enemy soldiers there were in the area, but attacks occurred almost every day and the base was on a high state of alert.

The original plan was for the SBS team to be airlifted into the Naka Valley to save the men humping all their gear. But intelligence warned that the enemy was dug in along the ridgelines at around 10,000 feet (3,000 metres). They were known to be armed with surface-to-air (SAM) missiles – American Stingers and Soviet SAMs – and would be on the lookout for a heavily laden chopper struggling to maintain altitude in the thin air. It was a tactic the mujahideen had used to great effect against the Soviets. They were sure to use it again.

There were other downsides to choppering in the SBS team. The peak they were aiming for was 12,000 feet (3,650 metres), which was close to the Chinook's operating ceiling. The helicopter would be laden down with men, weapons, ammunition and equipment, plus enough food, fuel and water for two weeks. Landing anywhere near the summit risked a crash landing in hostile territory, an option no one relished. Even if they went in at night, they risked alerting the AQT, which would compromise the mission from the outset.

The SBS team leader explained the situation to the CO of the fort, a Stetson-wearing American known as Commander Jim, over a cold beer. What was needed was some sort of transport to take them to the edge of the Naka Valley. From there they would 'yomp' (march full-laden), carrying all their own equipment and enough food and water for two weeks.

Commander Jim could scarcely believe his ears. Were these mad Brits really going to scale mountains 12,000 feet (3,650 metres) high, carrying two weeks' supplies? Worse, were they really planning to hide out in the rocks for ten days in an area crawling with AQT? Didn't they know that the Naka Valley was just eight miles (13km) from Shah-i-Knot – the Valley of the Kings – an AQT stronghold? Recent airstrikes on Shah-i-Knot meant that a large number of enemy soldiers had taken refuge in the Naka Valley. On top of that, to the north, under the OP they planned to set up on the ridge between the two highest peaks, was the terrorist training camp. After the US Air Force had flattened the place, did the SBS expect just to be able to walk out again? Was that really their plan? The SBS team leader confirmed that that was their plan and that it was pretty standard stuff for British Special Forces.

'They must make you guys pretty goddamn tough over there in England,' said Commander Jim, cracking another beer and producing a map. The SBS man pointed out their objective, a mountain peak about 15 miles (24km) from the fort, on the border with Pakistan.

'You guys are part of Task Force Dagger, aren't you?' asked Commander Jim.

'As far as I know we are, mate,' said the SBS man.

This was crucial, as the Pakistani government had given Task Force Dagger permission to chase the AQT into their country if necessary. Though the SBS, like the SAS, were not integrated into the command structure of Task Force Dagger, Commander Jim gave them the benefit of the doubt. He then explained that the roads leading to their objective were terrible. He could get boys from the elite 10th Mountain Division to give them a lift some of the way at night, with an escort of Humvees and Predator unmanned drones overhead. But the roads ran out about eight miles (12km) short of where they wanted to get to, barely in the foothills of the mountains the SBS men intended to climb.

It would take 24 hours to prepare the Predator. They would also have to start out in daylight across hostile country if they were to reach the drop-off point about midnight, giving the SBS team six or seven hours of darkness to make their climb. That meant they would have to make a fighting exit from the fort to make sure the AQT kept their heads down.

But the AQT were ahead of them. That night, they began a major assault on the fort using RPGs. Normally, an RPG is fired horizontally, aimed directly at the target, but the AQT realised that, by firing at a 45-degree angle, they could increase the range by around 300 yards (275 metres) and stand a good chance of lobbing the projectile over the walls of the fort. However, at that range, the RPGs were hopelessly inaccurate and rounds went off all over the place.

Woken by the cannonade at around 01.00, the SBS team rushed to the roof of the fort to join the US forces returning fire. Muzzle flashes were coming from a pile of rocks around 300 yards (275 metres) away, well within the range of the Diemaco assault rifle – a Canadian version of the M16 that was the weapon of choice of the SBS. As the firefight intensified, the two sides began exchanging heavy-machine-gun fire and the US forces started pounding the enemy position with mortars.

Commander Jim reckoned that they were under attack by some 15 AQT. They made these night-time assaults regularly to keep the Americans on their toes. But this time the commander wanted to hit back in force so that they would have an easier time of it when they ferried the SBS team out, so he called in an airstrike. As Commander Jim fed them the coordinates of the rock pile, two F-18 Hornet fighters came screaming in. Each dropped two GPS-guided 2,000lb (907kg) bombs, lighting up the sky, and when darkness fell again, the enemy was silent.

The next morning, a CIA man who spoke, Arabic, Farsi, Pashto and several other Afghan languages was choppered in. He was to collate the intelligence that was to be gained from the SBS mission. After he had met the team, the mission departure time was set at 16.00 hours the following day, leaving the SBS 24 hours to pack their equipment and complete the detailed planning of the operation.

From the point the roads ran out, there was eight miles

(12km) of pretty much uncharted territory up to the proposed site of the observation point. The team would have to climb from around 2,500 feet (around 750 metres) to 12,000 feet (around 3,660 metres). But it was not a smooth ascent: there were a series of ridges to scale. Allowing for the descent on the other side of each of these, they reckoned that they would have to climb around 15,000 feet (4,570 metres) in just seven hours if they were going to reach their destination while it was still dark.

There was another problem. Although men from Task Force Dagger were allowed to cross into Pakistan, they were to do this only if it was absolutely necessary. Pakistan was a fiercely Muslim country and the war was unpopular. Much of the population sided with the Taliban – who had their origins in the madrassas of Pakistan – and Osama bin Laden, rather than with the Americans or British. Delta Force's Afghan guide now pointed out that the SBS men's maps were wrong. The border had been moved and their mission would lead them some ten miles into Pakistani territory. While they agreed that he was probably right, they decided to ignore his advice. Their maps put the proposed site of the OP right on the border, but it was the only place that they would get a clear view over the training camp and the Naka Valley itself. Then they began packing their bergens, or rucksacks.

Little of the gear they had was standard-issue equipment. The SBS had a war fund and men going into action could call on it to buy the best kit available. During the day it would be hot high up in the mountains, but at night it would be bitterly cold. The men had bought thermal underwear and windproof Gore-Tex jackets.

Gore-Tex is an expensive, breathable, synthetic material that prevents water getting in from the outside, but allows sweat to get out. They each had a woolly hat, a thermal balaclava and gloves, thin cotton trousers, two pairs of socks and a poncho with a camouflage-pattern liner that could be used as a ground sheet or a sunshade. The Americans offered them fur-lined US Army-issue parkas, but they decided these were too bulky and heavy to carry.

The SBS men also had sleeping kit. The lighter clothing was packed at the bottom of the bergen with the heavier gear higher up. This made it easier to balance when walking with the pack in place. On top they carried food: a selection of British-issue 24-hour rations packs and US MREs – 'meals, ready to eat'. They sorted through these, discarding anything that had to be eaten hot, such as self-heating meals and hot-drink packs. The smell of hot food carries in thin mountain air and can easily compromise a mission. They then remade the rations into one-meal-a-day packs, planning to survive the rest of the time on chocolate bars and Brazil nuts, which are an unbeatable source of energy for their weight. They also carried sealable plastic freezer backs to piss and shit in. The smell of urine or faeces could also give their position away. Part of SBS and SAS training was to enter enemy territory and leave without anyone knowing they had ever been there.

Each man carried six bottles of water, which would give him 1.5 litres (2.6 pints) a day if the mission took six days, as now scheduled. They had been told to prepare for the mission extending up to 11 days, though they feared that such a tricky operation might take even longer. With all the heavy photographic and communications equipment they had to carry, not to mention their weapons and ammunition, they could not carry any more water and would have to depend on finding a spring or stream for extra water if the mission dragged on. As they were not expecting rain in eastern Afghanistan at that time of the year, they also carried two Katadyn pump-driven water purifiers. Each man also carried a personal medical kit and field dressings in case of injury, and baby oil to prevent the skin of the face and hands cracking. It is impossible to fire a weapon accurately with cracked hands.

Each man also carried tactical beacons that could be used as signal beacons in line of sight, or could be used to communicate with aircraft overhead. Each was programmed with the individual user's call sign so they could be identified. The pockets of the bergens were stuffed with compasses, binoculars, notebooks and pencils. A personal radio mike, which allowed each man to communicate with the rest of the team, was attached to their webbing. Night-vision goggles (NVGs) and other delicate equipment that might be needed in an emergency were packed on top.

Four of the six-man team carried Diemaco 5.56mm assault rifles, with Heckler & Koch 40mm grenade launchers that fitted on the barrel. Favoured by Special Forces, the launcher was accurate up to 300 yards (275 metres). At that range, a round could pass right through a man or, if it detonated, blow him in two. But they were heavy – bringing the weight of the Diemaco to 11.79 lbs (5.35kg) when fitted. As a rifle would have to be carried during the climb in case they met opposition, the grenade launchers were stowed in the men's webbing. One webbing pouch would be filled with 40mm rounds. Each man would also carry 16 magazines with three tracer rounds at the beginning of each to help the others identify the target. One magazine, marked with gaffer tape, was filled only with tracer in case of night-time contact, and a couple were filled with armour-piercing rounds in case they came up against any heavy weaponry.

The other two men carried Minimi SAWs – squad assault weapons. These were light machine guns favoured by US Special Forces. They also each carried a Swiss Sig Sauer 9mm pistol, two white-phosphorous grenades, two smoke grenades and one high-explosive grenade given to them by the Americans 'for luck'. Each man also carried an extra dozen boxes of ammunition for his main weapon, giving 500 rounds.

Infrared sights and laser devices were also carried. These were attached to the weapon as a night sight, or could be switched to steady laser mode to paint the target for smart bombs. On top of all that, team equipment – satellite phones, cameras, telescopes, secure communication equipment and numerous packs of spare batteries – had to be distributed between the men. Finally, they had a grab bag that contained everything they needed in an emergency, so, if necessary, they could ditch their bergen and make off. It contained a two-day ration pack, medical kit, ammunition and a personal radio. In all, their bergens weighed over 100lbs (45kg) and were packed so tightly that nothing could rattle, giving away their position when they moved. During a mission they were never to be unpacked, so they could make a quick getaway with their bergens. The grab bag was not to be raided either, since that would be all a man could take with him in an emergency.

But equipment means nothing if it doesn't work. When the men checked theirs, they found that the radio to give them secure communications back to headquarters was faulty, so they had to call Bagram to have a replacement Chinooked out. It was a vital piece of equipment. Normally it would be used to communicate directly with Poole but, as they were nominally part of Task Force Dagger, in this case they communicated with Joint Special Forces Command at Fort Bragg, North Carolina. They had to call in every 12 hours. If no communication was received after that time, attempts would be made to contact them by satellite communication and radio. If 24 hours went by, aircraft would be called in to search for them. If 36 hours passed, it would be assumed that the mission had been compromised and the men were dead, captured or on their way to the emergency rendezvous point. Helicopters would be sent to extract them and other aircraft would watch out for their tactical beacons in case they had been injured on the way and needed to be 'medevacked' out.

As they waited for the replacement radio to arrive, the men went over the communication and escape-and-evasion procedures again. Then, when the time came for the radio to be delivered, they went out to the loading zone. Coming over the horizon, they saw not a Chinook but an American C-130 Hercules. As they had been expecting a helicopter, they had not laid out a landing strip. Quickly, they laid down some flares, then realised that there were too many rocks for the C-130 to make a safe leading. The team leader popped a red flare to abort the landing and the C-130 flew overhead, but then it turned and, against all good sense, put down, disappearing into a cloud of dust. But a C-130 is a robust aircraft. Despite its rough landing, it remained unscathed and the radio was ceremoniously handed over.

Later that evening, as the SBS men were downing a bottle of Jack Daniel's they had brought from England, the CIA man came over to join them. They were a little concerned to see that all his equipment fitted into a small rucksack the size of the average soldier's day sack, and they wondered how he was going to feed and water himself, let alone keep himself warm. But the conversation grew raucous and nobody mentioned it.

The next day at 16.00 hours, they set off. The convoy raced out of the fort, but the enemy put up no resistance. For the first two hours of the journey it was light. Then the drivers and co-drivers, who had Kurtz machine guns resting on the laps in case of trouble, donned their NVGs and continued through the darkness. As they moved deeper into hostile territory, the Predators checked the road ahead. A running commentary was radioed back from the command centre, where operators were watching video beamed back from the drones in real time. Several times, AQT activity was spotted ahead and they stopped until the enemy had dispersed. Otherwise, the convoy diverted into dry riverbeds and wadis to avoid contact. Then, just before midnight, the trail ran out. The vehicles came to a halt and the SBS men dismounted.

After saying their goodbyes to the Mountain Division, they helped each other on with their backpacks, then marched the hundred yards (91 metres) up the mountain track. After finding cover, they dropped to the ground and signalled to their escort that all was clear, and the trucks turned and headed for home.

As the noise of the vehicles faded away, the SBS team sat silently, straining their ears for the slightest sound that might indicate the AQT was about. The drop-off was the most dangerous part of any mission, as it could easily alert the enemy to their presence. Meanwhile, as their eyes adjusted to the moonlight, the team leader scanned the hillside above for the easiest way up. They were not going to use their NVGs this early in the mission, as they ate up batteries and strained the eyes.

After a quarter of an hour, they got up and spread out into a patrol formation with the CIA man in the middle. Communication from now on was to be by hand signal only. Once they moved off, the silence was broken by the creaking of their heavy bergens, but there was nothing they could do about that.

They had hung their compasses from the back of their bergens, so that each man could follow the one in front by the slight luminous glow of the dial. After about an hour, they reached the top of the first ridge. From there they could see their objective towering 8,000 feet (about 2,440 metres) above them. Crossing a dry valley, they began to climb again. This time they had to scale a 60-degree slope of loose boulders and stones – an almost impossible task with a huge weight on their backs and a weapon in their hands. One man stumbled and slid 50 yards (46 metres) down the slope until he hit a tree. The others took a short break as he climbed back up to them.

Higher up, the terrain turned to smooth volcanic rock. Another man lost his footing, dropped his gun and slid down the slope until he smashed into a rock, which knocked him out. An avalanche of sparks followed him. With that noise and the fireworks display it had produced, any AQT in the area would be onto them. When the man came round, he pulled himself up and went to search for his weapon. He had broken one of the cardinal rules of Special Forces: never let go of your gun. Eventually, he found it, undamaged, though he wondered how the camera equipment in his bergen had fared.

The team leader faced a difficult decision. The only way they could continue up the hill was to stow their weapons – unthinkable for a Special Forces man – or don the NVGs. The goggles helped little. After another two hours, the men were tired out. Two others had fallen and one set of NVGs had been smashed to pieces. There were two more falls in the next hour but, despite everything, the British sense of humour carried them though. They could not help cracking up. Here were a team of elite SBS men in hostile territory crashing about like Keith Moon in a drum shop. Either the AQT were nowhere around or they were very unworthy opponents.

They had been on the move for six hours and were above the tree line when the sun began to come up. Although they were still 500 yards (457 metres) from the top of the next ridge, beyond it they could see the snow-capped peak that was their destination. The sight inspired them to further efforts. They were already at 9,000 feet (around 2,750 metres). They had 3,000 feet (915 metres) to go, which the team leader reckoned would take another three hours.

Once over the ridgeline, where their silhouette against the rising sun would have put them in danger, they stopped for a break. It was now light. No amount of hurrying would change that, so they had a rest and ate some chocolate to give them energy for the final ascent. As they continued the climb they came across a tiny spring, which rendered just about enough water to work the Katadyn filter. The team leader consulted his GPS and marked the coordinates. This was the only source of water they had seen on the ascent and it could be a lifesaver. They were on a hard routine, which meant no heating was allowed, so they could not risk lighting a fire even to melt snow.

As they continued the climb, the thin air left them gasping for breath, especially when they had to scrabble across loose scree. By the time they reached the peak at around noon, they were suffering symptoms of acute mountain sickness (AMS). Shortage of oxygen caused headache, nausea and vomiting. What they needed was rest and plenty of water, which in the circumstances they could hardly afford to indulge themselves with. But after a short break to scan the barren brown landscape of the Naka Valley beneath, they had to move on to find shelter. This was a risk, as AMS can prove fatal.

About a mile (1.6km) away were a pile of boulders and a thicket of pine trees that might provide cover. After 20 minutes, they reached it. It was the perfect place for an OP. It had clear views to the north and south, open arcs of fire across the surrounding ground, several escape routes and no obstacles to communication. While the other men rested, the team leader and the US Navy SEAL recced the surrounding terrain, checking for signs of human presence:

paths, goat droppings, any indications that people might use the area and that they might be discovered. After five minutes of searching, they had found nothing and assured themselves they were safe.

The place they had picked was a flat area of bare earth, just big enough for seven men to sleep there. To the north was a cliff that plunged vertically several thousand feet into the Naka Valley. The only entrance to the rock pile was to the south, where there was a gap between two boulders just big enough for a man to squeeze himself through. Outside this entrance, they set up three Claymore mines, enough to discourage uninvited visitors. A second sentry post was set up between two boulders at the western end of the post. A third was set up at the end of a gorge that ran parallel to the Naka Valley to the south. It was too precipitous and inhospitable to be inhabited, but a river snaked along it that might be sought out by goatherds.

At any one time, four of the six-man team would be on sentry or observation duty while the other two ate, slept or filed reports. The first thing they had to do was get oriented. From their maps they identified two hamlets of mud-brick houses that intelligence had identified as the centre of terrorist activity. Between them was wide, flat area where they had been told training took place. But nothing was going on there at the moment. It was 14.00, the hottest part of the day, when even al-Qaeda had to stay out of the sun.

The observers took 30 minutes on, 30 minutes off. Any longer would produce eye-strain and loss of concentration. Meanwhile, the CIA man set up a sophisticated listening device and satellite communications equipment, before putting a test call through to Joint Special Operations Command in Fort Bragg. Soon, he had established a two-way link. Using a small computer he could upload maps, notes, photographs and video footage to headquarters. At the same time, he could download intelligence from unmanned drones or manned observation aircraft circling above. The rest of the time he spent listening in to enemy signals. Occasionally alerted by a key phrase, he would scribble in a notebook.

When darkness fell the temperature plummeted, but those who were not on sentry duty still found it easy to sleep: they were exhausted from the long climb. But first they checked their guns for any water that might have got into them. If it froze, the gun could explode if it was fired. They also filled their sleeping bags with water bottles to prevent them from freezing. Even though they were exhausted, they were woken after just two hours' sleep by activity in the valley below. A number of Toyota pickups had arrived and their beturbaned passengers had lit a fire. However, they seemed unaware they were being watched, so those who were not on sentry duty went back to sleep.

In the morning, the team were still suffering the effects of AMS, though it was not bad enough to abort the mission. Flecks of blood had yet to appear in their spit – a sure sign it was time to get down from the mountain. As dawn broke, the valley below was obscured by cloud. Soon the sun burned it off and they could see the men below preparing themselves for a patrol. Armed with rocket-propelled grenades and Kalashnikovs, half of them set off towards the hills to the northeast; the other half moved to a patch of forest to the northwest.

A short time later, the CIA man spotted what he took to be a patrol 300 yards (275 metres) away, heading for their position. The team leader ordered his men to prepare for a fighting withdrawal. They were to pick up their grab bags and load them with ammunition. Firing would commence on his signal. Then, when he popped a smoke grenade, they were to begin their escape-and-evasion procedure and head for the emergency rendezvous point, where they would be picked up.

The men with Diemacos put on their grenade launchers and laid out the 40mm rounds around them. The situation seemed dire. If an enemy patrol engaged them here, they were probably done for. They were 15 miles (24km) inside hostile territory with no hope of an airlift out unless they got down the mountains again.

As they waited they could hear a man taking loudly in Arabic. Then he appeared. The CIA man had made a mistake. This was no patrol. It was just one man. He was talking into a huge Soviet-vintage radio and seemed oblivious of their presence. The SBS men were eager to capture or kill him, just to be on the safe side, but that was out of the question while he was still on the radio. The man strolled on, evidently unaware that he was in the gun sights of six trained killers. As he walked down off the ridgeline, he met some other men lower down and they all disappeared into the trees.

The SBS men could not be sure that they had not gone to get others. The man with the radio could have spotted them but pretended he had not, so that the AQT could come back in force. However, the CIA man had overheard his conversation and said that the man had betrayed no clue that he knew they were there. Believing they were probably safe, the SBS men decided to stay where they were and continue monitoring the situation.

By the middle of the morning, no terrorists had come to get them. However, several hundred young men and boys had turned up on the flat ground below and begun to do physical training exercises. They were unarmed, but the SBS men photographed them and made notes. By the time it grew hot, the trainees disappeared into what the SBS men took to be classrooms to be taught the finer points of terrorist attacks. With nothing happening below, the SBS men used the time to upload the digital photographs they had taken.

The following night, a Spectre gunship came over, making an infrared search of the valley. The SBS men were immediately worried that it might take them for the enemy and that they would be another victim of a blue-on-blue incident. However, it flew on without spraying them with 'friendly fire'.

The next day, after observing another PT session on the flat ground below, the team filed their first situation report. They had seen men with guns and young people training in what they had been told was a terrorist training camp. Everything, as far as they were concerned, was ready for the airstrike that was still four days away.

By Day Four on the mountain, the men's symptoms of AMS had lessened, but the cold and shortage of water as getting to them. At 08.00 hours, the team leader and his SEAL sidekick volunteered to risk heading down to the spring they had located on the way up to get more water. It was a long walk down a rocky path, but it would be a welcome respite from boredom.

On the way down the mountain, they saw an elderly goatherd shooing his charges along a path. The two men flattened themselves, but there was no cover to hide them. Although their standing orders on the mission were to assume any contact was hostile, they could not kill the old man in cold blood. If he spotted them, they would have to take him prisoner. As it was, he walked by seemingly oblivious to them and they let him go unmolested. It was, they knew, a risk.

Eventually, they reached the spring. While the SEAL kept guard, the SBS team leader filtered some 37 pints (21 litres) of water, which they carried back up to the OP. That, they decided, was the last trip they would make for water, since the mission had so nearly been compromised.

That afternoon several thousand people assembled on the flat ground between the villages under banners bearing verses from the Koran in Arabic. There were speeches and the SBS team assumed they were witnessing an al-Qaeda recruiting rally. They took more photographs and fired them off to Fort Bragg. Then the women down below began ululating. It was then that they realised that what they were witnessing was not an AQT meeting but a funeral. The majority of those present were women and children.

Reviewing everything they had seen, they realised that the PT exercises on the flat ground they had observed could be equally innocent. It could merely be a class of schoolboys being put through their paces, while the men they had seen out on patrol could merely have been looking for a lost goat. True, they had been armed, but that was commonplace in rural Afghanistan. What they were observing – and about to call an airstrike on – was not a terrorist-training camp at all, but a normal Afghan village going about its business.

They decided they would have to call the airstrike off, but when they tried to file a report they found their satellite communications would not work. The CIA man said he thought some wires had come loose during the climb. The SBS team leader reckoned he could fix it, but they would have to wait until the next morning when it was light.

After dawn, when he prised off the back of the communications unit, he found three wires had indeed come loose. They would have to be soldered back in position. Fortunately one of the SBS men had brought his tiny hex stove along with him, even though they were on 'hard routine'. As they now felt they were in no danger of being detected by the enemy – as the people they had been called in to observe were plainly civilians – they risked lighting it. The team leader used the stove to heat up the blade of his Leatherman multitool. (The Leatherman is essentially a penknife with up to 20 tools in the handle – the American equivalent of the Swiss Army knife favoured by many Special Forces operatives.) Then he used the remaining solder to reattach the connection and soon their satellite communications were up and running again. They filed their report and sat back to wait for a reply.

When it came, it appeared that Joint Special Operations Command was not convinced, since their report conflicted with their previous intelligence. They had decided to send in a Delta Force team to take a look for themselves, but they would not be there until the following morning.

By now the SBS team were low on water and, while they

waited, they began to notice the symptoms of dehydration that would severely impair them operationally. But they could not pull out now. First, they had to make sure that the airstrike was going to be called off. The lives of hundreds of innocent people depended on it. But desperate times call for desperate measures. The SBS broke out their medicinal kits and began fixing up saline drips. Taken intravenously, one bag of saline fluid was the equivalent of two litres of water.

That night, with no enemy presence in the area, the team leader called off the sentries and they all got a good night's sleep. Next morning the Delta Force team arrived, bringing water and rations. It seemed that their report had contradicted so much earlier intelligence that it had to be sent to the Oval Office and the then British Prime Minister Tony Blair for assessment. The Delta Force team quickly concurred that the two hamlets below were just that, not the biggest al-Qaeda training camp in Afghanistan. Then they left.

That afternoon, the CIA man with the SBS got confirmation that the airstrike had been called off. Snow began falling as they took their last look down at the Naka Valley, where they saw a bunch of kids playing. Then they too left the way they had come.

Twenty-four hours later, however, they were back in the Naka Valley, this time with the Delta Force patrol and transport, provided, again, by the 10th Mountain Division, along with Predators and a couple of F-18s providing top cover. As they pulled up on the flat ground between the two hamlets, the schoolkids came out to meet the visitors and were rewarded with sweets and chocolate bars. One of the boys then invited the SBS team leader to come and meet the village headman.

This turned out to be the old man they had seen herding goats when they were out getting water. He said that he had seen them but thought it was better to ignore them. He thought they had to be mad to spend days and nights on the top of a mountain in the freezing cold with no water. They explained that they were on a reconnaissance mission. If they wanted to know what was going on in the valley, the old man said, they should have come and asked him. He knew everything that happened in the Naka Valley. He said that he had seen a great many Taliban fighters passing through the valley. They were fleeing from the bombing of Shah-i-knot and were heading for safety in Pakistan. The men in the Toyota pickups who had lit a fire and camped for the night were some of them.

But the old man was suspicious too. The British had been in Afghanistan three times before, he said, and they had been beaten three times. Were they looking to be beaten again? What was more, when the British had come before, they had been a great deal smarter than the SBS men he saw in front of him this time. They would do well if they did not make fresh enemies among the Afghan people, pointing out that it was not very friendly of them to turn up at his village carrying so much weaponry.

The village leader then explained that he hated the Taliban. They had killed his son because they had caught him listening to Western music. The old man showed the SBS men arms caches hidden around the village where the fleeing Taliban had stored their weapons – Kalashnikovs, RPGs, machine guns, grenades and cases of ammunition.

The men then rigged the caches with explosives and blew them up.

The old man said he said he would fight the Taliban himself if he had been younger. As it was, the British and Americans must stay, otherwise the Taliban would come back. If they returned to find their weapons had been destroyed, they would take reprisals. He also told the SBS that, next time, they must come directly to his door like a friend, rather than sit out on a cold mountain overlooking the village deciding whether to bomb it or not. It seemed he knew what they had been up to all along.

Once back at the fort, the SBS men enjoyed a few more cold beers with Commander Jim before they were Chinooked back to Bagram.

CHAPTER THREE
OPERATION TRENT

Back at Bagram, the SAS had been cooling their heels. All they were being offered were hearts-and-minds operations, where they were to go out and provide medical aid to sick villagers. Worthwhile though this was, the SAS were itching for action. They wanted a crack at Osama bin Laden. The Americans, they felt, were relying – as usual – too much on airstrikes. It seemed the men of the 22nd SAS Regiment were not going to capture the world's most wanted man from a cockpit at 20,000 feet (6,100 metres). However, news filtered down that Tony Blair was pitching for a more active role for them.

The operation they were offered was an attack on a £50-million opium storage depot 530 miles (850km) from Bagram and 155 miles (250km) south of Kandahar in the desert region of Rigestan. Rigestan means 'country of sand' in Persian, so it would be the perfect desert operation for the SAS. This was an important military objective, as the Taliban used the export of opium to fund their operations. Intelligence reports indicated that between 60 and a hundred of the AQT's toughest men were well dug in around the objective, so the SAS men were going to be in for a fight. It was just the news they wanted to hear.

First, they assembled their fleet of Pinkies. They were not in good condition. Having come direct from deployment in Oman, they were caked with sand. This had got into the engines and eaten away at rubber seals and grommets. But they would have to patch them up the best they could, as they could not be properly overhauled until they returned to the UK.

But there was no way they could drive the 530 miles (850km) across hostile country to the objective. The Americans would provide six C-130 transports to get them there. They would also provide top cover in the form of two F-14 Tomcats and four of the heavier, carrier-based F/A-18 Hornets. However, close-air support would be provided for only one hour from 11.00 on the day of the operation. That meant that they would have to go in daylight.

The SAS did not relish this. They had been trained for night-time attacks, when the enemy were at their most vulnerable. An attack in the deserts of southern Afghanistan would kick up so much dust that the AQT would see them coming miles away during the hours of daylight. They could lose the element of surprise completely. On the other hand, the British government had pulled so many strings to get them an operation at all that they could hardly turn it down.

There was only one thing they could do: go in mob-handed. They would take both squadrons and make a full frontal assault, something they had not done since the Second World War. Again, this was not something that they had trained for in the SAS, which specialised in small-unit attacks. However, SAS men were recruited from other units, largely the Paras, where they were trained in these tactics. The possible consequences were monumental, though. They would be risking a large part of what even the Americans admitted was the best fighting force on Earth. And, if it went wrong, there would be a huge rift between London and Washington. As it was, the CO had just 24 hours to plan the mission. It would be called Operation Trent.

Key to the operation was to find a suitable landing zone (LZ). They had to get 120 men and 250 tons of supplies within striking distance of the target so they could arrive there at the same time as the air cover. But the area had not often been visited and rarely surveyed. They did not have any maps of smaller scale than 1:1,500,000. These did not even show the target, and the area of the LZ was just a blank. So the SAS would have to send in an eight-man HALO parachute team to find one. They would be jumping into hostile territory, hundreds of miles behind enemy lines. There were no friendly local forces in that area to assist them. They would be on their own.

Another problems was that there was no time to do a close reconnaissance of the target or set up OPs to get an accurate idea of what was going on there. All they had was the sketchiest of intelligence to go on. They would have no idea what the going was like underfoot, or under the tyres of their Pinkies. There was no way they could plan fields of fire, discover where the dead ground was or decide which weapons should be deployed where. Usually, SAS operations are planned meticulously. This time the men on the ground would have to make it up as they went along. Fortunately, SAS men are trained to use their own initiative.

But full frontal assaults were no longer part of the SAS handbook: they were for the infantry. British Army manuals reckoned that to make a successful frontal assault, you needed a superiority of three to one. Even with both squadrons deployed and taking the minimum estimate of the enemy, that would give them a superiority of only two to one. The whole operation seemed impossibly risky. But then SAS men expected to risk their lives. If they were concerned about danger, they would never leave Hereford. In this case, body-recovery procedures would be paramount. Ever since their involvement in the secret war in Yemen in 1964, the SAS had brought their bodies home, even if they had to fight to get them. In a village called Taiz, two SAS had been captured and beheaded, and their heads displayed on poles. The last thing they wanted to do was give the AQT a propaganda victory like that. Despite the odds, the SAS were determined to go ahead.

On the day of the attack, the assault force was briefed from aerial photographs in the hangar at Bagram. These showed the target some 12 miles (20km) north of the Pakistani border. The area was dominated by a geographical feature some 7,260 feet (2,213 metres) high. The ground between the LZ and the target appeared rocky, sandy and undulating. There were a number of laying-up positions and emergency rendezvous points. Some of the land might be cultivated and there was a chance that there were minefields in the area.

Intelligence indicated that the men guarding the depot were elite troops, trained in one of bin Laden's top training camps. They would be highly motivated and have no fear of death. They were well armed with Kalashnikov AK-47 assault rifles and RPGs, and were known to have stockpiled ammunition. Their morale would be high, as no Coalition troops had taken them on yet.

The area around the camp was to be regarded as a hostile environment. The only men on the ground before the main assault would be recceing the LZ. With no men near the target it would be impossible to tell whether the area was patrolled or what the defenders' daily routine might be. A single-track road led to the depot. This was used by lorries transporting the opium in and out of the warehouse, but it was not known whether there were sentry posts along the road, or whether it was mined or defended in some other way. Further, the rough terrain between the LZ and target was perfect for an enemy ambush. From the aerial photographs it was possible to see that the depot itself was surrounded by trenches and bunkers, which – as the SAS could hardly make a stealthy approach – would be manned by the time they got there. It was assumed that resistance would be stiff.

In fact, the depot seemed to be in the middle of an armed camp with numerous defensive features that ran from the 7,260-foot (2,212-metre) geographical feature in the north, some way to the south. It contained two large, single-storey brick buildings, one of which seemed to be the local AQT headquarters and was lit by electricity supplied by a generator. It was likely that the defenders could call on reinforcements. AQT forces were travelling south from Kandahar to escape the bombing. They wore no uniforms and would be dressed much like other Afghanis or Arabs. This could cause a problem, as there were also local nomadic tribes of Baluchi and Pashtun descent in the area, whose allegiances were unknown. While they could not expect the help of the locals once they were on the ground, they could not automatically assume everyone in the area was hostile.

As well as the four US Navy F/A-18 Hornets and the two F-14 Tomcats, the US would provide CH-47 Chinooks to medevac casualties out. That was all the information available. Now the SAS were given precise details of the objective of their operation. They were to destroy the enemy and the opium, recover what intelligence they could and establish a Coalition presence in al-Qaeda territory. It was vital that the enemy understand that there was nowhere in Afghanistan that British and American troops could not go.

The operation was to be executed in five phases. In Phase One, part of G Squadron's Air Troop would parachute into the area and secure the LZ. In Phase Two, the main force of SAS men would fly in from Bagram and deploy. In Phase Three, the advance party and the main force would move to the forming-up point (FUP), after a reconnaissance party on motorbikes had checked that it was clear of enemy and that there was at least one escape route in case they were attacked. The main force should reach the FUP – their last scheduled stop before the attack – before first light.

In Phase Four, A and G Squadrons would advance as close as possible to the opium depot by Pinkie. Then A Squadron would then dismount at advance to contact on foot while G Squadron would lay down a heavy blanket of fire to protect A Squadron's advance. The CO, RSM and the rest of the regimental headquarters would be on hand to assess the progress of the attack from the flank. Once the target was secured, they would destroy the opium and search for any intelligence. Then, in Phase Five, they would withdraw.

The officers commanding the individual squadrons then briefed the men on the route they would take and how they would form up in the convoy. This was planned to coincide with the order of attack. There were other questions to be answered. Would any deception be involved? What were the signals to fire? What would they do in the event of an ambush or, knowing American planes were about, friendly fire? Would they be taking prisoners? What should they do about civilians in the area?

Once thoroughly briefed on the rules of engagement, the men were given a schedule for the time of departure, return and post-operation debrief, along with the communication frequencies to be used throughout the mission. Then they synchronised watches, though there was still just under two days to go.

As the sun set at about H-hour minus 30, the HALO team packed its parachutes and taped up its bergen straps. These eight men would be dropping into Rigestan. They would be about 60 miles (97km) from the nearest friendly force, which was at Camp Rhino, a forward operating base set up at the Objective Rhino airstrip taken by the US

Rangers in the early days of the war. The land there was barren with sand ridges and dunes rising to a hundred feet (30 metres). They were to search for a suitable LZ and, when they had located it, hold it for 24 hours, if possible without being detected.

As it grew dark, they boarded the RAF Hercules that had been refitted for the jump and flown in from Oman. Each man was carrying 180lbs (82kg) of equipment. As well as their weapons and ammunition, and main and reserve parachutes, they carried bars of chocolate, field dressings, survival kits, GPS equipment and phials of morphine protected by masking tape and slung around their necks in case of injury. Each man carried a large-scale escape-and-evasion map with a message written in a number of local languages he could show to any friendly local if he got lost. It read:

> I am British and I do not speak your language. I will not harm you. I bear no malice towards your people. My friend, please provide me with food, water, shelter, clothing and necessary medical attention. Also, please provide safe passage to the nearest friendly forces of any country supporting the British and their Allies. You will be rewarded for assisting me when you present this number and my name to the British authorities.

After a last-minute briefing about what to do if the Hercules was hit by a SAM missile, the engines roared into life and the giant plane trundled down the runway. It was vulnerable to attack by a Stinger as it took off, but once they had gained altitude they were safe. At least the AQT had no air force.

As they gained height, the parachute-jump instructor (PJI) told them to put their parachutes on, then checked their straps. At 10,000 feet (just over 3,000 metres), he ordered them to plug into the C-130's oxygen console, which piped oxygen directly into their helmets. At 25 minutes into the flight, they were 27,000 feet – five miles, or 8,230 metres – from the ground. With 20 minutes to go before the jump, they switched their oxygen supply from the Hercules' console to the oxygen bottle they kept strapped to their bellies. It was a delicate and critical move. Any error at that point could leave the brain without oxygen, turning the man into a vegetable. It was a difficult procedure to switch pipes as the plane bumped up and down, but each man kept an eye on his oppo to make sure he did not get into difficulties.

When the plane reached the jump height of over 28,000 feet, the men's nerves were taut. Now they faced the five-minute free fall, then the parachute descent, which had its own dangers. The main chute was set to open barometrically at 3,500 feet (1,067 metres). If it failed, they would reach 3,000 feet (914 metres) travelling at 130 feet (40 metres) a second. At that speed, it would take the reserve another 1,000 feet (305 metres) to deploy, so they would have mere seconds to save their own lives.

They were also dropping into enemy territory. What would await them on the ground? If just one of them were killed or injured, the entire operation would have to be called off. No wonder the Air Troop required nerves of steel.

As the jump point neared, the rear of the C-130 opened and ice-cold air came rushing in. Once the ramp was locked in position, the men ran through a final check. Straps were given one last tug and they made sure once again that all their equipment – weapon, bergen, parachute, webbing – were secure. Then they put on their goggles and snapped the cyalume sticks on the backs of their helmets. These gave off a dull glow so that they could locate each other during the descent.

The base man – the man carrying the heaviest equipment and who would be the least manoeuvrable across the sky – would jump first. His equipment was checked by the PJI, while the Hercules' loadmaster checked those further back. The PJI then informed the pilot they were ready. Soon the red light came on and the base man inched towards the end of the ramp. When the green light came on, he flung himself backwards into the slipstream, followed in short order by the others. The PJI, who was strapped to the plane and wore a parachute just in case, leaned over the edge to watch them go. When he could not see them any more, the ramp was closed and the Hercules headed back for Bagram.

The eight-man HALO team falling from the aircraft reached terminal velocity – around 140 mph (225 kph) – in about ten seconds. Their goggles quickly misted up in the cold air so they wiped them the best they could. Diving blind, each man risked hitting another, possibly killing both of them. Searching for the green glow of another man below, they tried to stay within ten to 20 feet (three to six metres) of each other so that they would not be too spread out when they reached the ground. Only at 5,000 feet (just over 1,500 metres), did they separate to avoid getting whacked by one another's parachutes as they deployed.

At 4,000 feet (1,220 metres) they spread out their arms and legs to present the greatest resistance to the air. Then at 3,500 feet (1,067 metres), after falling for about two minutes, the barometric AOD – automatic opening device – loosened the main chute. As this deployed, they felt a reassuring jolt on the harness. At that height, there was enough oxygen to breathe, so they took off their masks, lifted their goggles and grabbed the steering lines that were Velcroed to the main risers. There was another two minutes to go. They checked around to see that everyone was at a safe distance – they needed to land close together, but not so close that their parachutes became tangled. Below, the rock and sand was coming up to meet them.

It was up to the lowest man to assess which way the wind was blowing. At around 200 feet (61 metres) they turned into the wind to slow their rate of travel over the ground. At 100 feet (30 metres), they dropped their bergens, since landing while carrying the weight of a pack would almost certainly lead to injury. They also loosened their main weapons, ready for action. Each man's bergen dangled on a long line. The sound of its hitting the earth prepared the man for landing, and the pack also provided a heavy anchor if the wind was high. Then the men pulled both steering lines to put the brakes on. A skilled parachutist can slow the parachute practically to a halt as he gently hits the ground. All eight men landed safely.

Silently, they dragged their parachutes away from the immediate vicinity of the drop. Then they formed up to give 360-degree coverage of the surroundings, searching in the darkness for lights, movement, recognisable shapes or straight lines that might indicate something manmade. At the same time, they were looking for cover and possible escape routes. This was a key part of any operation. Landing by parachute, even at night, meant that they could be seen from quite a distance. They were most vulnerable to detection – and attack – on landing.

After 15 minutes they began packing their parachutes away and sent a message back to Bagram, confirming that they had landed safely. It seemed that they had got lucky. The area where they had landed was flat, so they began checking out whether it would be a good enough LZ for the Hercules bringing in the rest of the assault force. Certainly it was large enough, so the crucial question was whether the soil was solid. The mission would be a disaster if one of the Hercules craft sank in soft sand. They had brought with them a device that looked like a rugby football with a spike on it. This was used to test whether the ground structure below the surface was firm enough to take the weight of a C-130. Then they had to mark out a runway. It had to be 900 feet (274 metres) long by 40 feet (12 metres) wide, facing, if possible, in the direction of the wind.

Next they had to find an observation point overlooking the LZ and the surrounding area so they could guarantee the safety of the landing party. It had to be big enough to give cover to two soldiers lying down. Nearby, they needed a laying-up point (LUP) for the others to rest. It would also have to give all eight a good defensive position if they came under attack. Both positions needed a good escape route and they should be close enough to minimise movement in the open needed to get between them.

The HALO team now split into two four-man patrols to search for suitable positions. The point man of each patrol looked for mines, booby traps and any sign of the enemy. The two men behind him scanned to the left and right, while the man at the back covered the rear. Every few minutes they stopped and listened for any sound of the enemy in the vicinity.

Once they had located an observation post (OP) and an LUP, two men were installed in the OP. Another two were put on sentry duty, while the remaining four rested, cleaned their weapons and ate cold rations. Again, they were on hard routine – no hot drinks, no cigarettes and no talking, except for whispering operational information.

About two hours after they had settled in, the sun began to rise. It lit a flat, forbidding landscape, but as least there were no enemy to be seen and no nomadic tribesmen who might give their position away. It was going to be a long day as they scanned the horizon to flank and rear.

At around the same time, the men back at Bagram began loading up their Pinkies. Each carried 18 jerry cans of petrol, six of water and rations to feed three men for ten days. They carried spare half-shafts and tyres for running repairs. Some carried sacks of rice in case there was a little hearts-and-minds work to be done. G Squadron's trucks were also weighed down with general-purpose machine guns (GPMGs), .50-calibre heavy machine guns, Mk19 belt-fed grenade launchers and Milan anti-tank missiles. As the fire support base, they would be going first, at around 18.00 hours.

The first flights would also carry eight motorbikes to patrol the LZ and reconnoitre the terrain on the way to the target. The Hercules would then turn round and come back to pick up A Squadron, who would leave five hours after G Squadron and arrive at around 01.00 the following day. Then the two squadrons would form up into a convoy and drive about 90 miles (145km) across the desert into the attack. The CO would go on the first flight, so he could organise things on the ground. The RSM would be on the second, bringing up the rear.

By 17.00 hours, the six US Hercules were lined up a good distance apart on the runway. This was done so that, if one was hit and exploded, the next would not be hit by the debris. The CO gave the men a final pep talk, after which they drove out to the Hercules. Each would carry either three Pinkies or two Pinkies and a French ACMAT truck. These heavy-duty transports – used by 42 countries – were employed by the SAS as mother ships, piled high with spare ammunition, fuel and water.

All the vehicles were reversed into the cargo hold and fixed down with chains around the axles. With the heavily laden vehicle on board, the planes were dangerously overweight. Each fully laden Pinkie alone weighed 3.5 tonnes, and each of the three-man crew carried 80lbs (36kg) of personal kit. The men wore standard desert DPM (disruptive pattern material), motor-cross goggles and the Arab headdresses adopted by the SAS when it was first started in North Africa in 1941. It took about 30 minutes to load each plane and they would leave at five-minute intervals.

Once the rear ramp was closed, the giant planes began trundling down the runway one by one. Airborne, the men had a cup of water. Some even sneaked a cigarette, although it was strictly against orders.

Two hours later the HALO team left the security of the OP and LUP and deployed around the makeshift airstrip. With five minutes to go they could hear the C-130's engines and turned on their infrared torches. These would be picked up by the Hercules' forward-looking infrared imagers, but no one on the ground could see them without similar equipment. Three minutes later, the men on the ground could see the first Hercules approaching. It had its lights off so they could see it only through their NVGs. At the same time, the loadmaster on board told the driver of the lead Pinkie to turn his engine on. Then he dropped the loading ramp. As the Hercules landed, all engines were racing. As the plane slowed to around ten miles an hour, the first Pinkie drove down the ramp, hitting the ground with a thump. It was followed by the other vehicles and motorbikes. They were all off in about ten seconds as the Hercules turned to take off again, clearing the runway just in time for the next plane to come in. Within about 30 minutes, the whole of G Squadron were on the ground and the planes were on their way back to Bagram.

The Pinkies quickly went into a defensive formation around the perimeter of the LZ with all guns pointing outwards. Someone might have heard the landing and, at any moment, the men might come under attack. They held this position while the motorcycle reconnaissance patrols were sent out to make sure that there were no enemy lurking in the surrounding territory.

Soon after midnight, the six C-130s came in again and by 01.30 hours A Squadron was lined up alongside G Squadron around the perimeter of the runway. After 20 minutes of watching and listening, they prepared to leave. They would be vulnerable if they stayed put for too long.

After a roll call that found everyone present and correct, the 40-vehicle convoy left the LZ and headed due south. A Pinkie armed with twin GPMGs led the way. The ACMAT trucks were in the middle of the convoy, as they were the most vulnerable, and the entire column stretched for about a mile and a quarter (2km). Ahead of them was at least an eight-hour drive. In the desert conditions of Rigestan, it would be hard to make 25 mph.

The first leg of the journey passed without incident. After about two hours, the motorbikes went ahead to reconnoitre an appropriate LUP where the men could have a rest. Once they reached the LUP, the Pinkies fanned out in a circular formation with the ACMATs in the middle.

With about one hour to go before sunrise, the motorcycles took off to reconnoitre the road ahead, then the Pinkies rolled out of the LUP. As the sun came up – making the column even more vulnerable – the terrain became tougher and the gradient steeper. This took its toll on the vehicles. With just two hours to go, one of the Pinkies armed with GPMGs broke down. There was no alternative but to leave it and its crew behind. They would be picked up when the convoy returned, after the fighting was over.

With only one hour to go, the opium depot was still not in sight. They were now in the foothills of the Brahui mountains. There was no sign of a track and the vehicles were getting bogged down in sand. There was still nearly two miles to go to the FUP when the convoy came to a halt. The terrain was now so craggy that al-Qaeda could be waiting to ambush them almost anywhere. The CO got out his tactical beacon (TACBE) and contacted the US fighters who were preparing to attack the opium depot. He asked them to fly directly over the column in their run-in to the depot. Then the column could simply follow their line in the target. The pilots were keeping an eye out for AQT patrols on the way.

The F/A-18s roared overhead and the convoy headed after them, directly over a sea of sand dunes. They gave the all-clear, so the column could forge ahead without worrying whether they were going to meet the enemy. With 30 minutes to go, the SAS reached the FUP. Again they stopped. The CO and his signaller went forward in his Pinkie to make an emergency close tactical reconnaissance. As he crested the next dune, the opium depot lay before him. He had planned to attack from the east, sending G Squadron in first to provide cover while A Squadron closed with the enemy, leaving the west side of the depot for the US ground-attack aircraft to strike. But the CO could see that this was now unworkable. The sand to the east side of the depot was too soft.

He turned back to the FUP and he issued new orders. The ground attack would be from the west. He contacted the US aircraft and informed them, telling them to make their run-in from the east. Then he gave the order to attack. G Squadron led the charge to the northwest. At first they were hampered by soft sand, but then they felt the tyres bite on a harder, rockier surface. To the south, they heard the whistle of incoming RPGs. Al-Qaeda plainly knew they were coming, perhaps alerted by the overflying F/A-18s. G Squadron were out of range of an RPG, fired horizontally. But the AQT were lobbing them at 45 degrees like mortars so the SAS men had to keep an eye skywards to see where they were going to land.

The range of the RPG meant that G Squadron would have to establish their fire support base about half a mile out (0.8km) from the depot. The officer commanding halted the convoy and the Pinkies skidded to a halt facing the target. They then began to lay down suppressing fire, pounding the al-Qaeda defences with their .50-calibre heavy machine guns, GPMGs, Mk19 belt-fed grenade launchers and Milan wire-guided anti-tank missiles. Any AQT personnel who had not reached their trenches soon lay dead.

The RSM – a veteran of the Falklands War – stayed back at the FUP. He was to guard the flanks and rear, ensuring the supply of ammunition and preparing to tend to casualties. Meanwhile, the CO rode up to the flank of the fire support base to direct the battle. The 14 Pinkies of A Squadron then swept around behind the fire support base and advanced on the western flank of the opium depot under the cover of the dust that had been kicked up by G Squadron getting into place. But soon enemy RPGs were raining down on them too. They also stopped about half a mile out. From there they would proceed on foot.

Now everything was set. The two SAS squadrons were in place for the assault. Then in came the F/A-18s with a thunderous roar. They fired Maverick missiles, destroying the depot and the £50 million worth of opium inside. Al-Qaeda's headquarters, though, had been spared. This was now to be the SAS's objective.

The huge explosion of the opium depot going up sent al-

Qaeda men rushing for cover, providing more targets for G Squadron. They laid down more fire to keep the scattering AQT men away from the headquarters that A Squadron were going to have to fight their way into. SAS mortar teams then started lobbing mortars at the defensive positions around the depot. Other teams lobbed mortars at the 7,260-foot (2,213-metre) geographical feature known as Spot Height 2213, which was on A Squadron's flank and could well harbour enemy positions.

Al-Qaeda were now reduced to firing their Kalashnikovs at G Squadron, even though the fire support base was hopelessly out of range. The RPGs were being reserved for A Squadron, who could risk going no further on board their vehicles. The lead vehicle skidded to a halt behind some rocks. The men dismounted and ran for whatever cover they could find. When the rest arrived, two men from each Pinkie were sent forward as an assault force. The rest stayed behind to give cover and protect their line of retreat.

Using classic infantry advance-to-contact drills, the assault force split into two-man teams. As one group 'went firm', holding ground and firing at the enemy, the second group advanced before itself going firm. This leapfrog manoeuvre is known as 'pepper-potting'. They had a lot of ground to cover, especially when weighed down with 50lbs (23kg) of kit, and they had to maintain momentum. Meanwhile, they were being pounded with RPGs and small-arms fire. At the foot of Spot Height 2213 they ran into two bunkers. Running up the slope to attack them would have been suicidal, so they called up a Pinkie and sprayed them with .50-calibre fire. But, as the bunkers were above them, they could not hit the enemy positions effectively.

With Spot Height 2213 and the bunker preventing A Squadron moving around to the north, they were faced with trenches facing east, west and south, filled with al-Qaeda. These were taking heavy fire from the fire support base, but that was doing little more than making the AQT fighters keep their heads down. The CO decided to move to get a clearer view of the situation. He could not move west, as that would have put him in a dangerous spot between the right flank of A Squadron and the left arc of the fire support base. Instead, he moved east. From there he could see the bunker on Spot Height 2213 that was impeding progress, so he ordered the fire support base to move forward 330 yards (300 metres), where it could put down heavy fire on the bunker as well as the trench system in front of the depot.

The US close-air support was available only for another 15 minutes so the CO decided to make use of it. A single F/A-18 came thundering in, scoring a direct hit on the top bunker. The large explosion caused a landslide that buried the lower bunker as well.

As A Squadron resumed their advance, the F/A-18 turned to strafe al-Qaeda's trenches with fire from their 20mm Vulcan cannons. These beltless, air-cooled cannons could fire at the devastating rate of 4,000–6,000 rounds a minute.

Although the pilots had been told that the attack had been switched from the east to the west, they had not been told of the fire support base's 330-yard (300-metre) advance. As he dropped to 2,000 feet (610 metres)on his run in, the pilot squeezed the electronic trigger. Falling short, the high-explosive rounds tore straight through G Squadron's position. The SAS men were stunned and cursed the Yanks for another blue-on-blue incident. But when they looked around, they found no one had been hit. By sheer luck the bullets had ripped through the earth between the Pinkies.

But another F/A-18 was on its way. The fire support base contacted the CO and, with seconds to spare, he radioed to the pilot, 'Check fire! Check fire!' Just in time, the strafing run was aborted. After a moment spent regaining their composure, the fight support base began firing again. The battle had been going on for an hour now – long by SAS standards – and it was far from over.

A Squadron were now nearly 550 yards (500 metres) from the depot and within the range of Kalashnikov fire. There was little dead ground. Only a few beds of dried-out streams gave any cover. Nevertheless, they continued their advance, taking out al-Qaeda fighters as they went. As A Squadron neared the target, the men at the fire support base stopped their cover fire for fear of hitting their own men. Instead the unit's snipers broke out their L82A1 Barrett's rifles. First used in the Gulf War, these were accurate over about a mile and a quarter (2 km) with explosive, armour-piecing shells. These soon found their mark, but al-Qaeda were not about to give up and one man from A Squadron, an ex-Para, was hit by a round from an AK-47. It was just a flesh wound and he made it to cover unaided, but al-Qaeda were overjoyed and began goading the SAS to come and get them.

Meanwhile, the RSM had grown restive at the FUP and

moved up to the CO's new position. There he got permission to go into action with five men from the headquarters party. They headed for the fire support base, where he picked up five volunteers from G Squadron. Splitting into two fire teams, they headed for A Squadron's right flank. As they pepper-potted forward they found the ground littered with the dead bodies of the enemy and empty cartridges cases.

As A Squadron reached the trenches, they found that they too were filled with dead bodies. Some of the survivors fled, only to be cut down. Others withdrew behind the wall of the command centre. The number of dead was now so high that survivors could use their bodies as cover. Taking no chances, the SAS men began clearing the trenches with grenades. At this point the RSM and his party caught up with them.

Next they had to take the mud huts al-Qaeda were taking shelter in. A group stayed back as a mini fire support base, while the others went forward to join the close-quarters battle the SAS are trained for. Meanwhile, the RSM and his men headed for the command centre but as he charged forward, the RSM was hit in the calf and went down. He was in excruciating pain and unable to move – and he was in the open in full view of al-Qaeda, where a sniper could easily finish him off.

A New Zealander from G Squadron rushed to his aid. Other men laid down smoke grenades and while bullets whizzed past him, the Kiwi managed to pull the RSM to cover. Although the RSM had been saved, the fact that he had been hit bolstered al-Qaeda's morale again. The SAS were now two hours into their biggest skirmish since the Second World War and they feared there would be more casualties.

Small pockets of al-Qaeda resistance dotted around the compound were still offering heavy fire. Men were pinned down. An SAS man charging forward was hit. He had been hit twice in the left knee, the rounds ripping through his flesh and bone. Two men from G Squadron raced over open ground, through Kalashnikov fire, to get him. Once under cover, they applied a field dressing, known as a shell dressing because it was used to dress large wounds. Fifteen minutes later another ex-Para fell. He had been hit in the wrist and the chest. Fortunately, the shot to the chest had ricocheted off a ceramic plate in his body armour. It had knocked him down, but done no serious damage.

The fire support base was now silent. A Squadron had moved into their arcs of fire, so there was nothing they could do but make tea. Like typical squaddies, there was nothing they liked more than a brew, even within earshot of battle. Meanwhile, the casualties were arriving back at the fire support base, where they were given morphine to dull the pain – ironic given the nature of their mission, as morphine is refined from opium.

A Squadron then attacked the mud huts, but one spectacularly brave – or daredevil – al-Qaeda soldier started firing RPGs at them. This encouraged the others to stand up and return fire. However, they were soon cut down in all their joyful exuberance and, as A Squadron closed in, the man with the RPG was killed too.

The SAS assault force continued pepper-potting forward, clearing al-Qaeda positions as they went, until they were within reach one of the mud huts. Their walls were already perforated with bullet holes but the SAS men weren't taking any chances. The first man lobbed a high-explosive grenade inside. The second fired a burst through the window. Then they went inside to check for booby traps and kill anyone who might have survived. Then came the shout: 'Building clear!'

The first hut was then used as a fire base to take the second. The same standard operating procedure was used. They used the same combination of stealth, high explosives and small-arms fire. Then they rushed inside, where they were struck by the smell of cordite and human excrement. Now the SAS had two fire bases for the final assault on the AQT headquarters.

Seeing that the battle was lost, some al-Qaeda men fled, only to be cut down by the snipers at the fire support base. There was no escaping the Barrett's heavy .50-calibre round, which could make a man's head explode like a watermelon.

The assault team were now using the Colt M203 grenade launchers fitted under the barrels of their Diemacos to fire 40mm grenades into the headquarters building. The building was then cordoned off with SAS men alert to any movement. Although the building seemed deserted, they could not be sure that among the dead all around there was not some surviving al-Qaeda soldier who might be willing to give his life for Allah – and they were still in range of snipers who might have taken cover on Spot Height 2213.

Now they faced a key part of the operation. The other objectives – destroying the opium, the depot and its defenders – could all have been done from the air. The justification for risking lives on the ground was to gather intelligence from the al-Qaeda headquarters. Even so, once inside, the search party were given just 15 minutes to go about their work. The reason for the hurry was that the CO was worried that al-Qaeda reinforcements might soon be on them. But the search team could not be hurried – and be safe. Before they fled, the enemy might easily have set booby traps. As the SAS men cleared each room, they kept a wary eye open for tripwires. They also used standard operating procedure for any corpse that had to be moved. Any one of them might be rigged with explosives, so the SAS man moving it would lie on the corpse and turn it over so the body would roll on top of him. That way, if an explosive concealed under the body did go off, the corpse would act as a shield.

Inside, the headquarters also smelled of shit and cordite. The place had been trashed. But among the debris in the room that appeared to have been used as a command post, they found two laptops and a mass of paperwork. These were loaded into grab bags and the building was evacuated. On the way out, as on the way in, the SAS men scanned every room and every corridor. Meanwhile, the CO called Bagram and set up a rendezvous a safe distance from the depot where a Chinook could pick up the casualties and medevac them out.

The assault team then exfiltrated the depot. But to return to their Pinkies, they had to make it back across the open ground they had fought their way over. Again, they had to overlap and cover each other. There was no assurance that there were no more al-Qaeda men around. Even a dying man on the battlefield might want to make himself a martyr by taking out an infidel.

After four hours of battle, the men of A Squadron found themselves back on their Pinkies without further casualties. The CO had decided against going back the way they had come. Instead, they would avoid the soft sand by heading further west. This would also keep them out of the way of al-Qaeda reinforcements coming in from Kandahar.

As the convoy headed off with the CO in the middle, the motorcycles spread out around them, searching for any sign of the enemy. The column reached the emergency LZ in time to meet the Chinook, which took the casualties off their hands. From there, they headed back to the LUP, picking up the men from the broken-down Land Rover on the way. They arrived at 17.30 hours and after they had covered their vehicles with camouflage and had a cup of tea, the debrief began. Each man was asked to recall as much of the action as he could. The CO would then compile this information into a comprehensive report on the operation, which would be filed back at Stirling Lines.

After some well-earned sleep, they pulled off at 09.00, stopping for a resupply of fuel and water dropped from an RAF Hercules. Meanwhile, the casualties were on their way back to the Centre of Defence Medicine at the Queen Elizabeth Hospital in Selly Oak, Birmingham, England, to be treated. Although the man with two rounds to the knee was the most serious case medically, for the men of the SAS the RSM's injury caused the most speculation. To be hit in the calf, the shot must have come from behind. That meant that the RSM had been shot by one of his own men. Either that or he had been running away – and no one would believe that of the RSM, a Falklands veteran.

Meanwhile, Central Command in Florida were delighted with the outcome and requested that the SAS make further anti-opium raids. However, A and G Squadrons were told they would be home for Christmas, but they did see action again. Another SAS man was injured after taking evasive action when a US Chinook tried to land on his Pinkie. Then, three days after Operation Trent, an SAS convoy were approaching a small fort they had been told was friendly. However, the two motorcyclists leading the convoy were fired upon. Swerving to avoid getting shot, they found cover and returned fire. Two of the men in the fort were killed. The rest surrendered.

By 18 December A and G Squadrons were back in Hereford. Watching the news, they heard of the shooting of prisoners at Qala-i-Jangi, and were appalled to hear the SAS being blamed. British troops were there, but they were with the SBS.

CHAPTER FOUR

THE BATTLE OF QALA-I-JANGI

On 23 November, an eight-man SBS team were deployed by Chinook to Mazar-e-Sharif, some 250 miles (400km) to the northwest of Kabul. The fourth largest city in Afghanistan, it had fallen – with the help of Special Forces – to the Northern Alliance under General Rashid Dostum, but it seems clear that after the city had surrendered, there had been a massacre of about 520 suspected Taliban supporters.

For diplomatic reasons, the SBS went into Mazar-e-Sharif in plain clothes in Land Rovers painted arctic white, as if they belonged to the UN – even though they had GPMGs mounted on them. Reporting to the US military headquarters housed in a schoolhouse closed by the Taliban, they were seconded into a quick-reaction force.

Their first task was to observe the surrender of 600

Taliban to General Dostum out to the east of the city. It was a sensitive operation, so the SBS men kept their jeans and T-shirts on and hid their faces behind *shemags*, traditional cloth headdresses folded round their heads. Heading out to Kondoz, which was still under siege by the Northern Alliance, they stopped at a fortified mound that housed a Northern Alliance checkpoint around a mile from where the surrender was to take place. They were not to go any closer, as Dostum feared that the Taliban might change their minds about surrendering if they saw British and American observers there.

Through binoculars they could see tense negotiations going on between the Taliban and Northern Alliance soldiers. After several hours, the Taliban began handing over their rifles, machine guns and RPGs, but they were not searched to see if they were carrying any concealed weapons. A US Special Forces officer explained that this was not deemed necessary as the Afghans took each other at their word. If, as a good Muslim, a Taliban soldier said that he had no concealed weapon, that was good enough. It was the Afghan way.

The 600 Taliban were to have been held at the airport, along with other detainees. But US were now flying military missions out of the airport and were understandably reluctant to have the place teeming with the enemy. Instead, the prisoners were to be held in the old fort of Qala-i-Jangi – which means 'the House of War' – eight miles (12km) to the west. The joint US-UK quick-reaction force waited at the checkpoint and saw a truck laden with surrendered arms – Kalashnikovs, heavy machine guns and rocket launchers – drive by. It was followed by truckloads of prisoners. It seemed the surrendered weapons were headed for the same destination, the armouries at Dostum's headquarters at Qala-i-Jangi.

The following day, carrying only side arms, the quick-reaction force were sent out on a bodyguard mission to protect a US Navy admiral who was flying in to inspect a hospital that had been damaged in an airstrike and needed rebuilding. On the way, the SBS men passed Qala-i-Jangi for the first time. It was a hexagonal fort with a tower at each corner, 500 feet (152 metres) from end to end. Its sloping ramparts rose 60 feet (18 metres) above the desert. On top of them was a mud wall that rose another 10 feet (3 metres) with battlements along the top. It was an impressive sight.

When their bodyguard duty was over, the force were on their way back to Mazar-e-Sharif when they heard the sound of gunfire. It transpired that the Taliban prisoners held at Qala-i-Jangi did have concealed weapons on them. Their plan had been to overpower their guards, storm the considerable armoury in the fort and rearm their comrades. Two CIA men had been in fort at the time, interrogating the prisoners, and were thought to be hiding somewhere in its labyrinthine fortifications.

The quick-reaction force were ordered back to Mazar-e-Sharif, where they armed themselves. As their presence in the city was supposed to be discreet, the SBS team had brought only their Diemaco assault rifles and 9mm Sig Sauer pistols. They loaded up with 15 thirty-round 5.56mm magazines for the Diemacos and three magazines each for their pistols, giving each man 500 rounds altogether. They had no grenades, machine guns or heavy weapons. Nine 5.56mm magazines were hung on their webbing. The rest were slung in grab bag with the pistol magazines, a knife, torch, NVGs, field dressings, a 24-hour ration pack and water. They also carried a communications kit and laser target-designators in case they had to call in an airstrike.

The briefing was sketchy. The Taliban, it was known, had managed to break into the armoury and were well armed. The two CIA men had been at the southern end of the fort when they had been attacked. One of them had called on a satellite phone, but did not know what had happened to the other one. After that the satellite phone had gone down. It was presumed that the man who had called was still alive, so their operation was primarily a rescue mission. (The quick-reaction force boasted just 21 men – hardly enough to take the fort.) The missing CIA men were named Johnny Michael Spann and Dave Tyson. Once they were rescued, the next priority was to contain the enemy and stop the prisoners breaking out.

The good news was that some other CIA men and Northern Alliance soldiers still held the entranceway to the fort. The bad news was that they could not expect any reinforcements. The Delta Force contingent of Task Force Dagger and the rest of the Northern Alliance were still fully committed in Kondoz.

Like the SAS in Rigestan, the SBS were going into action without proper intelligence. It was not the way they liked doing things, but lives were at stake. The odds were not good, either. There were eight SBS men, ten US Special Forces operatives and some 50 to a hundred Northern Alliance soldiers against 600 Taliban holed up in a seemingly impregnable fort. While the SBS men had no heavy weapons apart from the GPMGs on their Land Rovers, the Taliban were armed to the teeth. The consensus was that they were on a suicide mission. But then the previous year the SBS men had been with the SAS-led operation to rescue British soldiers captured by rebel forces in Sierra Leone, where they had been outnumbered five to one. Officially known as Operation Barras, it had been dubbed Operation Certain Death by Special Forces. Even so, they had still come through.

At the time, Sierra Leone was in the middle of a civil war. In late summer, while on a UN peacekeeping mission, a group of Royal Irish Rangers were on patrol in heavily armed WMIK Land Rovers when they were captured by a ruthless gang of rebels, known as the West Side Boys. The rebels contacted the British authorities, demanding various ransoms and concessions. To aid negotiations, the British supplied the rebel leader, Foday Kallay, with a satellite phone, but this also enabled them to pinpoint the West Side Boys' location. Negotiations led to a number of the Rangers being released, but the rebels held onto a further six, plus their Sierra Leonean liaison officer. Despite the initial breakthrough, further negotiations broke down and the rebels began to threaten the lives of their hostages.

MI6 had determined that the seven hostages were being held at Geri Bana, a small camp on the banks of a river delta, Rokel Creek. Across the creek at Magbeni, about 440 yards (400 metres) away, was a large rebel base. The stolen WMIK Land Rovers were also at Magbeni and their heavy machine guns could pose a threat to any rescue mission taking place at Geri Bana.

D squadron of the SAS, augmented by a number of SBS men, were secretly flown into Sierra Leone to prepare for a hostage rescue mission. However, when it was discovered that there could be hundreds of troops at the Magbeni camp, it was decided to bring in 1 Para as well. Using inflatable raiding craft under cover of night, SAS Boat Troop personnel and SBS marines delivered two combined observation teams upriver. Concealed in the jungle foliage, they began monitoring the two camps, listening in on the rebels' conversations using parabolic microphones. As the assault teams rehearsed their rescue plans, the OP teams sent back vital intelligence on the strength, disposition and morale of the enemy forces.

The inflatables dropping off the observations teams had run into sandbanks, which ruled out an amphibious insertion for the main force. The observation teams reported that both the camp holding the hostages and the main rebel base were surrounded by heavy foliage, which ruled out a land insertion. This meant they would have to use a direct aerial assault, which would be risky.

The objectives of the mission were to rescue the six Royal Irish Rangers and their liaison officer, recover or destroy the captured WMIK Land Rovers, suppress or chase off the rebel troops and capture or kill the rebel leader, Foday Kallay, a former Sierra Leone Army corporal. The assault force would be inserted by three Chinook HC2 helicopters flown by RAF Special Forces 7 Squadron. Two Chinooks would carry integrated SAS-SBS fire teams – 70 men in all – who would be landing at two separate LZs. The third Chinook would carry a support team from 1 Para. Further support would be given by two

Lynx Mk7 attack helicopters from 657 Squadron of the Army Air Corps, armed with mini-guns, and a Mil-24 Hind gunship manned by the Sierra Leoneans. At first light on the morning of 10 September, the aerial assault force went into action.

Since stealth was out of the question, the plan was to hit the hostage camp and rebel base with maximum speed and firepower. The hope was that this would catch the West Side Boys off guard so they had little time to react or kill the hostages. The three Chinooks arrived over their LZs simultaneously. The SAS-SBS fire teams fast-roped out of the choppers, while the helicopter gunships opened up on the Magbeni camp. The first wave of Paratroopers was inserted by the third Chinook, which quickly flew back to base to pick up the second wave.

The element of surprise worked. Many of the West Side Boys were asleep or nursing hangovers when the assault force suddenly appeared over the hostage camp. The downdraft from the Chinooks tore the flimsy tin roofs off many of their shacks and to add to their confusion, the SAS-SBS observation teams emerged from the jungle and engaged the enemy. In the resulting mêlée, the SAS rescue team found and secured the hostages, while the SAS-SBS fire teams went through their carefully rehearsed plan, seizing objectives, clearing buildings and setting up defensive positions.

Across the creek, a fierce firefight erupted at the Magbeni camp. The first wave of Paras set up mortars and pounded the rebel positions, holding the line until they were reinforced by the second wave, arriving in the returning Chinook. Now at full strength, the Paras pressed home their attack. The fighting was ferocious and the men, women and boy soldiers of the West Side Boys were no pushovers. Despite their lack of discipline or any real sense of tactics, they seemed to be completely fearless. It is thought that many were high on drugs and believed that they were protected by magical amulets. They fought hard and seemingly without care for their own lives.

The battle raged for several hours before it was deemed safe enough to call in the Chinooks to extract the hostages. They were flown out to the landing ship RFA *Sir Percivale*, moored in the capital Freetown's harbour. Most of the action was over by 08.00. After conducting mopping-up operations that saw the capture of Foday Kallay and the recovery of the Rangers' three WMIK Land Rovers, the last British troops pulled out at 14.00 the same day.

The SAS lost one man, named later as Brad Tinnion, an ex-bombardier. As the SAS had begun moving the hostages towards a helicopter, they had come under heavy fire from West Side Boys on the unsecured south bank of the creek. Trooper Tinnion was hit. He was dragged into the helicopter but was dead on arrival at the *Sir Percivale*. The Paras had had 12 wounded, one seriously. At least 25 rebels were confirmed killed, although the number may be much higher, as many may have been killed by gunship attacks along the tree lines. The captured Foday Kallay was later sentenced to 50 years in jail.

Operation Barras was judged a success. It was the first time that the SAS had worked with the SBS integrated into their fire teams. It was also the first time that the Paras had been deployed alongside UK Special Forces. This mission template, with Paras providing security and carrying out secondary raids for UK Special Forces, has become a standard in the current War on Terror, and its success in Sierra Leone was one reason for the creation of the Special Forces Support Group now in action in Iraq and Afghanistan.

Even though the SBS had come back from Sierra Leone unscathed, the men seconded to the quick-reaction force in Mazar-e-Sharif still felt a sense of trepidation as they prepared to take on the fanatics at Qala-i-Jangi. It was 01.05 when the quick-reaction force left the city, giving them just six hours of daylight. As they approached the fort they could see tracers and the occasional trail of an RPG. From half-a-mile away, they could hear explosions and the crump of mortars as battle raged. When they left the metalled road and took the track leading up to the fort's entrance, large 80mm mortars began slamming into the ground around them. Their white Land Rovers made an easy target. One hit and it would all over, so the drivers gunned the engines and began weaving. Minutes later the two Land Rovers, followed by the US SOF Humvees, slewed to a halt under the shelter of the 40ft (12-metre) arch of the entrance to the fort. Their vehicles were full of bullet and shrapnel holes, but amazingly no one had been hit.

They were greeted by a CIA man who seemed pleased to see them. He gave them a quick briefing on what he knew about the situation, shouting to make himself heard above the battle. He did not know which parts of the fort were still in friendly hands, apart from the entranceway and the tower above it, which offered a good view over both the fort's north and south compounds. The prisoners had been held in the south part, although the fighting had originally broken out in the north. There may have been some beleaguered Northern Alliance men holding out in small enclaves, but it was impossible to communicate with them as they did not have radios. Nor did the CIA have long-range communications with them, as they had been returning to the US military centre in Mazar-e-Sharif each evening to file their reports.

By then the uprising had been going on for some 18 hours. It had begun when one of the Taliban prisoners grabbed a senior officer of the Northern Alliance and pulled the pin on a grenade, killing both of them and injuring a number of other Northern Alliance men. Northern Alliance soldiers had then herded the prisoners into the dungeons beneath the fort but, in their haste, had not searched them. Later, another suicidal Taliban pulled the same trick with a grenade.

The following morning, as the two CIA men, Mike Spann and Dave Tyson, were interviewing an American who had been with the Taliban, all hell broke loose in the dungeons. Spann had headed for the entrance to the dungeon shooting wildly in an effort to quell the riot. When he had run out of ammunition, he had been brought down by a crowd of escaping prisoners and beaten savagely. It was thought he had died, but no one could be sure. Some members of the International Red Cross, there to oversee the fair treatment of the prisoners, had managed to escape with the help of Northern Alliance soldiers. Tyson had loosed off a few shots, raised the alarm and had taken refuge in General Dostum's headquarters at the north end of the fort. As he was not certain what had happened to Spann, he urged headquarters not to send in an airstrike. Then the batteries in his satellite phone ran out and the line went dead.

Key to holding the fort was the eastern tower above the entranceway. From there they could cover both the northern and southern compounds, so the SBS were tasked with securing it. They rushed up the stairs to find the top of the tower held by half a dozen National Alliance men, who were pleased to get some help, though they were a little bemused by the fact that the SBS men were in T-shirts and jeans rather than a proper uniform. The SBS joined in a furious firefight with the enemy below and quickly proved their worth. The prisoners from the south compound had broken through into the north one and were heading for Dostum's headquarters. From there, they would be in position to dominate the fort, so they had to be stopped. This was also Tyson's last known position and the quick-reaction force's primary mission was to find the CIA men.

The men on the tower now fired on the escaped prisoners heading for Dostum's HQ. Like all Special Forces men, the SBS fired off two shots at a time, making every round count. The Northern Alliance men, like regular infantrymen, fired in long bursts. Too long. This allowed the enemy time to take aim, and one Northern Alliance man fell dead with a bullet through his forehead. Another fell back with a bullet through his right shoulder.

The SBS team leader tended the wounded man, but with two casualties they would now have trouble stopping the Taliban reaching Dostum's HQ. What they needed was more firepower. Two SBS men ran down to the Land

Rovers and undid the bolts holding the GPMGs with their Leatherman multi-tools. They then hauled the two guns and a crate of ammunition up the tower. As they did so, the American Special Forces captain arranged an airstrike. Now they had enough firepower to suppress the escaping prisoners and organise a rescue mission.

As they got the GPMGs to the top of the tower, a second wave of Taliban broke through into the north compound and made for Dostum's HQ. The machine guns mowed them down, but the intense volleys of fire returned by the enemy were chipping away at the baked-mud battlements, robbing the defenders of essential cover. Soon there would be nowhere to hide on the top of the tower, but if they had to abandon the tower, the battle was lost.

Meanwhile the Taliban had taken cover behind three of Toyota pickups and were well protected. The SBS men had no grenade launchers or anti-tank weapons to take them out, so they aimed the GPMGs at the trucks' fuel tanks instead. One burst of fire and they exploded. For a moment, the enemy fell silent. Then the fighting began again with renewed vigour.

Despite the intense firefight, the SBS team leader kept his eyes peeled and spotted a Taliban fighter with his Kalashnikov slung over his back, attempting to scale the tower with a wooden ladder. He squeezed off a shot with his Diemaco, sending the climber tumbling to the ground. A second man started to climb, followed by a third. Both were dispatched the same way. Then the SBS man put a couple of rounds into the ladder's upright, smashing it in two and putting it out of action.

While the SBS held the tower, the American Special

Forces mounted a rescue mission intent on Dostum's HQ – Tyson's last known position. This would entail a dash across the north compound, where they would be exposed to enemy fire. But like the SAS and SBS, the US Special Forces and the CIA make it a point of honour not to leave their men behind. Even if Spann and Tyson were dead, their bodies would have to be recovered. It would be a risky mission, but an SBS man and his oppo, a SEAL seconded into the regiment, volunteered to go with them.

The rescue mission was even more dangerous than they had imagined. Just as their dash across the north compound had begun, mortar rounds began falling. They threw themselves to the ground. When they got up again and resumed their dash, a National Alliance man was blown into the air with one leg shredded. They had run into a minefield. Everyone froze, but standing still was not an option. Mortars began heading towards then again. Mindful of where they were falling, the men hurled themselves to the ground. Then they got lucky. A couple of mortars that had zeroed in on their position sank into the soft earth and failed to explode. But that was merely a stay of execution. Stuck out in the middle of the compound, they were sitting ducks.

There was nothing else for it. The SEAL jumped to his feet and ran towards Dostum's HQ. The others steeled themselves and ran after him. Somehow, they all made it to the comparative safety of a doorway. After catching their breath, they started scaling the wall with Taliban bullets pinging around them. When they reached the top, two RPGs smashed into the wall below them, injuring two Northern Alliance men and sending them tumbling to the ground. The SBS man and his fellow SEAL quickly returned fire, killing the men who had fired the RPGs.

Close-air support was now on its way. Two of the SBS men on the tower crawled forward under intense RPG and mortar fire, and with their laser target designators they illuminated the gateway the Taliban were using to get into the north compound and the pink building they were coming from. The team leader then radioed through the target coordinates to the pilot, but at the Americans' insistence, they also supplied their own coordinates. This was against SBS standard operating procedures but without them, the American Special Forces men explained, there would be no airstrike.

As they were dangerously close to the target, the team leader asked the pilot not to use their 2,000lb (90kg) GPS-guided joint direct-attack munitions (JDAMs), only their 500lb (227kg) laser-guided bombs. As the pilot lined up for this bombing run, the Taliban began to break out through the gateway again. The SBS tried to contain them with the GPMGs. Then the F-18 Super Hornet wheeled into sight. The men watched the bomb drop and threw themselves to the ground as it smashed into the gateway, silencing the Taliban there. The SBS men felt the shock wave roll over them, followed by rumble and shrapnel. Then they jumped to their feet and finished off the remaining men who had made it through into the north compound.

The fort fell silent. Then, after 30 seconds, the firing began again with renewed intensity. Taliban reinforcements had reached the bombed-out gateway and were pouring fire onto the men who had called in the airstrike. It seemed there was no stopping the Taliban. They were happy to make suicidal attacks. Sooner or later they would get through. In Sierra Leone, the SBS men had faced women and child soldiers pumped up on drugs who had had no concern for their own lives. As a foe, perhaps they were preferable to the religious fanatics of the Taliban. These men actively sought martyrdom.

The SBS men shared a last cigarette and prepared to die. Death they did not mind. In these circumstances, it was preferable to being captured alive. Taliban zealots were happy to torture those they considered *kaffir*, or a lowly infidel.

Now the Taliban began to burst through the ruins of the gateway again. Two SBS men on the tower alternated bursts of 60 to 80 rounds. This ensured that both guns did not jam or run out of ammunition at the same time. It also allowed the guns to cool, preventing rounds 'cooking off'. If one of the GPMGs failed on them, it would be all over. They had been fighting now for about an hour. Their only hope lay with a second airstrike that was now on its way.

Meanwhile, the rescue team were infiltrating Dostum's headquarters. But first they had to make another quick dash over open ground on an upper tier. What they needed was close-air support but the airstrike was still five minutes out. In the meantime, all they could do was hold their position and return fire.

Then they heard the F-18 roar overhead and when the bomb hit the gateway, the order came: 'Go! Go! Go!' They hit the ground running and raced across the open ground to Dostum's HQ. When, after the initial shock, the Taliban opened up again, they caught the rescue party in the open.

The highly trained Special Forces men fell flat on the earth and quickly turned to pepper-potting to continue their advance. The Northern Alliance men had not been taught this manoeuvre and fell like flies.

The SBS man shouted at the remaining Northern Alliance men, encouraging them to make for a baked-mud wall that offered a little cover. As he inched his own way towards it on his belly, bullets kicked up dust all around him. Some Northern Alliance men followed. They too reached cover, but now they were stranded. The intense Taliban fire was also chipping away at their protection. As with the other SBS men on the tower, their only hope lay in another airstrike.

The Northern Alliance men, like their Taliban enemy, were Muslims and happy to sacrifice their lives in the hope of entering paradise. This, however, was not part of SBS standard operating procedures. Instead they got on the radio to find out when the next airstrike was coming. The answer was that it was six minutes away. Could they hold out? It was then that the rescue team in the northern compound heard the reassuring sound of GPMGs from the tower blasting their attackers.

Although they were still pinned down, the rescue team began crawling on their bellies along the wall in the direction of Dostum's headquarters. They were halfway there when the mortar barrage started up again. The SBS man radioed to his colleagues on the tower to take the mortar crew out, but they could not locate them. But then relief was at hand as they saw the second 500lb (227kg) bomb flying above them. As it hit, they were on their feet, sprinting the last ten yards to the comparative safety of the stout mud wall outside the entranceway to the HQ. Moments later the Taliban machine guns opened up again. The enemy were unstoppable.

The SBS men were just contemplating the last dash to the entranceway when 30 Taliban came hurtling across the compound with cries of 'Allahu Akhbar' ('God is great'). The SBS man and his SEAL colleague turned and fired. The oncoming Taliban returned fire, holding their Kalashnikovs held at waist level. Although the Special Forces men were picking them off one by one, they were relieved when a GPMG opened up, scything them down.

One man who fell had pulled the pin on a grenade. When it went off, it detonated the others he was carrying and the rescue team leapt for cover. When they looked up, all that was left of the man was his pelvis and legs, and his fellow Taliban lay dead around him.

In the following lull, the rescue team contacted headquarters in Mazar-e-Sharif. Nothing more had been heard from the two CIA men. Then they heard from the SBS team leader on the tower who was acting as forward air controller. The next airstrike was ten minutes away, so they decided to postpone their final dash to Dostum's HQ until then. After what seemed like an age, they saw the bomb falling and began the dash. The Northern Alliance men, who were not so heavily laden with equipment, surged ahead, but their reward was a burst of machine-gun fire. The Taliban had a .50-calibre heavy machine gun zeroed in on the door to the HQ. The Special Forces men reacted quickly, diving for what little cover there was. Now they were between a rock and a hard place, caught out in the open with bullets pinging around them.

The Special Forces team had now been fighting for two and a half hours and the Taliban, despite their losses, still showed no sign of flagging. The SBS team leader called in four more airstrikes on the gateway, then another two on the southern compound of the fort. One laser-guided bomb hit the pink building where most of the Taliban were taking shelter. After each attack, there was a brief period of silence. Then the gunfire started up again. It was plain that no amount of airstrikes was going to deter the Taliban.

It seemed to the SBS team leader that the Taliban were managing to reinforce the men at the gateway from some hidden source. They must have a pool of men waiting in the corridors and dungeons under the fort where they were safe from the effects of the bombs hitting their fellow believers up above.

However, the bombing was having some effect. As the sun set, a Taliban ammunition dump began to cook off. For around half an hour there were no further attacks. But it seemed they had further caches of weapons. Mortar fire and gunfire then concentrated on the men on the tower. It seemed plain to the SBS that, for the mortar crew to zero in on them, the Taliban must have a spotter on some elevated position overlooking them. They looked but could not find him. Nor could they find the mortar crew, who moved between rounds to avoid being located. However this meant that the fire was not as accurate or as deadly as it could have been.

Nevertheless, it was time to move on. They headed around the battlements towards the tower on the northeast of the fort, halfway to General Dostum's HQ. On the way, they picked up more Northern Alliance men. These reinforcements had been sent back from Kondoz, where Dostum had the Taliban under siege. They zeroed their GPMGs on the ruined gate again and waited.

The rescue team outside Dostum's HQ then got a message from headquarters in Mazar-e-Sharif. It seemed that Dave Tyson had managed to escape from the fort and had turned up back at base, so the rescue mission was called off. Tyson believed that Spann had been killed but they had yet to find his body. The situation was now dire. The rescue team were getting short on ammunition. Dusk was falling. In the twilight it was going to be difficult to distinguish between friend and foe. They decided to pull out for the night and resume the search for Spann's body the next day.

But the SEAL was not happy. There was no proof that Spann was dead. He might be lying injured somewhere. Worse, he might be in the hands of the Taliban. While the other men were pulled out he raced back towards the western tower and began scaling it. The SBS man, his oppo, had no choice but to follow him. When they realised what was happening, the rest of the Special Forces rescue team also decided to follow suit and turned back towards Dostum's headquarters. While the main body of the team burst into the HQ, the SBS man followed the SEAL towards the western tower. Ahead he heard gunfire. His buddy was already involved in a firefight.

By the time the SBS man caught up, the SEAL had run out of ammunition and was continuing the firefight with a Kalashnikov he had taken from a dead Taliban. Under cover of darkness, the two men edged forward. They knew that on top of the northwestern tower was a Taliban position with a Dushka. The Dushka, or DShK M1938, is a Second World War-vintage Soviet heavy anti-aircraft machine gun that fires 12.7 x 108mm rounds. Mounted on wheels and with an armour-plated gun shield, it can also be used as a heavy infantry machine gun. (It took its name from the Vasily Degtyaryov, who designed the weapon, and Georgi Shpagin, who improved the feed mechanism. The K comes from *Krupnokaliberniy*, which means 'large calibre', while *Dushka* means 'dear' or 'sweetie' in Russian.)

The Dushka on the northwestern tower was now the pair's objective. They had gone just 15 yards (13.7 metres) when it opened up. But it seemed to be aiming at the wall behind them. Perhaps the Taliban had not spotted them, so they got to their feet and ran for the base of the tower, reaching its entranceway. This was the sort of manoeuvre they had been trained for. Covering each other, they made their way up the stairs of the tower. Above them, they could hear the machine gun loosing off suppressing fire into the gloom. As they burst out of the stairwell, they took the three Taliban fighters completely by surprise. The machine-gunner tried to turn his Dushka on them, but took a bullet to head. The other two were dispatched before they could react. It was a perfect Special Forces hit.

The SBS man now grabbed a Kalashnikov. His Diemaco was down to its last rounds but, like all Special Forces men, he had been trained to use enemy weapons, just in case. With the Taliban out of the way they now had the Dushka, too. The SBS man took over the gunner's seat, giving cover to the SEAL, who headed around the wall, still hell bent on finding his compatriot.

The SEAL was about 150 yards (137 metres) away when the SBS man saw a figure lurking in the dark and loosed off a burst from the Dushka to distract attention from his oppo. It worked, but the burst of fire warned the Taliban that the machine-gun post was in enemy hands and it now came under fire. But with the Dushka in his hands, the SBS man had enough firepower to take on anything they could throw at him.

When the enemy fell silent, the SBS man listened intently between squeezing out the odd burst of suppressing fire. When he heard sporadic gunfire from the direction of his SEAL buddy he grew worried. After a while the SEAL returned, ashen. He had found a body he took to be that of Mike Spann but, on his own and under fire, there was no way he could recover it.

The two men then withdrew to meet up with the rest of the rescue party. They had searched General Dostum's headquarters building and found nothing. With the SBS men from the battlements, they decided to return to base in Mazar-e-Sharif for the night and leave the Northern Alliance to do their best to contain the enemy.

In the ride back to town in the Land Rovers, everyone was quiet. They had been fighting for six hours and were exhausted. They were relieved to have survived – on several occasions they had thought that they faced certain death. But who knew what the next day would bring, or how long the siege would last?

When they reached the schoolhouse in Mazar-e-Sharif, it was dark. The first thing they did was break out more ammunition. If something at the fort kicked off during the night, they wanted to be ready. As they refilled their magazines, they assessed the day's fighting. The enemy they had been facing, they realised, were not Afghans. They were what the mujahideen used to call Arab Afghans – Egyptians, Saudis, Chechens, Pakistanis, Yemenis, Algerians, Sudanese and assorted Europeans and Americans – foreigners who had rallied to the Taliban's cause. Nor were they prisoners in any normal sense of the word. They had only pretended to surrender so they could stage this attack from inside the fort with the weapons stored there. They had not handed over all their arms, nor had they refrained from further fighting after agreeing to surrender in the honourable Afghan way. Some were skilled fighters, leaving cover to deliver a couple of shots, then disappearing before you could get a bead on them. The others were so suicidally fanatical that the ordinary Afghans among the Northern Alliance could not understand them. What had saved the day for the SBS was their training.

After a cup of tea, there was a debrief. The escaped CIA man, Dave Tyson, was on hand. He explained that he had escaped through a window at the back of General Dostum's headquarters, scaled the outer wall, then scrambled down the ramparts. It was the same way the Red Cross workers had got out before, but he had left it until the last moment when darkness was falling and he was certain that there was nothing more that could be done for Mike Spann.

It was now assumed that Spann was dead. This meant the quick-reaction force could change strategy. The Taliban, they knew, had more than enough weapons and ammunition, both those they had sneaked into the fort after surrendering and those from the arsenal that General Dostum had stored there. Irrigation ditches ran under the walls, so they had water, and they had food in the form of horses killed in the crossfire. This meant they could hold out for weeks. However, getting into the fort to get the weapons stored there made sense only if they then intended to break out as part of a grander strategy.

A CIA man gave his assessment. The AQT still held the south of their former stronghold Kandahar. There were some 6,000 AQT armed with heavy artillery in Kondoz. If they broke out and linked up with the forces from Qala-i-Jangi, they could take Mazar-e-Sharif. If they succeeded, the Northern Alliance would find themselves trapped between them and the AQT forces in Kandahar. This meant that the fighting force in the fort must be neutralised.

It was plain that the SBS-Special Forces team did not have nearly enough men to storm the fort. Nor did they have anything like enough men to besiege it. The only way they could thwart the enemy was to call in more airstrikes. That meant that they would have to go back into the fort the following morning and act as forward air controllers, directing the bombing raids. After liaison with Central Command, it was decided that these would start at 06.01 hours.

The best place to set up an OP was on the west tower, because it overlooked the whole of the south compound. As they had spent most of the previous day defending the eastern tower, this would give them the element of surprise when they went back in the morning. This would be the job of the Special Forces rescue team with the SEAL and his SBS oppo attached. The SBS guys who had occupied the eastern tower the day before would retake it and keep the enemy busy from that side too.

In the morning they awoke to hear that six Taliban had escaped from the fort during the night and raided a nearby village, slaughtering women and children. The men of the village had grabbed their guns, tracked down the Taliban, killed them and hung their bodies from the trees as a warning to others.

At 05.10 hours, the SBS-Special Forces team left the US military headquarters in Mazar-e-Sharif. Twenty minutes later they reached Qala-i-Jangi. This time they parked a few hundred yards from the fort, out of range of the Taliban's weaponry. From there they proceeded on foot, arriving at the walls just as dawn was breaking.

As the team tasked with retaking the eastern tower approached, they were warned by the Northern Alliance that the mortar crew who had given them so much trouble the day before had zeroed in on the entranceway to the tower. Once inside, the team relocated to the northeastern tower, skirting a large minefield on the way. On top of the tower they found a Soviet T-55 battle tank with its gun pointing towards the south compound. It had been driven up the ramparts by the Northern Alliance during the night, the crew explained. Although they were happy to have some extra firepower, the SBS were a little worried about having the tank on the tower as the fort had certainly not been built to carry that sort of weight and they feared that, if the tank loosed off a 100mm round, the recoil would bring the whole tower tumbling down.

By 05.45, the SBS had set up their GPMGs and their

communications equipment on the northeastern tower. The sun was not yet up, nor had the Taliban spotted them. The previous day's rescue team were now in position on the western tower. They had with them a Northern Alliance soldier who knew the layout of the fort well. He pointed out two targets they should hit. One was the pink building, General Dostum's stables, where the Taliban had taken shelter. The other was the main ammunition store. The SEAL painted them with his laser target designator, while the SBS man relayed the coordinates and identifying features. The stables were 250 yards (228 metres) away; the ammunition store 150 yards (137 metres). This was dangerously close, especially as the F-18 Hornet was armed with a 2,000lb (907kg) JDAM, which it had to drop first.

Exactly on schedule they heard the scream of the JDAM falling and took cover. The shockwave rolled over them, sucking the air from their lungs. Then they leapt to their feet and started letting loose with their Diemacos. They were met with an unexpected volley of return fire. Then they realised that the explosion had not been nearly as big as they had expected, given that the JDAM was to have landed so close to their position. A quick inspection revealed that the target had not been hit. Then they heard an English voice over the radio calling for a medic, and when they looked towards the northeastern tower, they saw it had been hit. Quickly they hit the radio and, in the nick of time, aborted a second airstrike.

The situation was confused. The main SBS team was supposed to be on the eastern tower, not on the northeastern one. The SBS man with the rescue team was a medic, so he and his SEAL oppo headed for the northeastern tower to find out what was going on. When they reached it, a terrible scene greeted them. The JDAM had hit the tank on top of the tower, killing the crew and all the Northern Alliance men around it – 20 men in all. Fortunately, fearing the weight of the tank would bring the wall down, the SBS and the American Special Forces men had spread out around the battlement away from the tower and the tank had shielded them from the full power of the explosion. Nevertheless, they were wandering around in a state of shock. One Special Forces man was plainly suffering from internal injuries. Some of the SBS men were buried under the rubble of the collapsed tower and were dug out alive.

The SBS man from the rescue team did what he could to patch up the wounded and they called for help. Within minutes a quick-reaction force from the 10th Mountain Division was on its way. They could not get there fast enough, as the Taliban seized the opportunity to fire on the wounded, who had neither the strength nor the weapons to fire back. When the quick-reaction force arrived, they quickly set up six M240 heavy machine guns to pump out suppressing fire while the wounded were evacuated. The rest of the Special Forces team accompanied them. Eleven injured men had to be taken out. The walking wounded were taken to Mazar-e-Sharif, while a helicopter was called to pick up the more serious cases. It would land about a mile outside the fort to medevac the stretcher cases out.

As they were getting the stretchers out of the vehicles ready for the pick-up, a news crew coming down the road stopped and began filming them. When asked to stop, the cameraman took the camera down but kept filming surreptitiously. The SBS and SAS are secretive organisations whose members and their families could face reprisals from the terrorist outfits they face. They need to keep their identities hidden and are naturally sensitive about being photographed or filmed. They also were on covert operations, which would be compromised if they had their faces all over the media, so one of the SBS covered his face with his shemag and walked up to the cameraman with a pistol in his *hand*. The news crews fled. Asked by a buddy if he would have shot the cameraman, he said no. He would have taken the man out into the desert to put the shits up him, then put a couple of bullets in his camera.

Once the wounded had been dealt with the team had to decide what to do next. Back at the schoolhouse in Mazar-e-Sharif, they assessed the situation. As if things had not been bad enough before, they were now seriously under strength. They had lost 20 Northern Alliance men, along with the firepower of their tank. Half the US Special Forces men were out of action, but the SBS men had come through with only a few minor cuts and bruises. The worst injuries were suffered by two men who had had their eardrums blown in. After a cup of tea, they felt better.

An officer with the US military police then turned up to debrief them. All blue-on-blue incidents had to be thoroughly investigated. The CIA stumped up $40,000 to replace the gear they had lost, plus $200,000 for a new laser target designator. They also went into prolonged negotiations with the Northern Alliance over their losses – including the T-55 battle tank the JDAM had destroyed.

The Northern Alliance also returned the Diemacos and other British gear they found in the rubble of the tower.

For the rest of the day, the Northern Alliance managed to contain the Taliban inside the fort unaided. There were sporadic exchanges of mortar and small-arms fire, but no serious attempt was made to break out. Perhaps the foreign Taliban were waiting for an outside force to arrive from Kondoz or Kandahar.

That night at 22.00 hours, a team of bruised and bandaged SBS men returned to Qala-i-Jangi. They watched as an AC-130 Spectre gunship circled over the fort, pounding targets with shells and large-calibre machine-gun rounds. Inside the fort, the Taliban mortar crew prepared to respond, only to receive a barrage of 20mm rounds. Then the AC-130 hit the main armoury, leaving the sky above the fort bathed in white light. As the Spectre flew off, the SBS men cheered.

The following morning they returned to the fort. They had expected to get a cold reception from the Northern Alliance, who had lost so many men in the blue-on-blue air attack. Instead, they were greeted warmly. The Northern Alliance knew it was the Americans who were responsible for their losses, not the British.

Even though they had received compensation for the lost laser target designator, the SBS men began digging in the rubble to see if they could find the old one. But then they came under fire. Although the Spectre gunship had taken out the mortar crew and the armoury, most of the Taliban fighters had taken refuge in the dungeons below the fort and survived the gunship's attack.

Meanwhile General Dostum had left the siege at Kondoz

to come to Qala-i-Jangi and take charge. He was appalled that the Taliban who had surrendered had not behaved honourably, as a good Afghan should. Breaking your word in such a manner was against all the tenets of Islam. Two captured Taliban commanders explained that the Afghan Taliban had behaved according to the Afghan code of honour. They had laid down their arms and returned to their villages. Those in the fort, who had broken the code, were foreigners. The Taliban commanders offered to try to re-establish the original surrender deal, but anyone who approached the fort was fired upon. As there was no other way to make contact with those inside, it was impossible to reopen negotiations. There was no alternative. It would be a fight to the death.

Dostum was also concerned about his horses, the cream of Afghanistan's cavalry mounts. He was furious when he heard that some had been killed and eaten, and the order was passed down that no one should risk killing any more horses in the crossfire.

For the rest of the day, there was little more they could do but contain the Taliban. The SBS men trained a GPMG on the window of a building where the Taliban were holed up and poured bullets through it. But it did little good. The Taliban simply kept their heads down when the SBS were firing, but popped up again when they stopped. The day ended with another stand-off and the forces returned to base at the schoolhouse at Mazar-e-Sharif. The SBS men spent that evening trying to think up new ways of breaking the siege, but failed.

The following morning, back at the fort, the Northern Alliance told the SBS that there were only a handful of

Taliban left inside. The SBS men knew this was not true. True, only half-a-dozen appeared above ground at a time, but the rest remained down below in the dungeons in case there was another airstrike. As they had no fresh ideas, the SBS resumed the strategy from the day before, aiming the GPMGs at the windows of Taliban refuges with the rest of the men sniping with their Diemacos.

As this was getting them nowhere, General Dostum decided to send his men in on a frontal assault with the SBS giving them cover. This, the SBS knew, would be suicidal. He would be sending men across open ground against an enemy that had good cover. Hundreds would be killed and nothing would be achieved. They tried to persuade the general that the infantry assault should be led by a tank. That way, his men would have some cover. The general was less than enthusiastic. He had already lost one tank and did not want to risk losing another. The SBS pointed out that the only heavy weapon the Taliban now possessed was an RPG. Only a very lucky shot with an RPG could take out a tank, especially if the tank kept front-on to the enemy positions. If it kept its distance it could hammer the Taliban with shells, which would at least keep their heads down until the Northern Alliance infantrymen got to them. Finally, the general saw the logic of the SBS's plan and a second tank was brought up.

As the T-55 trundled forward with Northern Alliance men taking shelter behind it, the Taliban rose to the bait, peppering the heavy armour plating on the front of the tank with small fire and RPGs – to no effect. Every time a Taliban put his head up to fire, an SBS sniper was on him. When the tank entered the south compound, it stopped and fired a shell into the main building where the Taliban had been taking refuge. It reloaded and fired again. The Taliban now had no choice but to launch a desperate counterattack. But it was too late. The shelling of the building blocked the entranceway to the dungeons below. Their main force was now trapped underground and anyone emerging from the rubble was cut down by the SBS marksmen.

Then the Northern Alliance troops moved in. Clearing away the rubble, they tried to enter the dungeons below, but anyone attempting to descend the stairs was shot at. By the time a dozen men had been hit, they pulled back behind the tank, then withdrew to tend the wounded.

The following day, the SBS resumed their positions on the battlements of the fort. The Northern Alliance began a second sweep, this time trying to locate the body of Mike Spann. As they did so, they came under fire from fresh enemy positions. It appeared that the Taliban had taken refuge in other underground chambers, some way from the main stronghold. The Northern Alliance responded by dropping grenades though the ground-level ventilation portals, followed by a burst of machine-gun fire.

Then a truck full of fuel drums was brought up. Diesel oil was then pumped into the basement and a phosphor grenade thrown in. A huge flame burst out of the entranceway. The idea was that anyone down below would be burned alive or asphyxiated. However, though many were killed by the grenade, the heavy diesel oil refused to ignite. Sporadic bursts of defiant gunfire could still be heard. However, the Northern Alliance had now located Spann's body and brought it with them when they withdrew again. A fellow CIA man covered it with an American flag and said a short prayer before it was loaded onto a truck and taken away. That evening at the schoolhouse in Mazar-e-Sharif, the SBS formed a guard of honour for Spann as his body was loaded onto a Chinook and flown out on the first leg of its journey back to the States. Afterwards, another CIA agent began questioning the SBS about whether they thought Tyson had done enough to help Spann. The SBS men disliked the implication of the questions and refused to cooperate.

The next morning, day six of the siege, the SBS drove back to Qala-i-Jangi and entered the south compound. It was a scene of utter devastation. Burned and mutilated bodies were surrounded by spent ordnance. Some of the dead still had their hands tied together. Beside them some 30 horses lay dead. The smell of death was overwhelming. The Northern Alliance were looting the bodies, a dangerous pastime as some had been booby-trapped with grenades that went off if the body was turned over.

Nor was the fighting yet over. Northern Alliance soldiers tasked with removing the bodies heard voices from an underground chamber and were cut down by a short burst of fire. Others rushed forward and dropped grenades down the ventilation shafts. There was a boom down below, but then came answering fire. The Northern Alliance emptied the magazines of their Kalashnikovs down the ventilation shafts and dropped in more grenades, but they had no way of knowing how effective this was, as no one was keen to go down below and check.

Over a cup of tea, the SBS figured out how to finish off the siege once and for all. The plan was to fill the entire basement of the fort with water. That way, the Taliban would either have to give up or drown. With the aid of the Northern Alliance, they diverted one of the irrigation ditches so it discharged into the basement. They left it filling the dungeons with freezing water all night and returned to Mazar-e-Sharif.

The next day the SBS were back at Qala-i-Jangi at 06.30 hours to find an old fire truck had been brought up to pump in more water. Eventually the survivors down below could stand it no longer. At 07.00, an SBS man spotted movement in the entranceway to the basement and raised his Diemaco. A bedraggled Taliban dragged himself up the stairway blinking into the light. The SBS man kept his finger on the trigger, but did not pull it. The man might have a grenade concealed under his clothing. Two Northern Alliance soldiers forced him to his knees and frisked him. They took his boots and cuffed his hands behind his back. He was followed by 12 more Taliban, making their way hesitantly up the stairway one at a time. Some were still clutching their Kalashnikovs. Others were blackened with diesel oil.

But no one knew how many more were still down there. At 10.00 hours, the SBS saw further movement on the stairs. One by one, 50 more Taliban emerged, some with shocking wounds. One man told his captors that he was an American. His name was John Walker Lindh and he was the so-called 'American Taliban' that Mike Spann had been interrogating before he was killed. Lindh had a bullet in his thigh and was taken to Mazar-e-Sharif for treatment and interrogation. Other prisoners taken said he had been present when Spann was tortured and finally killed.

Shipped back to the US, Lindh later faced ten capital

charges. In a plea bargain, he pleaded guilty to two in return for a sentence of 20 years with no parole. He also had to sign a secrecy agreement and drop all allegations of maltreatment and torture at the hands of the American authorities. In court, he pleaded guilty to being a member of the Taliban and carrying an AK-47 and two grenades, knowing it to be against US law. He is now serving his sentence in a medium-security prison in Indiana.

After being disarmed, the Taliban fighters were marched barefoot down a path to a waiting truck. Some were so exhausted that they could not make it that far and had to be carried on the stretchers the Northern Alliance had been using for removing the dead. Red Cross workers turned up and began distributing food, though most of the survivors were too weak to eat. One Chechen with a shrapnel wound to his leg continued mouthing off about killing the unbelievers, not realising that some of the Northern Alliance men could understand Russian. They told him in no uncertain terms to shut up. The Chechen then begged for someone to tend his wound. A Red Cross worker stepped forward to do so, but this provoked an angry reaction from the Northern Alliance. Why were these foreign workers feeding and tending these men who had tried to kill them just a few hours earlier? One Northern Alliance soldier threatened to smash the Chechen's head in with the butt of his rifle. The Taliban had killed his son, he said. His comrades restrained him.

In all, 86 Taliban gave themselves up. After the last one had emerged, Northern Alliance soldiers went down into the basement to check for booby traps. Then the SBS team leader went down to see for himself. At the bottom of the stairs he found corpses floating in the oily scum. It was dark and cold and the air was foul. No one knows how many men had died down there. Just 150 bodies were recovered and most of the 600 Taliban prisoners held at Qala-i-Jangi remain unaccounted for. Some of the bodies would have been obliterated completely by the bombing.

The Northern Alliance lost 50 men, including the 20 killed in the JDAM friendly fire incident. The US Special Forces had five men seriously injured. One had had his hip shattered. All had lost their hearing temporarily but regained it after their ruptured eardrums healed. They had black eyes from concussion and lacerations from shrapnel, but only one American, Spann, had been killed. All of the SBS men lived to fight another day.

When the world's media, who had been covering the siege of Kondoz, reached Qala-i-Jangi, questions were asked. Some accused the SBS of being complicit in a massacre of Taliban prisoners. Amnesty International called for an inquiry. There were also questions about the efforts made to rescue Mike Spann. His father felt that his son might still have been alive when the SEAL first spotted his body and that if a greater effort had been made then, he might have survived. The suggestion has also been made that Spann committed suicide rather than fall into the hands of the Taliban.

The official story is that former Marine Johnny Michael Spann had been alive when he fell into the hands of the Taliban. Both legs had been broken below the knee in a fashion known to be a favourite al-Qaeda torture method. He was kept live for some time. He had been shot twice in the small of the back, on either side of the spine, in a way that would deliberately cause pain rather than be life-threatening. Some time later he was killed by a bullet in the back of his neck, thought to have been inflicted when he was kneeling with his arms tied behind his back. His death would have been a long and painful one.

After an exhaustive inquiry, the JDAM friendly-fire incident was attributed to human error. However, in future the Americans would adopt the SBS's standard operating procedure of giving the coordinates only of the target, not of the friendly forces giving them, precluding the possibility that the pilot would mix them up.

For their part in the action at Qala-i-Jangi, the SBS men were awarded the American CGM – Conspicuous Gallantry Medal. The British are more secretive about their awards to Special Forces, rarely naming names unless the man concerned is dead, but the SBS commander and another man received high gallantry awards and two were mentioned in dispatches. The US Navy SEAL attached to the SBS received the US Navy Cross and the British Military Cross, which he received personally from the Queen. For their efforts to rescue two of their men, the CIA sent a telegram of praise for the SBS to the British government. General Dostum also sent his thanks.

By the time the siege at Qala-i-Jangi was over, the battle for northern Afghanistan was won and the SBS were tasked with providing security for the rebuilding of schools and villages that had been damaged in the fighting. The siege at Qala-i-Jangi raised the SBS's public profile worldwide, but it remains one of the most controversial actions of the war.

CHAPTER FIVE
TORA BORA

While Task Force Dagger and their Northern Alliance allies were closing in on Kandahar, the SAS were tasked with attacking a mountain hideout of mud-walled compounds and cave bunkers southeast of the city. A number of high-ranking AQT men were stationed there within easy reach of the Pakistani border in case they needed to flee. The SAS were also to take out an al-Qaeda training camp and headquarters in the same region. In cooperation with the Joint Special Operations Command in Fort Bragg and the Joint Special Operations Task Force base at K2 in Uzbekistan, the British Permanent Joint Headquarters in Northwood, Middlesex, had planned a classic search-and-destroy mission. SAS Sabre teams would be sent in to hit the complexes fast, killing anyone who resisted and taking prisoner those who complied.

From satellite photographs it was possible to identify four cave entrances at the first objective. Two four-man teams would hit it, with two 12-man teams to give covering fire and support. The main force was to be dropped by American Black Hawks on a ridge a little way from the complex. The men would then have to walk ten miles over rough terrain in their ceramic body armour, carrying a full load of ammunition, fragmentation grenades, belt-fed GPMGs, Diemacos, pistols and battlefield medical kits. Another 12 SAS men would be dropped six miles closer by small and stealthy MD-500 Little Bird helicopters. Armed with the shortened, silenced version of the Heckler & Koch MP5 – the MP5 SD3 – that the SAS favoured for close-quarters combat, they would act as an advance party reconnoitering the area.

When the advance party reached the complex, they identified five, rather than four, cave entrances. Through their NVGs, they could see a ventilation shaft, a VHF antenna and two satellite dishes. They could also see five defensive positions dug into the surrounding hills.

The main force arrived two hours before the operation was scheduled to start. The US Joint Force Air Component Command had offered the support of an AC-130 Spectre gunship, provided it was not needed by another team engaged in the area. Once everyone was in place, the troop sergeant major signalled ten minutes to go. It was still dark. No active infrared illumination was used in case the AQT had old Soviet night-vision equipment, but through their passive NVGs four snipers zeroed their cross hairs on the four guards, who appeared to be sleeping. The teams radioed in that they were ready.

The advance party was hiding just 20 yards (18 metres) from the main entrance to the cave. Suddenly an al-Qaeda man came stumbling out of the cave stopping just feet from them, before squatting down and answering the call of nature. He did not appear to have seen them, but they could not take that chance. Twenty 9mm rounds from two separate gunmen hit him, knocking him flat. The only sound was the noise of the Heckler & Koch bolt recycling. It carried through the thin mountain air to the ears of the other SAS men, who were in a state of high alert.

'Contact, repeat, contact,' whispered the advance party leader into his radio.

'Steady, lads,' answered the mission commander. 'One minute.'

But they did not have a minute. Twenty-nine seconds later, one of the sentries woke – stirred perhaps by the sound of the H&K or his comrade falling. He stood up and looked round. A bullet hit his head. It exploded. A second later, the other three snipers hit their targets and were acquiring a new one. The SAS troopers needed no order. The operation was now under way.

The assault teams hit the cave entrances at a full run. Two AQT men emerged firing their Kalashnikovs and were cut down by sub-machine-gun fire. One SAS man was injured, hit in the left shoulder and in the left side just below his ceramic armour. Inside, the cave was just 30 feet (9 metres) deep. Twenty AQT men were asleep side by side on rugs. They were quickly dealt with, and soon the assault team sounded the all-clear.

Outside, another bunch of AQT men emerged from a bunker the SAS assault team had not spotted, but the trooper commander on a nearby outcrop saw them. He alerted his men by radio and the AQT were cut down by machine-gun fire.

The assault team dragged their wounded man out of the cave and began first aid. One of them radioed for a medic from the support team and marked the position of the downed man with a beam of infrared light. The medic and his oppo were quickly on their way. They were still 150 feet (46 metres) away when AQT marksmen on the opposite hillside opened up, pinning them down and cutting them off fore and aft. Then they began lobbing RPGs. The troop sergeant major moved forward to the rescue the stranded Special Forces men while a machine gun provided covering fire.

Lobbed like mortars, the RPGs could not be aimed and fell indiscriminately. One hit the rocks over one SAS man's head, injuring him. He and his mate close by were stunned by the explosion, and two more men moved up to their aid. The AQT then attacked in force. They plainly expected to overrun the position easily and kill the SAS men, but they found that they were running directly into the muzzle flashes of two GPMGs, which spat withering fire.

Two hours later, the sun was up and the fighting was over. Twenty-two AQT men were dead and 17 captured, more than half of them wounded. Five had surrendered as soon as the fighting kicked off. Another six had been cuffed with plastic bindings inside the bunker directly the SAS assault teams went in. The rest had given up when they saw their colleagues being gunned down by machine-gun fire or the precisely aimed bullet of a sniper – though the snipers had had a difficult job because the muzzle flashes of the machine guns temporarily blinded their NVGs.

Four SAS men had been wounded. The troop medics on hand stabilised their condition and medevac helicopters were on their way to whisk them the 500 miles to a Royal Navy hospital ship in the Arabian Sea. Then the medics moved on to treating the wounded prisoners, while the rest of the force searched the area for other survivors or joined the picket to watch for any AQT reinforcements coming their way.

The SAS were involved in a number of these lightning attacks. Task Force 11's Little Birds – fitted with forward-looking infrared for night flying, engine-noise suppressors, air-to-ground rockets and 7.62mm mini-guns – would swoop on a target, inserting a six-man team to snatch key Taliban or al-Qaeda officials in the hope that one of them could be persuaded to reveal where Osama bin Laden or Mullah Omar was.

Later, Air Vice-Marshall Sir Jock Stirrup, head of the Permanent Joint Headquarters at Northwood, received a request from Central Command in Florida for more SAS and SBS men to assist American Special Forces searching the Tora Bora cave complex where Osama bin Laden was thought to be hiding. The Australian and New Zealand SAS would also be involved in the operation.

Tora Bora lies in the Tangai mountains, which separate Afghanistan from Pakistan. It is a lawless region, home to bandits and smugglers. The narrow roads there are cut into the sides of the mountains, dangerous for sure-footed pack animals and impassable for four-wheeled vehicles. The cave complex at Tora Bora had been used by the mujahideen as a base during their war with the Soviets. Just 31 miles (50km) west of the Khyber Pass and six miles (10km) inside the Federally Administered Tribal Areas of Pakistan, it is said to be a labyrinthine underground fortress on the scale of those built by Hitler under Berlin. According to US intelligence, there were underground ammunition dumps, command-and-control rooms furnished with the best communications equipment bin Laden's millions could buy, sleeping quarters, dining facilities and everything else an army needed to survive.

Despite the might of the Red Army, the Soviets had never managed to dislodge the mujahideen from Tora Bora. The US Army was unlikely to do any better, particularly as they feared taking casualties. Since US public opinion had turned against the Vietnam war, American politicians were terrified of televised coverage of body bags being returned home, so if bin Laden was there, he could continue to thumb his nose at the West indefinitely. But though the firepower of the US Army might not succeed against a fortress like Tora Bora, Special Forces might just be able to take it. And as their activities are largely covert, if they failed it would not be catastrophic in public-relations terms.

As the Taliban collapsed throughout the rest of Afghanistan, intelligence came in that al-Qaeda and the Taliban's foreign fighters were planning to make a last stand at Tora Bora. It had been bin Laden's headquarters during the jihad against the Soviets and it was where he had started al-Qaeda with his mentor, the radical cleric Sheikh Abdullah Azzam. It was Azzam who had invited bin Laden to come to Afghanistan from his home in Saudi

Arabia in 1979, although the two men subsequently fell out when bin Laden set up his own force of foreign fighters in 1988. Azzam was killed by a car bomb soon after. Bin Laden's foreign fighters became al-Qaeda – which means 'the base'. The base was Tora Bora.

By 10 December 2001, there were 50 US special operatives on the ground in the region. But for the final assault on Tora Bora, Central Command asked Jock Stirrup to transfer all available British Special Forces men to Tora Bora. MI6 gave their approval. If Osama bin Laden was in Tora Bora, they reasoned, the SAS should be there too. Permanent Joint Headquarters at Northwood decided they could spare two troops – half a squadron – of SAS men. These were flown in by US Task Force 160 Chinooks to join the Green Berets, who arranged safe houses for them. The SAS's primary role would be strategic reconnaissance, an SAS speciality, but they had already proved their worth in search-and-destroy missions against cave complexes and would be used as a rapid-reaction force if al-Qaeda were spotted trying to escape over the border. The SAS and Delta Force were tasked with hot pursuit into Pakistan.

While the SAS and US Special Forces got on famously, there was a rift between the British and Americans at government level. British Defence Secretary Geoff Hoon announced that if the British captured bin Laden, they would hand him over to the Americans only if they gave an undertaking that he would not face the death penalty. This was a requirement under the European Convention on Human Rights, but it did not sit well with the Americans, whose servicemen had been authorised by their commander-in-chief, President George W Bush, to kill bin Laden. But on the ground this rift was only notional. No SAS man intended to take bin Laden alive.

As they moved into the area of Tora Bora in December, the anti-Taliban forces recruited by the Green Berets took the ridgeline and a small village called Milawa when caves used by al-Qaeda for storing weapons were discovered. Four al-Qaeda men were killed by Special Forces snipers, but rumours circulated that bin Laden had escaped. It seems he had been warned by an al-Qaeda man who had run off with $5,000 he had been given for information. The unfortunate consequence for the man was that, in subsequent fighting, 20 members of his family were killed.

As the Special Forces moved into the region, they identified targets that were then bombed. It was thought that some 600 al-Qaeda men were killed, but this was speculation as it is hard to get accurate casualty figures after airstrikes. However, it is known for certain that large numbers of al-Qaeda men were killed by snipers.

Al-Qaeda then put out peace feelers. On the night of 11 December, they sent a radio message to the Northern Alliance offering to surrender. Negotiations were entered into and al-Qaeda agreed a ceasefire at 08.00 on 12 December. However, there were conditions. They would surrender only to United Nations personnel. Meanwhile, they tried to make another backroom deal and attempted to persuade the Northern Alliance to withdraw so they could fight the British and Americans. They had no wish to kill fellow Muslims, only the infidel.

Neither deal worked. The Americans would not accept any conditional surrender and they were footing the bill.

The National Alliance told al-Qaeda that they could indulge their foreign fighters' most fervent wish and arrange for them to visit Allah personally. Local anti-Taliban leader Hazrat Ali, who had 8,000 seasoned men in the area, added his own personal condition to any ceasefire with the AQT. It was that al-Qaeda must hand over bin Laden.

Hazrat Ali was one of a number of local warlords competing for the $25 million reward the US had offered for the capture of bin Laden. Unfortunately, the reward had rather confused things. Junior commanders held back good intelligence for fear that they would not get a slice of the reward and that all of it would be taken by the senior warlord. CIA and Special Forces men on the ground also pointed out to Washington that a cash reward was of little incentive to the Afghans, who measured their wealth in sheep, goats and Toyota Land Cruisers. It would have been better to offer to equip and supply any faction that caught bin Laden. That way everyone in that force would get a share.

To make absolutely clear to al-Qaeda that they were in no position to put conditions on their surrender, when the 08.00 deadline arrived, America sent in the B-52s, dropping smart bombs into the mouths of the cave where they were sheltering. Special Forces snipers were on hand to pick off those fleeing as they climbed up the surrounding mountains. For good measure, at 10.00, a 15,000lb (6,800kg) BLU-82 'daisy cutter' bomb was dropped at the entranceway of a cave complex, filling the valley with smoke and dust. This sent the surviving al-Qaeda men scuttling up towards the frozen mountaintops with everything they could carry. Once over the ridgeline they ran straight to an SAS team who were doing strategic reconnaissance along the eastern slope facing Pakistan.

To avoid any further blue-on-blue incidents, anti-Taliban forces were withdrawn at night, giving Special Forces equipped with night-vision equipment a free-fire zone where they could kill anyone they came across. They were armed with M24 7.62mm sniper rifles accurate up to around 2,900 feet (900 metres) and Barrett Light 50s, which can fire a heavy .50-calibre bullet some 3,280 feet (1,000 metres). Even at that range, the heavy shell could knock out a truck.

As the fighting around Tora Bora intensified, Prime Minister Tony Blair sent another 60 SAS men to Afghanistan, bringing their numbers up to 110. Alongside the Green Berets and Delta Force, they helped to clear out the remaining al-Qaeda men hiding in caves. Surgical strikes were made, using the close-quarters battle skills they had learned in their counter-revolutionary war training. At night, SAS snipers would pick off anyone making their way over the mountain passes. At least once they claimed to have had bin Laden in their sights, trapped in the small valley of Tora Bora, and the plan was to send one squadron into the valley to flush him out. When he headed for the furthest pass in an attempt to escape, the other squadron would be waiting to kill anyone who crossed their path. Delta Force were eager to join in and they were promised air support.

Although everyone involved in the planning of the operation was confident that it would succeed, the US commands in America pulled the plug. They knew al-

Qaeda had SAMs and they would not risk any planes coming in at below 12,000 feet (3,658 metres). (At that time, they did not have any attack helicopters or A-10 Warthogs – the first US plane to be designed specifically for close-air support – in the country.) This was extremely frustrating for the Special Forces, who felt that they were not being allowed to do their job. But because of that US fear of seeing men returning in body bags, there would be devastating political consequences if a jet fighter was brought down. It seemed that the Washington administration had not heard the SAS motto: 'Who dares wins.'

The stand-down was particularly hard for the SAS to bear, as they had friends in high places and it was perfectly possible for an SAS commander to put a call through to 10 Downing Street. But the US Special Forces rarely enjoyed similar privileges with the White House.

On 12 December, the fighting flared again, possibly initiated by a rear guard buying time for the main force's escape through the White Mountains into the tribal areas of Pakistan. Once again, tribal forces backed by US special-operations troops and air support pressed ahead against fortified al-Qaeda positions in caves and bunkers scattered throughout the mountainous region. Twelve British SBS commandos and one British SAS Royal Signals specialist accompanied the US special-operations forces in an attack on the cave complex at Tora Bora.

At 02.00 on 14 December, bin Laden was overheard on the radio. He was still in Tora Bora, though he was preparing to leave. A two-man sniper team were sent in. At 14.00 on 15 December, they radioed back that they had a positive identification on bin Laden. The entire team could have been there in half an hour, but the team leader refused to give the order without consulting high authority. When the request climbed the chain of command, it was denied. The operation was considered too risky. It could have been a trap and bin Laden was lost again.

Next time overflight surveillance spotted activity – 45 men entering a cave thought to be al-Qaeda's command control centre – Task Force Dagger's HQ contacted the SAS and sent them maps and pictures. The SAS men quickly prepared their kit. As they were going into a cave, they replaced their ball ammunition, which would ricochet off the walls, with ceramic rounds, which would shatter. They also abandoned their 'flash-bang' stun grenades for the more deadly high-explosive fragmentation variety. Two Delta Force men would accompany them – a liaison with the Joint Special Operations Task Force (JSOTF).

They planned to enter the cave at first light. That meant a long trek during the hours of darkness, but with the help of GPS, they were in position as dawn broke, having identified four tunnel entrances. One or two four-man teams would enter each, with additional teams remaining outside guarding the rear. They checked there was a bullet in the chamber, flicked off the safety and went in. Once inside they switched on their flash lights. The first team made contact immediately. Two sleeping al-Qaeda men awoke in the torch light, grabbed for their guns and were killed instantly. A third man was also cut down. By now every al-Qaeda man in the place was awake.

There were more al-Qaeda men than they had expected. Others were sleeping in bunkers on the other side of the slope, and they now took on the teams who were waiting outside the caves. The first SAS man to be hit inside the cave was dragged out, only to find himself under heavy fire from al-Qaeda on the next ridge. A second SAS man went down with bullets to his leg and hip. They called for close-air support, then cancelled it as al-Qaeda closed in. A 500lb (227kg) bomb on the al-Qaeda position would have hit the SAS too.

MD-500 Little Birds brought 24 more men with 7.62mm belt-fed GPMGs. But the only place close enough that was not under fire was two miles away, which meant a four-mile round trip over that rocky terrain. Then two more Little Birds came in. Once they had al-Qaeda in sight they gave the order for the SAS to take cover. After scything through the enemy with their mini-guns, risking small-arms fire and RPGs, they finished off with a couple of rockets each. Then they made off with requests for more ammunition ringing in their ears. The SAS were getting mighty low.

The fighting lasted for four-and-a-half hours. At the end, 38 al-Qaeda lay dead, 50 more were wounded and 21 captured – mainly Arab, Chechen and Pakistani. As well as the two wounded SAS men, ten more had bullets embedded in their armoured chest plates. The wounded men were flown back to Britain, while the prisoners were taken to the jail in Jalalabad and delivered into the tender mercies of Hazrat Ali.

Search-and-destroy operations continued but they did not find any massive underground fortresses, only small bunkers and outposts and a few minor training camps. As the caves were cleared out, it became clear that al-Qaeda did not have the sophisticated complexes that intelligence imagined. Most of the caves were shallow, sometimes with crude ventilation shafts. Munitions were stacked inside and there were mats for men to sleep on. Occasionally documents were found or laptops left behind that rendered some useful intelligence. The numbers on cases of Chinese, Russian and American ammunition were also good sources. The US ammunition, it turned out, had been brought from American manufacturers, using American money, by Pakistan, who had then shipped it on to the Taliban and al-Qaeda.

Despite the success of these missions and the intelligence they produced, the US commanders did not favour missions that put fighting men on the ground. Instead they preferred precision bombing. However, blowing up the cave entrances simply sealed the caves, along with any intelligence material that might be inside. No excavation operations could be undertaken easily in that remote area. Indeed, it would have been almost impossible to get the earth-moving equipment necessary to that location. Osama bin Laden could have been dead in one of the caves and no one would have known about it. (It is thought bin Laden and his main force escaped through the White Mountains into the tribal areas of Pakistan.) Instead tribal forces, backed by US special-operations troops and Coalition air support, attacked fortified al-Qaeda positions in caves and bunkers throughout the region.

During the attack on Tora Bora, one SAS man – the RSM – won the Conspicuous Gallantry Cross, awarded 'in recognition of an act or acts of conspicuous gallantry during active operations against the enemy'. It has been awarded just 15 times since its introduction in 1993. Despite having been seriously wounded, the RSM took on the enemy armed only with his commando knife. He had been hit at least twice by enemy fire, yet somehow managed to get back to his feet and continue fighting, before resorting to his knife as the conflict descended into savage hand-to-hand contact. The medal was presented in a private ceremony with the Queen in 2002. The citation praised his 'outstanding leadership in drawing his knife and charging the enemy, inspiring those around him at a time when ammunition was running low and the outcome of the battle was in doubt'.

By 17 December 2001, the last defenders had been overrun and the area secured. Four SAS teams were left behind to mop up. Other teams were inserted into the Kandahar area to the south, near the Pakistani border, where they assaulted Mir Wais Hospital after remnants of the Taliban and al-Qaeda barricaded themselves in. Another team were assigned to protect Gul Agha Sherzai, who had regained his position as governor of Kandahar after the Taliban vacated the city on 7 December. Sherzai was dismissed as 'warlord of the year' by Robert Fisk of the *Independent*.

CHAPTER SIX
OPERATION ANACONDA

With the decline of the Taliban as a fighting force that held territory, the role of Special Forces changed. They began interdiction (taking out enemy lines of communication) and search-and-destroy missions, making commando-style raids, usually under cover of night, on villages suspected of harbouring members of al-Qaeda or Taliban personnel. The Special Forces of all the Allied nations got involved. A SEAL unit called Task Force K-Bar, which was led by a Navy commodore and included German, Canadian, Danish and Norwegian Special Forces personnel, was involved in raids and surveillance in southern Afghanistan. The British SAS were employed in operations along the Kwaja Amran mountain range in Ghazni and the Hada Hills near Spin Boldak. They went in at night by helicopter, storming villages, using stun grenades and grabbing suspects, who were whisked away for interrogation.

In early March 2002, the US Special Forces Group's Task Force 11, Task Force Bowie and Task Force Dagger, along with the Australian and New Zealand SAS and the German KSK, led elements of the US 10th Mountain Division, 101st Airborne Division, British Royal Marines, Canada's 3rd Battalion, Princess Patricia's Canadian Light Infantry and the Afghan National Army together in Operation Anaconda, an Allied push to clear al-Qaeda and Taliban forces out of the Shahi-Kot Valley and Arma Mountains southeast of Zormat.

It began on 1 March, when US Special Forces infiltrated the area and set up OPs. Teams India and Juliet, taken primarily from the Delta Force, were to take positions at the north and south ends of the Shahi-Kot Valley, where they could watch the approaches from Gardez. The third team, Mako 31, a SEAL unit, were tasked to set up an OP on a geographical feature known as the Finger, where they could observe the LZ for Task Force Rakkasan – the 187th Infantry Regiment of the 101st Airborne, who got their nickname 'Rakkasan' (from the Japanese for parachute) during their occupation of Japan after the Second World War. On their way, the SEAL unit saw a group of Afghan fighters with a Russian Dushka in a position that would have threatened the Chinooks bringing in the first wave of US troops. They made plans to destroy the emplacement at D minus one hour. Any earlier and the enemy would have been able to replace the Dushka, and they would have been warned that an attack was coming.

The following day US and Afghan forces began to

sweep the Shahi-Kot Valley to root out rebel forces regrouping in there. At around midnight, the units of Task Force Hammer loaded their vehicles and left their base in Gardez for the valley. Task Force Hammer consisted of a large force of Afghan militia led by Zia Lodin and the Special Forces A-team Texas 14/ODA 594. The road was in poor condition and several soldiers were injured when their trucks overturned. It was then decided that the trucks should switch on their headlights to see where they were going, although this would destroy any element of surprise.

Further down the road, a convoy led by Army Chief Warrant Officer Stanley L Harriman of the 3rd Special Forces Group split off from the main force and set out for its assigned OP. An AC-130 aircraft called Grim 31, which was providing fire support and reconnaissance for the assault, spotted them but due to a problem with the plane's navigation system, the aircrew failed to identify the convoy as American. As a result, Grim 31 engaged the column, killing CWO Harriman and wounding several US Special Forces and Afghan militia before orders were sent telling it to break off.

The main body of Task Force Hammer reached its start line around 06.15 hours and waited for what they had been told would be an aerial bombardment lasting 55 minutes. In fact, only six bombs fell before one got stuck in the launch bay of a B-1B Lancer on its run. While the next bomber waited for the B-1B to get permission to jettison the bomb and go round again, both planes and the two F-15E Strike Eagle fighters accompanying them received orders telling them to cease the bombardment.

There may have been some confusion here, and this order may have been the one telling Grim 31 to cease fire.

With the men already demoralised by the lack of air support, Task Force Hammer's trucks were raked with accurate enemy mortar fire at key points along the road. Plainly, al-Qaeda had been expecting an attack, and the anti-Taliban Afghans suffered more than 40 casualties. Indeed Task Force Hammer's attack stalled even before they entered the valley, due to unexpectedly heavy small-arms and mortar fire, and the close-air support they had been promised was assigned to Task Force Anvil on the other side of the ridge.

At 06.30 hours on 2 March, the first wave of Rakkasans and Mountain troops were landed by helicopter along the eastern and northern edges of the valley to await the fleeing fighters at their assigned blocking positions. However, they came under fire almost immediately and were pinned down by heavy mortar fire throughout the day. Instead of the 150 to 200 fighters they had been expecting, they found between 500 and a thousand dug in on the high ground surrounding the valley, and the first wave of Rakkasans and Mountain troops had brought just one 120mm mortar with them. They received fire support from the Apaches of the 3-101's aviation brigade but after suffering 28 killed, they were airlifted out that night.

It was not all bad news. Throughout the day, the Special Forces reconnaissance teams who had infiltrated the area the previous day called in airstrikes from B-1s, B-52s, F-15s and F-16s, inflicting heavy casualties on hundreds of Taliban and al-Qaeda fighters. The Australian SAS provided in-depth operational intelligence and Signalman

Martin 'Jock' Wallace was awarded the Australian Medal for Gallantry.

A hundred Australian SAS men were involved in Operation Anaconda. 'We landed early in the morning and walked straight into an ambush,' said Wallace. In fact, they were put down on top of an al-Qaeda stronghold, a tunnel complex about which they had had no intelligence. Seconds after touching down, they were caught in a withering crossfire and Wallace had a rocket-propelled grenade fired straight at him. 'The round hit the ground and slid through the mud,' he said. 'It basically chased us up the hill as we ran from it and it just lay there steaming in the ground as we were scrambled for cover.'

If it had gone off, he would almost certainly have been killed. But though Wallace and his comrades had survived, there was another problem. The American soldiers with them had dropped their backpacks as they ran for cover in the opening attack. These packs contained their ammunition and radio equipment and were in full view of the al-Qaeda machine-gunners. The US troops now had no hope of recovering this vital gear.

Fortunately, Wallace had not dropped his pack. He had kept hold of his radio, so they could communicate directly back to Bagram. Even so, the odds were not good.

'Al-Qaeda got on to the western ridge,' said Wallace, 'which meant that they were behind us, so the guys who were shooting at the al-Qaeda on the eastern ridge were now taking rounds in the back.'

SAS commander Colonel Rowan Tink, who was listening on the radio link as al-Qaeda closed in, was convinced that they were not going to get out alive. Using their knives and their bare hands, the SAS men began to dig in. Al-Qaeda then began mortaring them, targeting the only mortar the Coalition force had.

'I was just lying there, watching them out of the corner of my eye,' said Wallace, 'and about five or six of them disappeared in a puff of grey smoke. It was basically a direct hit on the American mortar from the al-Qaeda mortar.'

The survivors were badly injured. 'We had guys with chest injuries,' said Wallace who, like all SAS men, had had some basic medical training. 'There were open fractures, basically fragmentation wounds, some over their entire bodies.' It was clear that he would have to go out there, pull the injured men to safety and dress their wounds. Putting himself in harm's way, he moved out under fire, collected some of the wounded and dragged them back into the comparative safety of the dry creek bed where they had found cover. It was this action that won him the Medal for Gallantry.

Al-Qaeda laid down heavy fire and fought more fiercely than had been anticipated. 'These guys were definitely committed and they were there to fight to the death – and we accommodated them,' said Wallace.

According to Colonel Tink, the assumption that the ground commander of Operation Anaconda, General Hagenbeck, and his staff had made was that, at worst, his men should be facing a stalemate in that position. 'This was perhaps a little bit overoptimistic,' said Colonel Tink. 'On the afternoon of the first day there was no doubt that we knew we had a real battle on our hands.'

Even Hagenbeck realised they were in trouble. 'The

medics had called for air evacuations,' he said. 'In fact, on one occasion, the helicopters were en route and I had to turn them around in mid-air to take them back out of there because it was clear to me that they would be shot down.'

By then, 30 Americans had been wounded and now lay in the creek bed with Signalman Wallace for some protection. Things were so desperate that a B-52 bomber was called in to hit the al-Qaeda positions, though barely a few hundred yards separated them from the American and Australian soldiers. It was a dangerous situation.

'I was lying on my back watching the B-52s come overhead,' said Wallace, 'and you could see the bomb-bay doors open and the bombs as they started to fall. You're just hoping that they're going to be on target and not on your position. When you're dropping things from 30,000 feet [9,144 metres] and they're not laser-guided, it's definitely a recipe for disaster.'

When the bombs hit, Wallace could feel the initial shockwave coming through the air and the ground, followed by the noise of the shrapnel whistling overhead. Undeterred, al-Qaeda continued their attack and the Americans and Aussies were now running low on ammunition. A lot of their machine-gun ammunition was in the backpacks that they had dropped, and these packs still lay in a position so exposed to enemy fire that was impossible to retrieve them. The Americans had completely run out of 7.62mm ammo for the heavy machine guns. Their only mortar piece had been taken out, so they were basically down to personal weapons. Meanwhile, the enemy kept up their withering attack.

'Probably the heaviest fighting was around last light,

when they managed to dominate both of the ridge lines and launched a ground assault from the north,' said Wallace. 'By the end of that they had set up a machine gun in the south, so they had us surrounded. That was probably the scariest part of the whole day.'

For 18 hours, machine-gun fire, mortars, RPGs and SAMs hammered the encircled troops. It was estimated that the Coalition forces were up against a thousand AQT fighters, outnumbered ten to one. 'There was no chance of reinforcements: they would have been cut to pieces by the surrounding force,' said Wallace.

American Apache attack helicopters tried to rocket the al-Qaeda positions. But the entire hillside basically opened up with small-arms fire, and that was the last they saw of the Apaches. 'They copped a caning and then limped off the battlefield,' said Wallace. Only when darkness fell were the AC-130 Spectre gunships allowed in. 'It was a survival situation,' he said. 'Without air cover, we would have been wiped out.'

Relying on his intensive training, he helped direct a strike by AC-130 gunships on the enemy.

'We were able to divert enough firepower to keep the al-Qaeda from massing their forces and overrunning them,' said General Hagenbeck. 'So, all the way up to the time that they were extracted, we were concerned about that, but you need a little luck on your side, and we had it that day.' That air power and the greater capacity for the coalition soldiers to fight effectively at night saved them, he said. At midnight, a fleet of Black Hawks lifted them out. Battle-damage assessments estimate that they left behind 500 AQT dead.

While the Australian SAS were acquitting themselves so well in the Shahi-Kot Valley, the SBS were back at Bagram, where they watched in some frustration as ranks of US Special Forces men lined up to board a fleet of helicopters that would take them out on Operation Anaconda. However, the deployment began with a disaster. When the Special Forces men hit the ground, they found they were dropping straight into snow up to their waists and were pinned down by the heavy machine gun nests AQT had hidden under rock outcrops. As the casualties were medevacked out, the SBS at Bagram found themselves being pulled into the field hospital as the Americans urgently needed trained medics. US Rangers, who had been the first in, were coming back with their arms and legs all shot up within the first few hours.

The following evening, Lieutenant Colonel Blaber, commander of Task Force 11, was told that two SEAL teams commanded by Lieutenant Commander Vic Hyder were on their way to Gardez. The SEAL teams, Mako 21 and Mako 30, were to establish an observation point on the peak of Takur Ghar, which commanded the Shahi-Kot Valley. They needed to be inserted by helicopter before dawn. It was suggested that they be dropped some 4,260 feet (1,300 metres) east of the peak.

They were supposed to have set off at 11.23 hours on 3 March, but one of the Chinooks broke down. The delay meant that the SEALs would have to be dropped on the peak itself, otherwise they would not reach it by dawn. An AC-130 gunship reconnoitred the peak and saw no enemy activity, but was called away before the two Chinooks carrying the SEALs, Razor 03 and 04, arrived.

At around 02.45 hours, Razor 03 landed on the peak and was struck in the left-side electrical compartment by an RPG. As the stricken helicopter took off, Petty Officer First Class Neil Roberts fell out of the open ramp. Razor 03 tried to return and retrieve him, but the damage prevented proper control and the helicopter crash-landed some four miles (6.5km) away in the valley.

Roberts managed to activate his emergency beacon. His only weapons were a pistol and two hand grenades; his light machine gun had not fallen out of the chopper with him. The men on the helicopter saw three al-Qaeda fighters begin moving in on him. Roberts crawled towards better cover, engaging the terrorists with the pistol and grenades, but he soon ran out of ammunition. Nobody knows exactly what happened next. Images broadcast by a Predator unmanned aerial vehicle showed the three men dragging him away. A rescue team later recovered his body. Roberts had died from gunshot wounds.

Soon afterwards, Razor 04 arrived at the LZ to drop the other SEAL team, Mako 30. As soon at the SEAL team hit the ground they too came under fire. A US Air Force combat controller, Technical Sergeant John A Chapman, was hit and two SEALs were wounded. Mako 30 were forced off the peak due to their losses and called the quick-reaction force at Bagram airbase for help.

The quick-reaction force consisted of 19 Rangers, a tactical air-control party and a three-man US Air Force special tactics team. It was carried by two Chinooks, Razor 01 and Razor 02, and led by Captain Nate Self. Due to difficulties with satellite communications, Razor 01 was directed to the hot LZ on the peak by mistake. At around

06.10 hours, Razor 01 reached the LZ and immediately came under attack. The right-door mini-gunner, Sergeant Phillip Svitak, was killed by small-arms fire, and then an RPG hit the helicopter, demolishing the right engine and forcing it to crash-land. As the quick-reaction force left the helicopter, Sergeant Brad Crose, Specialist Marc Anderson and Private First Class Matt Commons (promoted posthumously to corporal) were killed. The rest of the force and the surviving crew took cover in a hillock and a fierce firefight ensued.

As Razor 01 was landing on Takur Ghar, Razor 02 had been diverted to the town of Gardez. It now rode in with the rest of the quick-reaction force and Lieutenant Commander Hyder, arriving at 06.25 hours. With the help of close-air support, the small force was able to consolidate their position on the peak. However, fog had closed in in the Shahi-Kot Valley, which meant the Predator surveillance drones were often useless.

Fortunately, a six-man Australian SAS team had infiltrated the day before and remained undetected. They, however, were having trouble with the bitter cold. 'Quite a few of us are Queenslanders and had never seen snow before until we went to Afghanistan,' said one of the men. 'The novelty wore off after about five minutes.'

On a nearby peak, dozens of Rangers were trapped and under fierce attack. The Australian team reported the situation back to the Coalition command tent, where the feeling was close to despair. 'These men were way behind enemy lines,' said Colonel Tink. 'They were isolated on the top of the mountain. Clearly, they had been engaged by some heavy machine guns and, at that particular stage, we were unsure how long they'd be able to survive. We knew they had dead and wounded there.'

Luckily for the Rangers, the SAS were in place. 'You had to have someone there on the ground,' said General Hagenbeck, 'that could see and hear and smell and pick up the sense of the battlefield of what was going on. We were very much dependent upon the Aussies, certainly in that part of the battlefield.'

The Australian SAS team coordinated a constant barrage of bomb and rocket attacks on the advancing fighters, and called in multiple airstrikes to prevent al-Qaeda from overrunning the downed helicopter. The enemy counterattacked at midday, mortally wounding Senior Airman Jason D Cunningham. Under the direction of the Australian SAS, AC-130 Spectre gunships were brought in to give close-air support. Even then, the al-Qaeda barrage was so intense that US troops could not be medevacked out during daylight hours for fear of another downed helicopter.

Finally, at around 20.00 hours, the quick-reaction force and Mako 30 were rescued from the peak of Takur Ghar. Along with the survivors, the helicopters carried the bodies of seven Americans – Roberts and six of his would-be rescuers. Eleven more were wounded. The ridge was named Roberts' Ridge by the US troops in memory of their fallen comrade. The SBS men working as medics back at Bagram were particularly affected, as the SBS and SEALs often swapped personnel and consequently knew each other very well.

The Australian SAS men continued to provide this niche capability to the Americans during Operation Anaconda.

'We were able to remain deep behind enemy positions undetected for long periods of time,' said Colonel Tink, 'and provide them with valuable information, which was very detailed. In fact, a number of reports I handed over, I remember various Americans being amazed at the detail we were able to provide on dress, equipment, activities, where these people were positioned, et cetera, et cetera.'

The value of this specialist support did not go unnoticed. 'I tell you, I would not have wanted to do that operation without the Australian SAS folks on that ridge line,' said Hagenbeck. 'I mean, they made it happen that day.'

By the time the Aussies returned to base, word had got around. 'It was almost embarrassing, to the point where the Americans were so glad of our help,' said one of the patrol. 'You might go to a meal night in a mess, there might be a hundred people in front of you, all Americans, and all of a sudden they would step aside, maybe even applaud, and push you to the front of the line. We were looking pretty wild and woolly, but we were taken aback by it and a bit embarrassed.'

Despite all the Americans' fancy gadgets, the SAS had proved their worth again. 'I think there's one important lesson I took out of Afghanistan in regard to technology,' said Colonel Tink, 'and that is, at the end of the day, the technology has to be designed to *support* the man, not *replace* the man. And I think we demonstrated that through our reconnaissance and surveillance capacity.'

Shortly after the fiasco on Roberts' Ridge, the US set up a revenge mission to punish al-Qaeda. US Delta Force troops led the payback, and invited several men from DEVGRU – the Naval Special Warfare Development

Group, formerly SEAL Team 6 – to join them, as Roberts had been one of their men. An SBS man on secondment to the SEALs was on this assault. A US Predator was following an al-Qaeda convoy and the ambush team were dropped on the ridgeline along its route. When they spotted the five-vehicle convoy in the valley below them they opened up with everything they had. The AQT fighters who managed to get out of the vehicles were hardly able to raise their weapons and return fire before they were taken out.

Once the firefight was over, the Delta and SEAL ambush force went down to search the 20 or so bodies. There were few Afghans among them: most were Arabs or Chechens. Several of the dead were wearing US Army webbing, which the Americans angrily ripped off. But one of the al-Qaeda men was still alive and as a US soldier turned him over, the wounded man detonated a grenade. Luckily, his body took the brunt of the blast, which caused few injuries to the ambush force.

The Americans also retrieved a US Army GPS and a night-sight from the dead. When the serial numbers were traced, it turned out that they had been taken from US soldiers killed or captured in Somalia, during the US military intervention in Mogadishu in 1993.

By 12 March, US and Afghan forces had swept through the valley and cleared it of remaining rebel forces, and on 18 March Operation Anaconda was declared officially over. But that was not the end of the hunt: on 15 April 2002 Operation Mountain Lion began in the Gardez and Khost regions.

Then, on 18 August, the Army Rangers and other

coalition Special Forces joined the 82nd Airborne Division on Operation Mountain Sweep. They mounted five combat air-assault missions on the area around the villages of Dormat and Narizah, south of the cities of Khost and Gardez. The troopers found an anti-aircraft artillery gun, two 82mm mortars and ammunition, a recoilless rifle, rockets, RPGs, machines guns and thousands of small-arms rounds. They also detained ten people.

A week after the end of Operation Mountain Sweep, reports surfaced in the *New York Times* that some US Special Forces commanders wanted to quit the futile search for Osama bin Laden. Indeed Special Forces forward operating bases (FOBs) were regularly coming under attack. The base three miles northeast of Sarabagh had been under more or less constant bombardment during March. By mid-May, reportedly six rocket attacks had been made at Orgun-e, Khost and Miran Shah.

And so it went on. A US Special Forces soldier was killed while on patrol in Paktia on 19 May. On 17 June a Special Forces patrol was fired upon near Tarin Kot. The same day, another team of 20 US Special Forces troops and 40 Afghan soldiers came under small-arms fire near Shkin in the Birmal region of Paktika. On 22 June, a rocket landed near the US Special Forces in Khost. Before dawn on 3 September, four 107mm rockets landed close to US Special Forces operating in southeastern Afghanistan and, between 11.00 hours on 15 September and the early morning of the next day, at least ten rockets fell upon the Khost bases, where more than a thousand American troops were based.

Then, in early September 2002, ex-Taliban soldiers tried to assassinate President Karzai in Kandahar. The 46 US

Special Forces troopers guarding him managed to wrestle one of the two attackers to the ground, but two innocent Afghans were killed in the fracas.

Eighteen months later, a CBS camera crew were given access to the 19th Special Forces Group's base in the hostile Pesch Valley, an isolated place near the Pakistani border. Osama bin Laden had been seen in the valley a few months before, just before the unit entered the area. By that time the Special Forces had dropped their aggressive role. Now they concentrated on making friends, although when they met the local elders, they reminded them that they were still looking for bin Laden and that they would pay good money for him.

When the Special Forces had first arrived in the area, they had been rocketed every other day. After five months, attacks came only every two or three weeks. Green Berets medics helped local people who were sick or injured, and they began building schools. Although they maintained an artillery post on top of a nearby mountain, they were beginning to find that locals were helping turn in arms caches. As well as killing, winning hearts and minds is what Green Berets, like the SAS, were trained for.

That summer, on 17 June 2004, two New Zealand SAS soldiers were wounded in a pre-dawn gun battle in central Afghanistan. The NZ SAS had begun operations assisting in the War on Terror in Afghanistan in late 2001, making three six-month rotations of between 40 and 65 soldiers before withdrawal in November 2005. Secrecy surrounds much of their operations in Afghanistan, but according to a New Zealand government summary sheet released in July 2007, the NZ SAS soldiers routinely patrolled enemy territory for three weeks or more at a time, often on foot, after being inserted by helicopter. Radio New Zealand news said the service had maintained a 100 per cent mission success rate. There were 'casualties on both sides' during firefights, though no New Zealanders were killed.

In 2004, Prime Minister Helen Clark reversed the normal policy of keeping SAS troop deployments secret. While not going into detail, she said that they would be working with soldiers from other countries and contributing their skills in reconnaissance, surveillance and tracking. Some 50 NZ SAS troops would be sent to Afghanistan at the beginning of April for 'long-range reconnaissance and direct-action missions'. The deployment was for a period of six months. The New Zealand SAS were to join 11,000 US troops in a coordinated hunt with 70,000 Pakistani soldiers along the Afghanistan-Pakistan border for top al-Qaeda and Taliban leaders.

More of the story came out because NZ SAS man Corporal Bill 'Willy' Apiata, a Maori from North Island, was recommended for the Victoria Cross. As a result, the New Zealand government took the unprecedented step of releasing the name of a serving SAS soldier, though not the full details of the event or the names of his fellow SAS men. 'The granting of a Victoria Cross is such an extraordinary event that it would be impossible to maintain the confidentiality of the identity of Corporal Apiata,' said Defence Minister Phil Goff. 'We came to the judgement that it was better we announce his name and the circumstances of his winning the award, rather than risk the highly probable outcome that it would be leaked somewhere down the track.'

The nature of the heroism that won Apiata the VC was revealed in the citation:

Lance Corporal (now Corporal) Apiata was, in 2004, part of a New Zealand Special Air Service (NZSAS) Troop on patrol in Afghanistan, which laid up in defensive formation for the night. At approximately 03.15 hours, the Troop was attacked by a group of about 20 enemy fighters, who had approached by stealth using the cover of undulating ground in pitch darkness.

Rocket-propelled grenades struck two of the Troop's vehicles, destroying one and immobilising the other. The opening strike was followed by dense and persistent machine gun and automatic-rifle fire from close range. The attack then continued using further rocket-propelled grenades and machine gun and rifle fire.

The initial attack was directed at the vehicle where Lance Corporal Apiata was stationed. He was blown off the bonnet by the impact of rocket-propelled grenades striking the vehicle. He was dazed, but was not physically injured. The two other vehicle crew members had been wounded by shrapnel; one of them, Corporal D, was in a serious condition.

Illuminated by the burning vehicle, and under sustained and accurate enemy fire directed at and around their position, the three soldiers immediately took what little cover was available. Corporal D was discovered to have sustained life-threatening wounds. The other two soldiers immediately began applying basic first aid.

Lance Corporal Apiata assumed command of the situation, as he could see that his superior's condition was deteriorating rapidly. By this time, however, Lance Corporal Apiata's exposed position, some 70 metres in front of the rest of the Troop, was coming under increasingly intense enemy fire. Corporal D was now suffering serious arterial bleeding and was lapsing in and out of consciousness.

Lance Corporal Apiata concluded that his comrade urgently required medical attention, or he would likely die. Pinned down by the enemy, in the direct line of fire between friend and foe, he also judged that there was almost no chance of such help reaching their position. As the enemy pressed its attack towards Lance Corporal Apiata's position, and without thought of abandoning his colleague to save himself, he took a decision in the highest order of personal courage under fire.

Knowing the risks involved in moving to open ground, Lance Corporal Apiata decided to carry Corporal D single-handedly to the relative safety of the main Troop position, which afforded better cover and where medical treatment could be given. He ordered his other colleague, Trooper E, to make his own way back to the rear.

In total disregard of his own safety, Lance Corporal Apiata stood up and lifted his comrade bodily. He then carried him across the 70 metres of broken, rocky and fire swept ground, fully exposed in the glare of battle to heavy enemy fire and into the face of returning fire from the main Troop position. That neither he nor his colleague were hit is scarcely possible. Having delivered his wounded companion to relative shelter with the remainder of the patrol, Lance Corporal Apiata re-armed himself and rejoined the fight in counterattack. By his actions, he removed the tactical complications of Corporal D's predicament from considerations of rescue.

The Troop could now concentrate entirely on prevailing in the battle itself. After an engagement lasting approximately 20 minutes, the assault was broken up and the numerically superior attackers were routed with significant casualties, with the Troop in pursuit. Lance Corporal Apiata had thereby contributed materially to the operational success of the engagement. A subsequent medical assessment confirmed that Corporal D would probably have died of blood loss and shock, had it not been for Lance Corporal Apiata's selflessly courageous act in carrying him back to the main Troop lines, to receive the immediate treatment that he needed.

Corporal Apiata modestly said that he was just doing his job.

Further details of the New Zealand SAS's contribution come from a US Navy Presidential Unit citation awarded in December 2004. It was given for the 'extraordinary heroism' of the units that comprised the Combined Joint Special Operations Task Force South and Task Force K-Bar between 17 October 2001 and 30 March 2002, covering the period of Anaconda. One of these units was the Special Air Service of New Zealand. The citation said SAS units had helped neutralise Taliban and al-Qaeda in

> extremely high risk missions, including search and rescue, special reconnaissance, sensitive site exploitation, direct action missions, destruction of multiple cave and tunnel complexes, identification and destruction of several known al Qaeda training camps, explosions of thousands of pounds of enemy ordnance. They established benchmark standards of professionalism, tenacity, courage, tactical brilliance and operational excellence while demonstrating superb esprit de corps and maintaining the highest measures of combat readiness.

The New Zealand SAS left Afghanistan when the British 16th Air Assault Brigade took responsibility for pacifying Helmand province in January 2006. Naturally, British Special Forces found themselves in employment again, among them the Special Reconnaissance Regiment (SRR), whose formation had been announced by Defence Secretary Geoffrey Hoon on 6 April 2005. The secrecy surrounding the SRR is even greater than that surrounding the SAS or SBS, but it is known that the British Army's newest unit recruits from all UK regiments, and that it is the only British Special Forces regiment to allow women in operational roles. Operatives also need to be proficient in Arabic and Farsi.

It is thought that the SRR's main role is to support SAS and SBS operations by providing close-target reconnaissance, surveillance and 'eyes-on' intelligence. It absorbed the 14th Intelligence Company – also known as 'The Det' – a special plainclothes surveillance unit created in 1973, specifically for operations in Northern Ireland. The skills learned there were thought to be useful in the war against terror.

The SRR has been involved in several controversial operations in its short life. Following the London bombings in July 2005, the SRR was deployed on the streets of the capital to counter the terrorist threat. It was reported that members were involved in the surveillance operation involving the Brazilian Jean Charles de Menezes. The electrician was mistakenly thought to be connected to the 7 July attacks and trailed to Stockwell tube station by SRR operatives. As he boarded the train, he was fatally shot by police. The official Independent Police Complaints Commission report into the Stockwell incident does not mention the SRR, instead identifying the surveillance operatives involved as being from SO12 (Special Branch) and SO13 (Anti-Terrorist Branch), both now combined into SO15 Counter Terrorism Command.

Back in Afghanistan, on 27 June 2006, two members of the UK Special Forces, Captain David Patten of the SRR and Sergeant Paul Bartlett of the SBS, were killed during covert operations in the Sangin Valley, a notorious Taliban sanctuary in the province of Helmand. Along with a third man, they were ambushed while returning from a night patrol when insurgents hit their armoured 'snatch' Land Rover with an RPG. The soldiers left the vehicle and the two died in the ensuing hour-long firefight. The third Special Forces man was severely injured.

Other SBS soldiers had called in a quick-reaction force of paratroopers from the nearby joint British-Afghan military base at the town of Sangin, but it too came under fire from the Taliban. British commanders also called in 105mm light artillery and air support from RAF Harrier jets, Apache attack helicopters and an American A-10 Warthog ground-attack fighter. The provincial police chief said 12 Taliban were killed and 20 were injured in the attack.

Two months later, in September 2006, the SBS joined US Special Forces on the Canadian-led Operation Medusa to drive the Taliban from the strategically important Panjwayi district of Kandahar province. It was reported that the SBS were at the vanguard of a large-scale attack by conventional forces. The SBS were supported by another relatively new British unit, the Special Forces Support Group (SFSG), which has also seen action in Iraq. Formed largely around 1 Para, who had worked alongside a joint SAS-SBS mission in Sierra Leone, they were to act as a cut-off group (or blocking force) while the SBS attacked. However, their efforts were hampered by tragedy. An RAF Nimrod spy plane crashed while supporting the operation, killing all on board, including members of SBS Signals Squadron and their SFSG equivalents.

In May 2007 the SBS had better fortunes when they led the raid on the Taliban military leader Mullah Dadullah. He was a highly valued prize in the War on Terror, and a sophisticated operation was put into place to find him. Two months earlier, a controversial prisoner exchange had taken place. An Italian reporter named Daniele Mastrogiacomo, along with his two Afghani assistants, had been taken hostage by the Taliban. In a much-criticised move, the Kabul authorities agreed to Dadullah's demands that they release two senior Taliban commanders held in custody in exchange for the safe return of the journalist and his aides.

Although the authorities seemed to be giving in to terrorist demands, it was in fact a classic military deception. It turned out that the top-secret US electronic surveillance unit Task Force Orange had been able to tag the two Taliban commanders, perhaps by means of trackers inside their bodies. As a result, satellite-phone conversations between the commanders and Dadullah were monitored and traced. By May, Task Force Orange had pinpointed Dadullah's location. He was holed up at Bahram Chah in the south of Helmand province, close to the border with Pakistan.

Some 50 commandos from SBS C Squadron were given the mission to storm Dadullah's stronghold. First, a reconnaissance party approached the area in a Supacat 6x6 all-terrain vehicle. The team quickly determined that an airstrike on Dadullah's mud-walled compound would not guarantee that he was taken out, so C Squadron would go in and finish the job.

Along with a party of Afghani soldiers, the men of C Squadron, were loaded into two RAF Chinooks. They came under fire from Taliban defenders as they were inserted into the area but once on the ground, they made a classic infantry attack on the compound, pepper-potting towards the objective. One group went firm and provided covering fire as another group pressed forward, before going firm themselves. The 20 Taliban defenders put up a fanatical defence with rifles, machine guns and RPGs, but after a four-hour battle the SBS were able to clear the compound, suffering only four wounded. Dadullah was killed in the attack. He had been shot twice in the torso and once in the head in a typical 'double-tap' favoured by Special Forces operators.

The Taliban evened the score when an SBS commando was cut down in a hail of bullets in July 2007 in the remote province of Nimruz, which borders Iran. He was flown to a field hospital but died of his wounds. However, it was said that as many as 30 AQT fighters were killed in the assault, which was backed by attack helicopters and jets. The target – 'a significant Taliban commander' – was said to be among the dead.

In September 2007, two Italian soldiers, possibly intelligence operatives, were believed to have been captured by Taliban militia. An operation to free them was put into motion once intelligence had pinpointed the location of the hostages, close to Farah, in western Afghanistan. A force of SBS commandos from C Squadron was loaded onto four Lynx Mk7 helicopters. Armed with .50 calibre rifles, airborne SBS snipers covered the assault teams as they swooped down on the militia, who were moving the hostages in a convoy of 4x4s. As the snipers disabled the vehicles by shooting through their engine blocks, other SBS men were inserted onto the ground to engage any kidnappers not already taken out. Nine AQT fighters were killed as the hostages were recovered, although the two were injured in the operation.

Then, in February 2008, the SBS reportedly took out a senior Taliban figure, Mullah Abdul Matin, in a shoot-out at Gereshk, in Helmand province. Matin, his lieutenant Mullah Karim Agha and a bodyguard were travelling across the desert on motorcycles when the SBS were dropped into his path by helicopter after a tip-off on his whereabouts. Matin opened fire with an AK-47 but was cut down in a hail of bullets, along with his two accomplices. Troops recovered night-vision goggles, grenades and a detonator.

Matin had been a deputy of the Taliban chief Mullah Omar. He had organised several suicide bomb attacks on British convoys, killing two British servicemen and wounding a dozen in the previous 18 months. His men had also murdered of dozens of Afghan civilians. As Lieutenant Colonel Simon Millar, British Forces spokesman in Helmand, said at the time, 'Mullah Matin's been a priority target for some time. He commanded fighters and reported directly to the highest Taliban levels of command. He's responsible for the kidnapping of local nationals, had links with the narcotics trade and had provided security to the traffickers.'

Three months later an SBS team took part in a mission to recover sensitive electronics gear from an unmanned RAF Reaper spy drone that had crashed in Afghanistan. An RAF Harrier jet was scrambled to blow up the £50-million Reaper with a laser-guided 1,000lb (454kg) bomb. 'There was no way we could take even the slightest risk of the Taliban getting hold of any parts,' a senior military source said.

When George W Bush visited Britain in June 2008, he asked once again for help of British Special Forces in a final attempt to capture Osama bin Laden before the President left the White House. It seems he wanted to be able to say that, as well as killing Saddam Hussein, he had also killed or captured bin Laden and so had left the world a safer place.

The SBS are not new to the frontier region of northern Pakistan. Operating on intelligence provided by the Special Reconnaissance Regiment and its US counterpart, the Security Coordination Detachment, the Special Forces have been assisting Delta Force on operations in for some time, including regularly crossing the border from Afghanistan after securing the permission of the Pakistani government.

These operations involve the use of Predator and Reaper unmanned aerial drones fitted with Hellfire missiles that can be used to take out specific terrorist targets. America rarely acknowledges the use of Predator and Reaper drones, but admitted that a strike was made on a suspected al-Qaeda safe house in the Pakistani province of North Waziristan earlier in June. Villagers said the house was empty.

At the time of writing, bin Laden has evaded capture for nearly seven years, but sources believe he is in the Bajaur tribal zone in northwest Pakistan. A Pentagon source said Special Forces were rolling up al-Qaeda's network in Pakistan in the hope of pushing bin Laden back towards the Afghan border, where the Coalition forces, bombers and guided missiles are lying in wait. 'They are prepping for a major battle,' he said.

PART TWO
ON THE
HIGH SEAS

CHAPTER SEVEN

TAKING OUT THE TERROR SHIP

In the months following 9/11 and the British-backed invasion of Afghanistan, Britain braced itself for a terrorist attack. Neither the Afghans nor Saudi radicals such as Osama bin Laden had much time for the British and an attack was believed to be only a matter of time. Just three months after 9/11, on 22 December 2001, the British secret service became aware of a cargo ship steaming towards the UK. Named the MV *Nisha*, it was believed to have been primed as a massive chemical weapon, and crewed by 16 terrorists as a massive suicide attack on London at Christmas.

The *Nisha* was said to be carrying some 25,580 tons (26,000 tonnes) of sugar and headed for the Tate & Lyle sugar refinery in Silvertown, east London, some four miles from the City. However, she had recently been seen in the

Red Sea and off the coast of Somalia, where she was thought to have picked up members of al-Qaeda who operated in that area. She had also stopped off at Mauritius to pick up her cargo. The island had recently been plagued by terrorists allied with the Lebanese faction Hezbollah and it had come to the attention of Mauritian police that two Hezbollah operatives had recently bought a large quantity of the pesticide Lannate. In turn, the Mauritian authorities had told the local CIA bureau chief that the Lannate had left the island on the *Nisha*.

The active ingredient in Lannate is a chemical called methomyl, which is highly toxic – not just to spiders and ticks but to humans. Fields where Lannate has been used to kill pests must be sealed off for seven days before it is safe to return to them. Intelligence agencies had already identified methomyl as a chemical terrorists could use as a crude nerve agent. Sugar, meanwhile, is highly flammable and often used in homemade explosives. If terrorists were to detonate the sugar in the hold of the *Nisha* at the Tate & Lyle refinery with the wind coming from the east, deadly methomyl would be blown across the City of London, killing tens of thousands and paralysing one of the world's foremost financial centres. The resulting economic chaos would be felt worldwide. The losses of the brokers's offices in the World Trade Center on 9/11 would be a pinprick by comparison. The *Nisha*, it seemed, was one great big improvised nerve-chemical bomb.

When the CIA bureau chief in the Mauritian capital of Port Louis contacted CIA headquarters in Langley, Virginia, they in turn contacted their counterparts in MI5 and MI6, who duly passed the intelligence on to the

Above: General Tommy Franks, head of US Central Command, briefs the press in March 2003.

Below: An RAF Hercules C-130 transport plane in 2005.

Above: *USS Carl Vinson* launches an F/A-18 in October 2001.

Below: On board the *USS Harry S Truman*, 2,000-pound Joint Directional Attack Munitions (JDAMs).

CIA agent Mike Spann was killed in Afghanistan.

John Walker Lindh – the American Taliban.

Above: A US bombing raid destroyed this Al Qaeda training camp in Tora Bora in December 2001.

Below: An AC-130 Spectre gunship.

New Zealand SAS man Corporal Bill Apiata, whose identity was revealed when he won the Victoria Cross.

General Sir Peter de la Billiére in 1990.

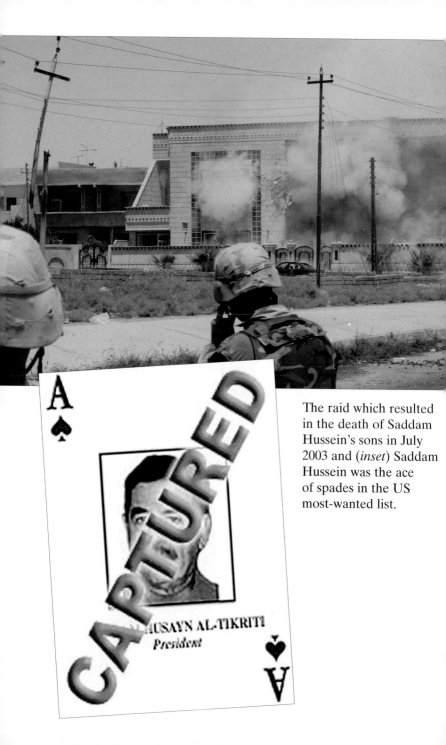

A ♠

CAPTURED

...HUSAYN AL-TIKRITI
President

♥ A

The raid which resulted in the death of Saddam Hussein's sons in July 2003 and (*inset*) Saddam Hussein was the ace of spades in the US most-wanted list.

British government. As the order to take out the *Nisha* had come from the highest level in Whitehall, Special Forces were given permission to use 'any means necessary' to halt the ship.

As the *Nisha* turned into the English Channel, the SAS and SBS were alerted. Men who had just returned from chasing AQT around Afghanistan were awoken at 06.45 hours and ordered to assemble at their headquarters in Poole, Dorset. They had been intending to enjoy a happy family Christmas, and this was not the news they wanted to hear.

Earlier that morning, the company sergeant major had received a call from the Cabinet Office briefing room, where military officers and government ministers assess any threat to national security. He put out the word and by 08.30 hours the SBS began to assemble. There were only a handful of them, as two of the three combat squadrons – M and Z – were in Afghanistan. The regimental HQ was also there, the first time it had been deployed overseas. The remaining men of C Squadron had been left behind in Blighty as a counter-terrorist squad. As this was a seaborne operation, the SBS were in charge, but to take the *Nisha*, they would need an assault team of about 70, so they were promised the support of 26 SAS men from Hereford.

Although there is a healthy inter-unit rivalry between the SAS and SBS, they often train together for just such a seaborne assault, using HMS *Rame Head*, a former Second World War escort ship moored off Whale Island in Portsmouth. Twice a year there is a joint exercise on a moving vessel – a fast hydrofoil Seacat ferry. One of these exercises usually takes place just before Christmas when conditions are likely to be at their worst. This, however, would be the first time they were to undertake a direct-action assault (DAA) on a vessel at sea for real.

The only time the regiment had come close was in 1972, when blackmailers had threatened to blow up the cruise liner *Queen Elizabeth II*. The liner was then in the mid-Atlantic with 1,438 passengers on board, and a ransom of $350,000 was demanded. As the *QE2* circled a thousand miles from Britain, men of the SBS – along with an SAS sergeant and a bomb-disposal expert – were parachuted into the Atlantic from an RAF Hercules. The bomb-disposal expert, Captain R Hacon Williams, was not parachute-trained, so he had to be given instruction en route. The team had to make their jump into a rough sea and were then picked up by lifeboat. Once on board the liner, they were rushed to the ship's captain, who briefed them while their equipment was mustered, and an RAF Nimrod provided secure communications with the team's British base. The suspect packages – two suitcases on the boat deck and four large containers in the car deck – proved to be harmless, and the FBI eventually picked up the hoaxers.

Every member of the jump team received the Queen's Commendation for Brave Conduct, and the exercise provided valuable experience in inter-service cooperation. After this incident, some bomb-disposal experts were parachute-trained and the SBS kept a team on standby for future operations of this type. But 29 years on, none of the men of the *QE2* operation were still on active service with the regiment. Furthermore, their training had been boarding a friendly ship that was stationary. This time, they would be attacking a hostile ship that was making good headway through the water.

By 17.00 hours on 22 December, the mixed SBS-SAS squadron had assembled at Poole. Normally, the men would have at least 24 hours to plan and prepare for such a mission, but the MV *Nisha* was only 200 miles away from London. She was making 16 knots and at that speed, she would reach her target in 13 hours. But there was even more urgency than that. As the ship's cargo was thought to be deadly to anyone downwind if it went off, they would have to get to the *Nisha* before she got close to the coastline of Britain. Consequently, they were to hit the vessel the following morning. The mission would be called Operation Ocean Strike.

Inflatable rubber assault-boats, weapons, ammunition and specialised assault equipment were loaded into 20 souped-up Mercedes-Benz vans. With a police escort, the convoy set off at high speed for RAF Yeovilton in Somerset. Once there, they took over one of the hangars, where they would bed down for the night. Intelligence agents from MI5 and MI6 had come up with plans of the *Nisha* that the Special Forces could use, and a makeshift operations room was set up with naval charts and aerial photographs pinned to the walls. Meanwhile, the SBS men prepared the explosive charges they were going to need to gain entry to the ship.

With the regimental headquarters in Afghanistan, it fell to the company sergeant major to give the briefing. Their mission was to stop the ship and arrest the terrorists. They would hit the *Nisha* just before first light in international waters off the coast of Sussex. It was vital that the ship be stopped before she reached the Thames estuary.

They would attack simultaneously from above and below: the SAS would be lowered from helicopters while the SBS would come alongside on their rigid inflatables. The aim was to swamp the opposition with firepower. A photograph of the vessel was flashed on a screen. The *Nisha* displaced around 17,000 tonnes unladen and stood 80 feet (24 metres) out of the water at the stern. It was a flat cargo ship about 450 feet (137 metres) long with five cargo holds and a superstructure four storeys high at the back. The SAS boys coming in on the Chinook would land on its roof. Snipers onboard two following Lynx attack helicopters would take out any opposition. The SAS were to break into the crew's cabins and neutralise them while they were still in their beds.

Meanwhile, the rigid inflatables would be launched over the horizon from the frigate HMS *Sutherland*. After scaling the starboard bow using hook-and-pole ladders, the SBA men would search the cargo holds from bow to stern. Each four-man team would have a man from the EOD – Explosive Ordinance Disposal – unit to deal with any bombs they came across. Sixteen men from the Joint Nuclear, Biological and Chemical Regiment would be standing by with a full NBC decontamination unit. Holding cells for any prisoners had been set up at the army base on Thorney Island in Chichester Harbour. Finally, following the Lynxes with the snipers on board, there would be four Sea King helicopters carrying a command-and-control team, along with men from Special Branch and HM Customs and Excise (now amalgamated with the Inland Revenue and called HM Revenue and Customs).

After the briefing, the men being lowered onto the roof of the bridge drew straws to see who would go first. Then, at 23.00, the regimental doctor came round with 'nerve agent pre-treatment set' (NAPS) tablets – thought by some to have been responsible for Gulf War syndrome. But there was no reluctance to take them, as the men genuinely faced the threat of chemical agents. The unit's medics were also given two phials of atropine, an antidote to nerve gas. After that, the assault force tried to get their heads down, but the NAPS had left them restless and irritable.

Despite the dangers of a daylight assault, the British government thought that boarding a merchant vessel in international waters in the middle of the night might appear a little heavy-handed. But the SBS wanted the cover of darkness for their attack, so a compromise was reached. Officially, daytime starts at 05.30 hours, but in December it is still dark at that time, so the initial assault could benefit from the cloak of the night to retain the element of surprise. The follow-up would take place after dawn broke, so the British government could maintain that it had been a daylight raid.

At 04.55 hours, two Chinooks took off from RAF Yeovilton, each carrying a squadron of Special Forces. The trip out to the *Nisha* was to take 35 minutes, but it was going to be a rough ride and the run-up hazardous. The weather had closed in. Cloud cover had descended to 150 feet (46 metres). There was a 30-knot wind and a 15ft (4.5-metre) swell. Travelling at 120mph (193kph), the lead Chinook with 30 men on board had to fly low enough to stay under the *Nisha*'s radar sweep but high enough to miss the tops of the waves. This would have been hard enough in daylight, but the pilot was flying on instruments. They had NVGs, but their images were obscured by the green glow of sea spray. Behind the lead Chinook came the two Lynxes carrying the sniper teams and the four Sea Kings carrying command and control and back-up, spread out in a V formation.

At 05.27 hours, the lead pilot caught sight of the *Nisha*'s flashing navigation lights. They were still four miles (6.5 km) out. The Special Forces men braced themselves. A Chinook has no armour plating, so it is vulnerable even to small-arms fire. If a helicopter was downed and sunk in the middle of the Channel, the emergency air bottles the men carried strapped to their chests would have been no good to them. The water was so deep they would have run out of air before they reached the surface.

The men put on their respirator masks and checked that there was a round in the chamber of their main armament. Most carried Heckler & Koch (H&K) MP-5 9mm machine pistols, the Special Forces' weapon of choice for close-quarters battle. Others carried pump-action shotguns, which were good for blowing off doors, or H&K G3 sniping rifles, the shortened version with the retractable stock. After flicking off the safety catch, the men put on thick leather gloves to protect their hands from rope-burns as they lowered themselves to the ship.

With minutes to go, the men got to their feet. They were wearing coal-black counter-terrorist gear made from fire-retardant rubberised cotton. This was flexible enough to run in and waterproof enough to go diving in. The tight hood covered their heads and the respirator their faces. Not only was this practical dress for an attack, but its appearance had the added advantage of intimidating the enemy. Hanging from their webbing were stun grenades known as flash-bangs and canisters of CS gas. As well as their main armaments, they carried knives strapped to their chests, a Sig Sauer 9mm pistol on the hip and backpacks full of explosives.

At 05.30 hours, the lead Chinook flared out into a hover. The men in the back could feel the icy wind as the side door was flung open and they could see the *Nisha* pitching below them. When the Chinook descended to about 50 feet (15 metres), the helicopter's loadmaster kicked out the ropes. The descent looked impossible. The pilot had to hold the helicopter steady so the ropes didn't tangle. Below, it was only just possible to make out the unlit roof of the bridge the men were to aim for. Under normal circumstances the mission would have been aborted but the threat was so great they knew they had to go ahead.

Gradually, the pilot eased the helicopter in close enough for them to make the descent. This took a minute, more than enough time to rouse any terrorist on board. Then came the cry of 'Go! Go! Go!' As the helicopter pitched wildly in the high wind, the men grabbed the ropes and flung themselves out of the door. The descent towards the pitching ship was hair-raising and most made a heavy landing.

The first man on board saw a lighted door below him, and one of the crew came out and began climbing the stairway up to the roof. The SBS man had not had time to take off his heavy gloves, so he could not get his finger into the trigger guard. His weapon was useless, and direct action was called for. As the crewman reached the top of the steps, the SBS man took a swing at him, knocking him off the ladder. He fell onto the steel deck below with a heavy thud and did not get up.

The SBS man then took off his gloves, unclipped his MP-5 and started down the steps. The rest of his four-man team were now right behind him. At the bottom of the stairway, they stepped over the unconscious crewman and approached the door that led to the bridge. This was the most dangerous part of the operation. While the rest of the men on board might be asleep in their bunks, the bridge was bound to be manned and by now they must have known someone was coming. Busting though the door, the lead SBS man shouted, 'Get down! Get down!'

At the back of the bridge were three men who froze in shock at the sight of four men in black pointing sub-machine-guns at them. The lead SBS man strode across the bridge, grabbed the first man and threw him face down on the floor. The other two soon got the idea and were face down on the floor. They were Asian in appearance and appeared to have been interrupted while enjoying a game similar to dominoes at a table. The fourth man on the bridge appeared to be the captain. One of the SBS team put a pump-action shotgun to his head and ordered him to maintain the present course. The man was too frightened to do anything, so the SBS man took his hands and put them on the wheel, indicating that the captain should continue dead ahead. Then he told him in words and gestures to slow the ship to a halt. By then, 60 seconds had elapsed.

Then the team heard the boom of a shotgun in the crew's quarters below. Quickly they cuffed the men with plastic strip, and with the bridge secure, called the command-and-control unit, giving a brief situation report. Leaving two men in charge of the bridge, the SBS team leader and his oppo headed back out on deck. As more gunfire sounded, the two men dragged the unconscious man on the deck under shelter, cuffed him and headed down the stairway to the floor below.

From the lower decks, they could hear the sound of grenades going off. A blast blew open a doorway and they charged in. A second team had already taken the radio room. A third had secured the third floor and a fourth had hit the crew's quarters. Meanwhile the Chinook had pulled away, allowing the Lynx helicopters to take up their positions on either side of the *Nisha*, where their sniper teams could give the seaborne assault force cover.

The assault force in their inflatables had now arrived at the bows. Despite the mountainous seas, they managed to scale the sides of the ship and climb down into the front hold, where they began their search. From there, they managed to break though the sealed hatch into the next hold, then the one after. Just two minutes into the assault, the ship was crawling with black-clad figures.

The two SBS men from the bridge had taken off their respirators – the face-masks had steamed up in the cold night air – when they saw a wispy white vapour emerging from a stairwell. Gas! Quickly they pushed their respirators back into position, but it was too late. One man vomited into his face-mask and searched frantically for a phial of atropine, thinking he'd been hit with nerve gas.

But then he realised he recognised the smell from exercises. It was CS gas, let off by the fourth team in the crew's quarters on the floor below.

The fourth team had used a shotgun to blast a door off its hinges, then lobbed in the CS canister. Two crewmen were rudely pulled from their beds in their underwear and cuffed with plastic strip in the corridor. Soon the companionways were full of men in various states of undress with their hands cuffed behind their backs. With the aid of powerful torches, the Special Forces men combed the bowels of the ships, using explosive charges to blow open storerooms. They found a workshop that could have been a bomb-making factory, but this they would leave to one of the EOD teams to deal with.

Believing any danger to have been neutralised, the troops bundled their prisoners outside before they succumbed completely to the effects of CS gas. Lined up face down on the open deck, they could breathe freely, but they were now in danger from exposure to the cold. So the troopers went back into the cabins to grab blankets and coats for them.

After 15 minutes, the entire ship was secured. As dawn was breaking the Sea Kings dropped off the EOD teams and a Special Branch anti-terrorist squad. A Customs and Excise launch pulled alongside and a replacement crew from the Royal Navy took control of the ship. Just 30 minutes after arriving on the *Nisha*, the Special Forces were winched off the ship and flown back to Thorney Island. They were then taken to RAF Yeovilton and back to Poole for a debrief.

Two of their men had been injured in the assault. One was

hit when a fire extinguisher he had hurled at a door bounced back, and the other was bruised by a CS canister that had rebounded. The crew suffered nothing more than cuts and bruises. The *Nisha* was taken to Sandown Bay on the Isle of Wight, where she was searched for five days. In the nothing suspicious was found, but the episode was described to a House of Common's Select Defence Committee as 'a successful run-out of the counter-terrorism machinery'.

PART THREE
IRAQ

CHAPTER EIGHT
DESERT STORM

On 2 August 1990 some 100,000 Iraqi troops – with six divisions of the elite Republican Guard – invaded neighbouring Kuwait. The Kuwaiti forces were unable to repel the invaders and within a few hours Saddam Hussein had achieved his object of seizing the small, oil-rich state, which he considered to be a province of Iraq hived off by the British during the First World War. Possession of Kuwait greatly expanded Iraq's short coastline, and Saddam and his henchmen began looting the state of its considerable financial resources. When the United Nations Security Council passed a resolution demanding that Iraq withdraw, Saddam refused to comply. As the invasion posed a threat to Saudi Arabia, the world's largest oil exporter, which lay next door, the United States, its NATO allies, Egypt, Syria and other Arab nations put together a coalition to expel Saddam Hussein from Kuwait. Thus began the military build-up of 700,000 men known as Operation Desert Shield.

This greatly annoyed one Osama bin Laden, who had returned to his native Saudi Arabia a hero of the jihad against the Soviets in Afghanistan. He and his Arab legion had expelled the Red Army, it was said, and ultimately brought down the mighty Soviet Union – although, in fact, his foreign fighters had made only a minor contribution to the struggle. With the Iraqi army in Kuwait, bin Laden had met the crown prince and offered his Arab fighters to King Fahd to defend Saudi Arabia. Instead, King Fahd turned to the US and NATO. This meant that foreign, non-Muslim troops would be stationed on Saudi territory. Bin Laden was appalled. The presence of infidels, he argued, defiled the sacred soil of the 'land of two mosques' – the holy cities of Mecca and Medina. His vocal criticism of the Saudi monarchy provoked government attempts to silence him and he eventually fled to Sudan.

Meanwhile, Saddam Hussein continued to defy the United Nations and the Coalition launched Operation Desert Storm in what would become the First Gulf War. The Coalition commander, General Norman Schwarzkopf, was an old-fashioned soldier who had little time for Special Forces. During the build-up to the war, he saw no role for them. However, the commander of the British Forces, Lieutenant-General Peter de la Billière, was a former commander of 22 SAS and he tried to convince Schwarzkopf that the very special skills of the British Special Forces would be useful.

In August 1990, D and G Squadrons of 22 SAS were

already on manoeuvres in the Gulf region, perfecting their desert-warfare skills. 'We had been operating in Oman with a batch of our new four-wheel-drive vehicles called light-strike vehicles – LSVs – which were designed specifically for rough terrain,' one SAS man recalled. 'We had spent weeks putting them through a series of punishing tests. They were good, although their suspension couldn't survive a fall from a Chinook helicopter from an altitude of a hundred metres, which we discovered when one was accidentally dropped. Still, there isn't much kit that can survive that kind of treatment. We were roughly acclimatised by the time we touched down in Saudi, though none of us were prepared for the piss-poor weather we would encounter later on operations.'

Nevertheless, they were on hand to put their training to good use. 'So there we were,' he said, 'a motley crew with bergens and weapons walking across the tarmac to a group of waiting trucks. Around us, an army of multinational air force personnel worked feverishly on their aircraft. We didn't know what the high command had in store for us, so all we could do was train for any likely operation that might crop up.'

No immediate role was seen for the SAS, as the Green Berets had already taken on the role of border reconnaissance. It was then proposed that the SAS join Delta Force in rescuing the hundreds of foreign nationals being held hostage as part of Saddam Hussein's 'human shield'. There had been some 800 Britons in Kuwait when he attacked, and there were another thousand in Iraq who were being held around vital Iraqi military, government and industrial targets, whose loss to Allied air attack would have severely damaged Iraq's ability to wage war.

By mid-November, Special Forces command had earmarked some men from the SAS, SBS and an RAF Special Forces section to join US units for the evacuation raids, although no formal plan had been approved. Helicopter insertion and extraction and amphibious raids were all considered, but all had huge risks involved. In fact, any plan would have proved impractical as the hostages were held in various locations all over the country. Suddenly, however, on 6 December 1990, Saddam Hussein released the hostages. It seemed that the SAS would no longer be needed, increasing their frustration.

Even so, the build-up of UK and US Special Forces in Saudi Arabia was continuing apace. This opened the possibility of their extensive use behind enemy lines before the main ground forces were ready for offensive action. However, the US high command seemed to have no task for them in the short term except for a number of 'penny packet' operations. This was thought to be because Schwarzkopf had gained a poor impression of Special Forces during his time in Vietnam.

'At first Norman Schwarzkopf had opposed the idea of deploying Special Forces behind enemy lines,' said de la Billière, 'on the grounds that there was no task that could not be carried out by the Allies' overwhelming air power or, later, by the conventional armoured forces. I myself was not prepared to recommend Special Forces unless two conditions were fulfilled: one was that there must be a real, worthwhile role for the SAS to perform, and the other that we must have means of extricating our men in an emergency.'

General de la Billière finally succeeded in persuading Schwarzkopf that Special Forces should be given a chance to prove themselves. After being on standby for months, men from A and B Squadrons left to join D and G Squadrons in the Gulf shortly after Christmas 1990. 'By late December 1990, the majority of the regiment had been deployed in the Gulf, including some blokes from R Squadron, the reserve,' said one man who was there. 'However, because no specific role had been assigned to us, patience began to wear a little thin.'

Soon, the British Special Forces group in the theatre numbered some 700 men, including elements of the SBS and RAF Special Forces aircrew. Of the total, the SAS contributed 300 men, making this the largest deployment of the regiment since the Second World War. In the end, G Squadron was not used, because a squadron was needed on counter-terrorism duty back in the UK. The task now was to find a worthwhile mission for the others to undertake.

By mid-January 1991, de la Billière decided the SAS could be effective in creating diversions ahead of the main attack, destroying Iraqi communications facilities and tracking down the mobile Scud missile launchers that had so far eluded both satellite reconnaissance and airstrikes. Heavily armed desert fighting columns were duly formed to infiltrate Iraqi territory and carry out search-and-destroy missions. By destroying just about anything they could find, they aimed to force the Iraqis to deploy large forces to track them down.

There were four columns in total – two drawn from A Squadron and two from D Squadron – and these now underwent intensive training in the United Arab Emirates. Each column consisted of between eight and 12 Type 110 Land Rovers, armed with a Browning .50 calibre heavy machine gun, GPMGs, American Mk19 40mm grenade launchers and Milan anti-tank missiles. They would carry some 30 men and be protected by motorcycle outriders. With them would be a short-wheelbase Mercedes Unimog open truck. This would be used as the 'mother ship', carrying the bulk of the supplies, fuel, ammunition, NBC equipment and spare parts. The columns were to go into action at night, laying up during the day to avoid detection. In the end, all four SAS columns stayed inside Iraq for the full duration of the war, operating under the control of the Special Operations Command of Central Command (SOCCENT), an Allied organisation coordinated by the Americans.

Just before dawn on 17 January, eight Apache attack helicopters destroyed the Iraqi air defence radars, creating safe corridors in which aircraft could fly. The Coalition air forces then targeted the Iraqi command-and-control infrastructure. Iraq, completely unprepared for such an attack, suffered substantial damage to its infrastructure and a devastating blow to its morale. Desperate to retaliate, Saddam Hussein turned his Scuds on Israel and launched 12 missiles into the suburbs of Tel Aviv. Miraculously, most inhabitants avoided injury, but the consequences could have been devastating.

The missiles that had reached Israel had carried conventional warheads. However, the idea that the next batch might carry chemical or biological agents caused widespread panic. Israel threatened to invade Iraq and destroy the Scud sites. It also declared that it would respond with a nuclear strike on Baghdad if Iraq used unconventional warheads. For United Nations commanders this was a nightmare situation. If Israel became involved in the war, it would cause a massive split between the Western members of the Coalition and their Arab allies. The whole war plan would be destroyed – something that Saddam Hussein was well aware of.

The SAS were immediately ordered to find and destroy the mobile Scud launchers, using road-watch patrols and mobile fighting columns. Eight-men SAS patrols were dropped by helicopter far behind enemy lines. They were to set up static OPs to survey the main supply routes for the movement of Scud launchers and call in airstrikes to destroy them. As a result, Israel put on hold its threat to retaliate.

After being carried into Iraq, the first patrol requested that their helicopter wait while they surveyed their surroundings. The flat terrain, they decided, offered too little cover, making it dangerous to continue their mission, so they returned to the waiting helicopter. The second patrol, having considered their surroundings, also reckoned it was too risky to continue. They had not asked their helicopter to wait, so they decided to drive back to the Saudi border in the only vehicle they had with them. Before departing, they requested an airstrike on a nearby mobile radar station, but the US A-10 aircraft mistook them for the target. Realising the mistake, the pilot managed to pull away just in time and went on to destroy the intended objective.

Other teams were more successful. However, the area in

which the SAS were working was suffering its most severe winter weather on record, and the men were ill prepared for the conditions they faced. Standard-issue desert kit gave them little protection from the snow, sleet, rain and freezing night-time temperatures, and the men developed frostbite and hypothermia.

The desert units were resupplied by a temporary formation, known as E Squadron. This was a convoy of ten Bedford four-ton trucks with a heavily armed SAS Land Rover escort, whose orders were to meet up with the fighting columns at a rendezvous point some 86 miles (138 km) inside Iraq. The convoy left Saudi Arabia on 10 February and reached the RV at 15.00 hours on the 12th. In a huge operation, more than 390 NCOs attended a mess meeting of warrant officers and sergeants called by the RSM. The vehicles were serviced or repaired, and prisoners handed over. The convoy returned to Saudi Arabia, reaching base on 17 February.

There was no amphibious role to assign to the SBS, but they wanted to get involved anyway. As a result, a line was drawn down the middle of Iraq, with the SAS's area of operation to the west and the SBS's to the east. As well as searching for mobile Scud launchers, the SBS had a special mission to perform. Their sector contained a mass of buried fibre-optic cable that provided the Iraqi high command with intelligence and frontline reports. The location of the main junction was just 32 miles (52 km) from Baghdad.

On 22 January, with barely time for their usual work-up, 36 SBS men embarked on two Chinook helicopters from No. 7 Squadron's Special Forces Flight and flew into Iraq.

The team carried 400lbs (180kg) of explosives and was heavily armed. They were venturing into an area full of nomads and desert spies, close to Iraqi air and ground forces. As the helicopters landed, they disengaged their rotors but kept their engines running for a quick escape.

The SBS men quickly found the communications cables. Digging down, they pulled out a length to take back with them for analysis, then placed explosives along the exposed area. When the charge was detonated, it took out a 40-yard (36-metre) section of the cable. Within 90 minutes the SBS had destroyed what was left of the Iraqi communications grid while suffering no casualties. The lieutenant leading the team grabbed one of the cable route markers and presented it to General Schwarzkopf on their return.

The most famous SAS patrol of the First Gulf War had the call-sign Bravo Two Zero. On the evening of 22 January 1991, eight SAS men, loaded with equipment and supplies for an extended stay, were flown into Iraq by Chinook. As well as hunting down Scuds, their tasks were to observe the main westerly supply route and sever underground communications cables that ran between Baghdad and Jordan.

Once on the ground, the patrol travelled some 12 miles (20 km) from the LZ, but after finding shelter in a small cave, they discovered their radio was not working. Soon afterwards, they made contact with the enemy. After vicious firefight, the patrol was forced to withdraw and head for the Syrian border some 75 miles (121 km) to the west. On the way, the patrol suffered injury and hypothermia, and the men became separated. As a result, three died, one escaped but four were captured. They endured weeks of beating and horrendous torture, but at the end of the war they were released with the other POWs and returned to the regiment. The patrol was immortalised in two books: *Bravo Two Zero*, written by its sergeant-commander under the alias Andy McNab, and *The One That Got Away* by Chris Ryan, the patrol member who reached the Syrian border.

Other SAS units fared better and used laser designators to mark targets for airstrikes, ensuring pinpoint accuracy. By the end of the war, they had helped take out numerous communications facilities and, it is estimated, destroy about a third of Iraq's Scud launchers.

Despite dangerous terrain, dreadful weather, radio problems, enemy action and intelligence, the Regiment lost only four soldiers. In recognition of their contribution, members received 55 medals for gallantry and meritorious service, and General Schwarzkopf gave the SAS with his personal commendation.

The SBS kept a lower profile. However, at the end of the war, they were chosen by General de la Billière to reclaim the British embassy in Kuwait. The buildings, it was feared, might be booby-trapped or even harbour a suicide squad of Iraqi troops, and the SBS had to work on this assumption. On 27 February 1991, they flew into Kuwait and set up a temporary base at the airport. The next day they went in. As two Chinooks hovered over the embassy, the SBS team belayed down to the roof of the embassy, throwing stun grenades through the windows and blowing down the famous front door designed by Edwin Lutyens. It is thought that the SBS were involved in other operations during Desert Storm, but so far these have remained a secret.

While the British Special Forces had to shoehorn themselves into Operation Desert Storm, the Americans found themselves a role from the beginning. Iraq had invaded Kuwait on 2 August 1990. By 31 August, the headquarters unit of the 5th Special Forces Group from Fort Campbell, Kentucky, had moved to Saudi Arabia to begin its initial mission to support the Saudi Arabian forces. The 1st Battalion, led by Lieutenant Colonel Jerry Thompson, followed. By 14 September, the 2nd Battalion under Lieutenant Colonel 'Ironman' Davis was in the country, and it was followed by the 3rd Battalion under Lieutenant Colonel Mike Shaw. The 1st Battalion were based on the east coast, near Dharhan, and operated out of King Fahd International Airport, while the 2nd and 3rd Battalions were stationed at King Khalid Military City.

The first task was to set up their FOBs, arranging their living quarters and their operational, communications and support centres. They needed ranges and manoeuvre areas to acclimatise the troops and prepare them for combat. They also had to develop defence and evacuation plans for the base. This presented a problem, as King Khalid Military City was isolated and there was a shortage of heavy weapons.

On 13 October 1990, Special Operations Team-A 505 under Captain Ken Takasaki were the first Special Forces unit into action, deploying along the Saudi–Kuwait border with a Saudi Special Forces unit under Captain Prince Fahd, a graduate of the US Special Forces and Rangers course. They patrolled the border from the town of ArRuqi approximately 37 miles (60 km) eastwards, setting up bases in border forts called *mazekahs*. The rest of the border was patrolled by US Special Forces and Coalition units, using Humvees armed with Mk 19 machines guns, night-vision devices and communications equipment. These units were the eyes and ears of the entire Coalition force. The *mazekahs* also provided outposts for Iraqi deserters to surrender to. Leaflets and loudspeakers were used to lure deserters over the border; they were then interrogated and provided invaluable intelligence.

The 5th Special Forces Group continued their border missions until 10 February 1991, when they were replaced by scouts and lead elements from regular units then in theatre. Even when Operation Desert Storm was under way, this border mission was no soft option. There were several firefights with the enemy and some close calls. On one occasion Captain Dan Kepper's detachment was forced to make a quick exit from its *mazekah* and flee in their Humvee under intense ground fire. They managed to escape without loss of life, though their vehicle was damaged. However, even this hasty retreat provided valuable intelligence on the tactics employed by the Iraqis.

Special Forces played another vital role. They acted as liaison with the Arab members of the Coalition. Every Arab unit that went into action had Special Forces troops with it. Thanks to their language skills, they were able to provide General Schwarzkopf with vital information about the Coalition forces' ability and willingness to fight. Stationed on the brigade and battalion boundaries between Egyptian, Syrian and Saudi units, they played a valuable role in integrating units from different nations into a single force.

On 13 January, airborne intelligence discovered that Iraqi forces were moving up to the border, so Schwarzkopf ordered the US 1st Cavalry Division to move up to counter them. This meant moving through Syrian positions at night. The 2nd Battalion of the 5th Special Forces Group were called in to expedite their movement without the two Coalition partners mistakenly coming to blows. Young American soldiers could easily have mistaken the Syrians for Iraqis, especially as they were both equipped with Soviet T-62 tanks.

Once Operation Desert Storm got under way, there were many other incidents where units had to pass through the positions of different nations. Thanks to the Special Forces, not one incident of fratricide was reported.

Special Forces men also provided Arab troops with protective measures against the supposed threat from Saddam Hussein's chemical weapons, coordinated fire support and tactical operations. A Special Forces detachment was sent to the 35th Kuwaiti Armoured Brigade to train them in mine-clearing, Iraqi defensive tactics, aircraft and armoured-vehicle identification and tank-killing techniques. When the Kuwaitis received Yugoslav M-84 main battle tanks, Special Forces troops taught them how to operate and maintain them and, as the 35th Brigade led Joint Force Command, North, into their homeland, Special Forces soldiers went along as advisers.

The 2nd Battalion of 5th Special Forces Group turned their three line companies into four companies to divide themselves between Egyptian and Syrian armoured and commando divisions. They claim to have been responsible for the capture of 8,700 Iraqi prisoners of war.

Once the air war had started, Schwarzkopf also sent US special operations teams deep into Iraq to look for Scuds, as a backup to British Special Forces who were providing intelligence and briefings on the conditions there. These missions were extremely dangerous, as the entire country was an armoured camp and even areas that looked empty on the map turned out to be heavily patrolled by Iraqi units sent out to capture downed Coalition pilots. As the war progressed, SAS men joined with US Special Forces into fighting groups that constantly harassed the enemy, tieing up large numbers of Iraqi soldiers who otherwise would have been available to face the main forces as they came across the border.

While the 2nd Battalion of the 5th Special Forces Group moved forward with their Egyptian and Arab units, the battalion's main headquarters stayed behind in King Khalid Military City to collate incoming intelligence. During the Allied offensive, the Special Forces detachment also coordinated close-air support. The entire Arab force were dependent on US air cover and they needed English speakers to call in airstrikes. Two Special Forces medical sergeants performed a combat amputation on an Egyptian soldier while under intense indirect fire. Another Special Forces soldier crawled into a minefield to drag a wounded Egyptian soldier to safety under artillery fire. One Special Forces Battalion Commander and two of his officers made a close-quarters battle assault on an Iraqi command post, clearing the position. They later received awards for their valour.

Ahead of the main force, there were Special Forces on

reconnaissance missions hundreds of miles deep into Iraq. These teams, supported by the XVIII Airborne Corps and the VII Corps, were placed near the highways to report any attempt by Republican Guard reserves to counterattack or retreat. Special Reconnaissance units had been in training for this task since early October 1990 in flat areas in Saudi Arabia that resembled Iraq. The teams worked on their patrolling techniques, immediate-action drills and reconnaissance procedures. The construction of hide sites was a primary concern. Due to the barren terrain in which the teams would be operating, they would have to rely on ground OPs dug rapidly during the hours of darkness. Problems soon became obvious. Where would they put the dirt and sand they had excavated? What could they cover the hide site with once it was almost finished? What materials best camouflaged the viewing ports? These problems were gradually solved team by team as they conducted mock infiltrations and rehearsals.

Special Reconnaissance teams were also dropped by helicopter to hunt for Scuds in areas hundreds of miles from friendly forces, and where they were surrounded by enemy troops. After poring over dozens of aerial reconnaissance photographs for power lines, towns and areas where dogs and camels might alert their owners, the teams were ferried in on the MH-60s and MH-47s of the 3rd Battalion of the Special Operations Aviation Regiment. The pilots were old hands at special-operations flying, coming in at 20 feet (six metres) off the desert floor at 140 knots in the dead of night to drop off the teams at isolated LZs.

Having been set down, the teams then had the problem

of finding somewhere to hide as daylight approached. In some places there was no vegetation, hills or small folds in the ground for miles. The ground was usually hard, covered with just a dusting of sand. But where the ground was softer, along the Euphrates River, for example, there were other problems. Soft ground and water meant agriculture, and teams deployed there found themselves surrounded by inquisitive farmers.

On 23 February, the day before the ground attack, eight more Special Forces teams flew into Iraq, but were unable to find hide sites in the barren terrain. One MH-47 delivered two A-teams. One radioed for immediate extraction. The area where they had landed was completely featureless and nothing like the terrain they had prepared for. The other hung on for three days, communicating via satellite. Some were extracted, but others were captured.

The same day, 23 February, three soldiers from Detachment A-532 of the 1st Battalion under Master Sergeant Jeffery Sims were dropped off by an MH-60 from the 160th SOAR (Special Operations Aviation Regiment). After crossing the border at 21.00 hours, they landed at 22.00 hours at a position north of the Euphrates, less than 100 miles (160 km) from Baghdad. They had less than five hours to prepare their hide sites, and there were less than eight hours to go before the XVIII Airborne Corps and the VII Corps would cross the border. Unfortunately, the helicopter landed in a ploughed field with furrows almost three feet (nearly a metre) deep and their boots sank into the loose earth. They were greeted by the sound of barking dogs, though this seemed to alert no human interest.

By first light, Master Sergeant Sims and his men had hiked to their hide sites and dug in. On their way, a 50-car railway train had rolled close by their position, a fact they communicated by satellite direct to the XVIII Airborne.

When the sun came up, the local people awoke. Farmers and sheep herders began walking around near the hide site. No one had expected so much foot traffic. One shepherd walked within a foot of the peephole, but took no notice and walked on. They had another close scrape when another sheep herder with a dog came dangerously close. Then, at around 14.00 hours, their luck got worse. A small girl and a man who appeared to be her grandfather stopped in their tracks, staring in the direction of the hide. The old man edged closer, then the girl ran towards the site. Slowly lifting the lid, she stared wide-eyed at the Green Berets inside. As the three men aimed their silenced pistols at her head, the old man started yelling, 'The Americans are here! The Americans are here!' to shepherds close by.

The team had already been compromised, so shooting two civilians would serve no purpose, especially as one was a little girl. The Green Berets let her and the old man go and radioed for extraction. Then they ran to a ditch some 550 yards (500 metres) away, where they intended to make a stand. Within 30 minutes, Iraqi troops had begun arriving by truck along the highway. The team began firing at the enemy soldiers, knocking them down one by one. Their rifles were set on single shot to preserve precious ammunition.

Then two busloads of troops arrived and armed civilians began moving around their flanks. Several village men stood on an old masonry wall surrounding a stone house nearby, waving their hands to indicate Sims's position. The Green Berets picked one of them off, but soldiers and villagers were now creeping up the irrigation ditches. The team hit several of them and they retreated, but more buses carrying soldiers arrived. It was plain that the Green Berets could not hold them off for ever.

Then, an hour and a half after they had been discovered, an F-16 Eagle roared overhead and, at Sims's direction, dropped cluster bombs and thousand-pounders into ditches just 300 yards (275 metres) from Sims's position. Then an MH-60 flown by Chief Warrant Officer Randy Stephens and Chief Warrant Officer John Crisufulli arrived, having crossed 240 nautical miles or 444 kilometers in broad daylight. Under an intense barrage of small-arms fire, Sims and his men dashed for the helicopter, got on without injury and were whisked back to Saudi. It was the only hot extraction in daylight carried out during Desert Storm.

Another Special Reconnaissance mission was led by Chief Warrant Officer Chad Balwanz, commander of Detachment A-525. His eight-man team were inserted on a tributary of the Euphrates, on a mission to monitor traffic along Highway 8 from Baghdad to An-Nasiriyah. After infiltration they dug two hide sites, but by morning the area was swamped by civilians, including throngs of small children playing nearby. At one point the children found themselves right on top of the hide sites and, meeting the Green Berets eyeball to eyeball, fled screaming. The team had plainly been compromised.

The team moved to a new position, planning to move

further south at nightfall to establish another temporary hide site. For two hours, they carried out surveillance on the road. Then the children returned. Adults followed, some carrying weapons. After them came Iraqi soldiers. Then four large trucks came screeching down the road and more Iraqi soldiers poured out. Balwanz counted more than a hundred. In the next ten minutes he and his team managed to pick off some 40 enemy soldiers. Then a US Air Force F-16 arrived and soon Balwanz was directing airstrikes dangerously close to his own positions. Nevertheless the team held out and, at 20.00 hours, an MH-60 of the 160th SOAR managed to pull them out. Not one member of Balwanz's team was killed or wounded.

Between them, Master Sergeant Sims's Detachment A-532 and Chief Warrant Officer Balwanz's Detachment A-525 had accounted for an estimated 250 to 300 enemy dead and wounded. Other Special Reconnaissance missions were not so dramatic. All the other teams infiltrated without any fuss, dug their hides, and counted vehicles and soldiers. It was tedious work but they remained undiscovered.

US Special Forces also conducted direct-action missions during Desert Storm. Most were of a sensitive nature and details remain classified. General Schwarzkopf forbade the Special Forces sneaking into enemy territory before the air war started and rejected many proposed operations after the bombing started. The main objective of the few direct-action missions that were launched involved disrupting enemy communications. Americans joined the SBS in the operation to cut the fibre-optic cable that ran from

Baghdad to southwest Iraq. According to an after-action report, this was 'a totally successful operation in that the infiltration and exfiltration was perfect and no enemy activity was encountered'.

Another direct-action mission followed a request by the two Army Corps for soil samples so they could assess the capacity of the area to carry heavy traffic. The Central Intelligence Agency had warned General Schwarzkopf's generals that the tanks and trucks they wanted to send across southern Iraq for the 'Hail Mary Play' might become dogged down in the sandy terrain.

General Schwarzkopf recognised that he was short of detailed intelligence on the weather and terrain in the region and allowed six-man Special Forces teams to be helicoptered covertly into Iraq to scoop up soil samples for analysis in Riyadh. The teams also carried camcorders and digital cameras that transmitted photographs back to headquarters. The soil samples showed that the ground was firm enough for tanks and the pictures gave commanders a close-up view of their intended battlefields.

US Special Forces were also tasked with search-and-rescue missions to recover downed pilots. The 2nd Battalion of the 5th Special Forces Group took it upon themselves to train for this role in September and October, and duly took over from the US Air Force, who did not have an effective programme.

As aircraft were needed for CSAR (combat search and research), Special Forces again called on the 160th SOAR for assistance, as their MH-60 Black Hawks and MH-47 Chinooks were equipped for deep insertions. They began training together, developing new tactics and manoeuvres. Their plan was to infiltrate a rescue team and a Humvee up to two hundred miles behind enemy lines with the MH-47 setting down while the vehicle made the recovery. Special Forces teams established a good rapport with the pilots of the 160th SOAR as they spent long hours practising rescuing downed airmen. They also sawed down stretchers to fit on the MH-60s and procured communications devices for the Special Forces security teams.

When the air war began, CSAR units positioned themselves in FOBs. On 17 February, a US F-16 suffered engine failure 40 miles (65 km) behind enemy lines and crashed. At 18.15 hours, AWACS (airborne warning-and-control system) aircraft in charge of the operation put out the call. Within minutes two modified MH-60 Black Hawks from the 3-160th SOAR were in the air. They were equipped with night-vision devices and carried security teams from the 2nd Battalion of the 5th Special Forces Group armed with AT-4 handheld rocket launchers and M16/203 assault rifles. By 20.00 hours, Chief Warrant Officer Thomas Montgomery had located the pilot as enemy vehicles were closing in on him. Montgomery called AWACS for support, then picked up the pilot, Air Force Academy football star Captain 'Spike' Thomas. As they made their escape, Iraqis fired SAMs at the retreating helicopter, but onboard jamming devices and emergency evasive action left the missiles far behind. Minutes later, an F-16 was on station to take out the enemy vehicles. This was the only CSAR mission conducted at night using night-vision guidance.

The Special Forces did not have to carry out as many

CSAR missions as they expected. It had been predicted that 40 aircraft would be lost on the first night of the air war. In fact only three were downed, and the Coalition lost only 52 planes during the entire war. Twenty-two pilots and crew survived their shoot-down. Of these, 14 were captured immediately, while eight evaded capture – two for more than 24 hours. Of the seven CSAR missions launched, only three were successful. Nevertheless, knowing that the Special Forces were on hand to ride to the rescue boosted the morale of the air crew.

US Special Forces also played a key role in the liberation of Kuwait City. The plan was for the US Marines to hold their position on the outskirts while a vanguard of Kuwaitis, Syrians, Egyptians and other Arab forces drove into the capital. This meant that the only American troops into the city in the first wave were the Green Berets with the Arab units. One of the Special Forces' responsibilities was to see that the Kuwaitis did not retaliate against Iraqi prisoners for the atrocities that had been committed during the occupation. The Coalition did not want any atrocities of its own on its hands.

As the Allies entered the city, the Special Forces expanded their role beyond merely 'advising' the Arab forces. With the help of Kuwaiti resistance fighters who had remained in the city during the occupation, Special Forces troops began clearing areas of booby traps and mines. Members of the resistance also guided Special Forces teams to key Iraqi headquarters buildings and torture facilities, where they collected five truckloads of documents indicating violations of the Geneva Conventions.

As Special Forces teams had accompanied Arab units

who certainly overstepped the mark when it came to retaliation, they came under criticism from the international press who had followed. As a result, Special Forces teams were withdrawn from the Arab units, but not before they had helped the Egyptians secure their embassy. US Special Forces also retook the US Embassy in Kuwait City.

At a press conference at the end of the war, General Schwarzkopf singled out Special Forces for special praise. This surprised his staff, as he was known not to be a fan and had left half of the Special Forces commands back in the US. He had also doubted the usefulness of the SAS at the beginning of the war. Now he thanked them personally. 'What you've done is never going to be made public and we can't make it public,' he said solemnly. Then he added, 'You kept Israel out of the war.'

By the end of the war, both the SAS and the SBS had been involved in the destruction of many communications facilities and, it was estimated, eliminated about a third of the mobile Scud launchers. General Schwarzkopf conveyed more generous praise privately in a letter dated 9 March 1991 – ten days after the ceasefire. It was written on the headed notepaper of the 'Office of the Commander-in-Chief Operation Desert Storm, United States Central Command, APO New York 09852-0006' and marked 'SECRET'. Addressed to 'Sir Patrick Hine, Air Chief Marshal, Joint Headquarters, Royal Air Force Wycombe, Buckinghamshire HP14 4UE, it was sent 'Thru: Sir Peter de la Billière KCB, CBE, DSO, MC, Lieutenant-General, British Forces Commander Middle East, Riyadh, Saudi Arabia'. It read:

Subject: Letter of Commendation for the 22d
Special Air Service (SAS) Regiment

1. I wish to officially commend the 22d Special
Air Service (SAS) Regiment for their totally
outstanding performance of military operations
during Operation Desert Storm.

2. Shortly after the initiation of the strategic air
campaign, it became apparent that the Coalition
Forces would be unable to eliminate Iraq's firing
of Scud missiles on Israel.

The continued firing of Scuds on Israel carried
with it enormous unfavourable political
ramifications and could, in fact, have resulted in
the dismantling of the carefully crafted coalition.
Such a dismantling would have adversely affected
in ways difficult to measure the ultimate outcome
of the military campaign. It became apparent that
the only way the Coalition could succeed in
reducing these Scud launches was by physically
placing military forces on the ground in the
vicinity of the western launch sites. At that time,
the majority of available Coalition forces were
committed to the forthcoming military campaign
in the eastern portion of the theatre of operations.

Further, none of these forces possessed the
requisite skills and abilities required to conduct
such a dangerous operation. The only force
deemed qualified for this critical mission was the
22d Special Air Service (SAS) Regiment.

3. From the first day they were assigned their missions until the last day of the conflict, the performance of the 22d Special Air Service (SAS) Regiment was courageous and highly professional. The area in which they were committed proved to contain far more numerous enemy forces than had been predicted by every intelligence estimate, the terrain was much more difficult than expected and the weather conditions were unseasonably brutal. Despite these hazards, in a very short period of time the 22d Special Air Service (SAS) Regiment was successful in totally denying the central corridor of western Iraq to Iraqi Scud units. The result was that the principal areas used by the Iraqis to fire Scuds on Tel Aviv were no longer available to them. They were required to move their Scud missile firing forces to the north-west portion of Iraq and from that position the firing of Scuds was essentially militarily ineffective.

4. When it became necessary to introduce United States Special Operations Forces into the area to attempt to close down the northwest Scud areas, the 22d Special Air Service (SAS) Regiment provided invaluable assistance to the US forces. They took every possible measure to ensure the US forces were thoroughly briefed and were able to profit from the valuable lessons that had been learned by earlier SAS deployments into western Iraq. I am completely convinced that had the US

forces not received these thorough indoctrinations by SAS personnel, US forces would have suffered a much higher rate of casualties than was ultimately the case. Further, the SAS and US joint forces immediately merged into a combined fighting force where the synergetic effect of these fine units ultimately caused the enemy to be convinced that they were facing forces in western Iraq that were more than tenfold the size of those they were actually facing. As a result, large numbers of enemy forces that might otherwise have been deployed in the eastern theatre were tied down in western Iraq.

5. The performance of the 22d Special Air Service (SAS) Regiment during Operation Desert Storm was in the highest traditions of the professional military service and in keeping with the proud history and tradition that has been established by that regiment.

Please ensure that this commendation receives appropriate attention and is passed on to the unit and its members.

Signed:
H Norman Schwarzkopf
General, US Army
Commander-in-Chief

CHAPTER NINE
BACK TO IRAQ

During the Second Gulf War, the US, Britain, Australia and Poland put on the ground the largest special-operations force since the Vietnam War. In northern Iraq particularly, there was a huge special-operations presence. At the time of the invasion, as many as 80 per cent of the combat forces of the 53,000-strong US Special Operations Command – including Navy SEALs, Army Green Berets and Rangers, and Delta Force operatives – found themselves committed in Iraq and Afghanistan.

After Tora Bora, the SAS had returned home to Britain, but, in the run-up to the Second Gulf War, America again asked for their help. President George W Bush particularly wanted the British SAS on board. General Tommy Franks, who was now in command of the invasion of Iraq, was aware how close the SAS had come to nailing Osama bin

Laden and the remnants of his al-Qaeda forces in Afghanistan. When they slipped away into Pakistan, he blamed overcautiousness from the US Special Forces.

The multinational contribution to the invasion of Iraq was the responsibility of Brigadier General Gary L 'Shooter' Harrell. He had commanded the Special Forces hunting for cocaine baron Pablo Escobar in Colombia in the early 1990s and had been with Delta Force during their disastrous attempt to capture the warlord Mohamed Farrah Aidid in Mogadishu in 1993, which resulted in the notorious 'Black Hawk Down' incident.

The British element was closely integrated into the US Joint Special Operations Command, alongside the 75th Rangers and the 1st Special Forces Operational Detachment Delta – the Delta Force. They were supported by the 160th Special Operations Air Regiment with 14 Chinooks, 18 Sikorsky MH-60 Pave Hawks, seven MH-6 Hughes Little Birds and Hercules MC-130s, along with other helicopters and air-to-air refuelling tankers for search-and-rescue missions. The British component was 215 SAS men from B, D and G Squadrons, along with their pink Land Rovers and SAS-trained signallers and support groups, plus M Squadron of the SBS, who were with 3 Commando Brigade of the Royal Marines on board HMS *Ark Royal*.

British Special Forces were also supported by the Joint Special Forces Aviation Wing – the 657 Army Air Corps Squadron with six AH-7 Lynx helicopters, along with eight CH-47 Chinooks from the 7th Squadron of the RAF, based at Odiham, Hampshire. The Hercules aircraft of RAF Special Forces Flight of 47 Squadron would carry the SAS to their dropping-off points, and a former commander of the SAS – Lieutenant General Cedric Delves – was sent to MacDill Air Force Base in Tampa, Florida as Special Forces liaison officer with US Central Command.

General Franks also wanted the Australian Special Forces on board. He was well aware of their contribution to the war in Afghanistan after their CO, Lieutenant Colonel Rowan Tink, had been awarded the US Bronze Star for bravery. The Australians contributed a hundred men from their 1st SAS Regiment with the 4th Battalion of the Royal Australian Regiment, a commando unit who would act as a quick-reaction force to extract the SAS if they got into trouble. They were supported by some 250 airmen and women and maintenance crews deployed with a squadron of 14 F/A-18 Royal Australian Air Force Hornet fighter aircraft, some 150 personnel deployed with three RAAF C-130 Hercules transport aircraft and some 150 personnel deployed with two P-3C Orion maritime patrol aircraft.

The Australian Special Forces Task Group itself was some 500 strong. These included an advance party of an SAS squadron, CH-47 Chinook troop-lift helicopters and personnel from 5th Aviation Regiment, and specialist troops to deal with the threat of weapons of mass destruction (WMD) drawn from the Incident Response Regiment based at Holsworthy, New South Wales. They would also be on hand to rescue downed airmen or evacuate the wounded. Rather than be integrated into the command structure of the American Special Forces like the British, the Aussies maintained their own Special Forces Forward Command to ensure that the Australian

SAS were always commanded by Australians. However, it was located within the headquarters the US Special Operations Command.

Other Coalition members also supplied Special Forces troops. Poland provided commandos from the Polish Operational Manoeuvre Reconnaissance Group – the *Grupa Reagowania Operacyjno Manewrowego*, or GROM – and Canada sent its specialist Joint Task Force Two.

The Americans also supplied three battalions from the 5th Special Forces Group based at Fort Campbell, Kentucky – 2,000 men in all – and the US Navy Special Warfare Wing. This consisted of the US Navy SEALs and DEVGRU. They had their own air arm, the 16th US Aviation Wing, with MH-53 Pave Low helicopters for CSAR missions and Hercules MC-130, some of them kitted out as Spectre gunships. Then there were the 8th US Psychological Operations and the 9th Civil Affairs Battalion (Airborne) to win over the hearts and minds of the Iraqi people.

When the US Special Forces went into Jordan in late 2002, the SAS went too, joining their American colleagues at Azraq airbase. This was to be their FOB. By October they were in the west of Iraq, where they were to undertake an 'area denial mission' so that Saddam Hussein could not rain down Scud missiles on Israel, as he had attempted to do during the First Gulf War. There, the SAS, backed by Royal Marines of 45 Commando, were in the vanguard of the freewheeling war in the Iraqi western desert. Along with a squadron from Australia's Special Air Service Regiment, Poland's GROM and US Special Operations Forces, they set out to neutralise any Scud missile batteries threatening Israel. This was done under a secret agreement with Israel, which had already deployed it own Special Forces teams or *sayerets* in the region. Again, for political reasons, the Israelis had to be removed and replaced by Coalition Special Forces.

The British and Americans found little opposition. One officer has called western Iraq a 'Special Forces playground'. They attacked airbases, roads and communications sites in fast-moving Land Rover patrols, and undertook covert forward reconnaissance. During the initial air attacks, they directed the bombing and they undertook 'psyops' – psychological operations – to encourage those who opposed Saddam Hussein's regime to rise up. These ran entirely separately from the CIA and MI6 operations to contact opposition groups and gather intelligence in the Kurdish region and around Basra.

In the south, Special Operations personnel gave aid to the conventional forces and, in the cities, help to the anti-Ba'athist Shi'ia elements. Meanwhile, the Green Berets, Delta Force and the CIA were training the Kurdish Peshmerga guerrillas in the north. US Special Forces were also working closely with the Kurdish fighters there in their efforts to bring down the regime. The SOF also helped bring in the 173rd Airborne Brigade, and marked and called in Coalition air power on regime targets. Special-operations forces were also responsible for attacking a number of specific targets such as airfields, sites thought to house WMD, and command-and-control headquarters. Coalition Special Forces teams were also used to capture isolated oil wells, both onshore and offshore. It was vital to keep them from being sabotaged so that oil pumping could resume once a new government had been installed in Baghdad.

The British were determined not to have a repeat of the disastrous Bravo Two Zero mission. Their Pinkies would be airlifted by helicopter or Hercules into the country, then they would infiltrate as near as possible to their objectives. They would also have the designated combat air support of two RAF flights of G7 Harriers. Also on call at Azraq airbase were ten F-16 Fighting Falcons and a National Guard contingent of A-10 Warthog dedicated ground-support aircraft.

Even as the main forces went in, there were hundreds of Special Operations forces already in the country, laid up in positions where they could observe the Iraqi Republican Guard or key military installations. That figure rose rapidly as the glare of the international media turned to the build-up of the main UK and US ground forces, allowing Special Forces units to conduct a shadowy war in the west and north. Unofficially, US and Allied Special Forces were given freedom of action to operate anywhere inside Iraq. They were a key component of the air war, guiding smart bombs onto Saddam Hussein's headquarters and palaces. The SAS and SBS were also used as pathfinders in support of the British infantry assaults in the south in the early days of the war.

But the British Special Forces were becoming drastically overstretched. The SAS's headquarters at Stirling Lines was practically deserted. As well as the three squadrons they had taken to Iraq, more men had been drafted in from the R (Reserve) Squadron as well as 21 and 23 SAS, the territorial regiments. Other men came from the

Revolutionary Warfare wing, the HQ Squadron and the regiment's training wing. Only A Squadron, who had seen the latest fighting in Helmand province in Afghanistan, remained behind in the UK in case of emergency.

On 15 March, the SBS, Royal Marines commandos and US Navy SEALs went in to capture and secure oil platforms in the Gulf and the oil fields around Basra. Dropped into the sea by helicopter at night, they had to swim in full kit to the legs of the platform, scale them using ropes and magnetic pads, and then storm the platforms with MP-5SDs and stun grenades. They did not know whether the platforms were manned, whether those who might be on board were armed, or whether the platforms were booby-trapped. On one platform taken by the GROM, the phone began to ring. The team froze, fearing the telephone might be rigged to detonate explosive charges. After a while it stopped and the Polish officer commented that it must have been a wrong number – to everyone's great relief.

By March 2003, the Australians were in-theatre, getting acclimatised and training for their eventual commitment. Their job would be to conduct special operations in the western desert, where they were to prevent the Iraqis using the WMD they were believed to have, and to deny them the use of ballistic missiles once more. Otherwise, they were to conduct harassment missions on command-and-control centres and to deny the Iraqis freedom of movement in the theatre. They would also have to work closely with the British SAS and the US Delta Force, and to liaise closely with the RAF and the USAF, on whom they depended for close-air support.

The SBS, Royal Marine Commandos and US Navy SEALs took key positions around the Al Faw peninsula before the main force arrived, and led the attack on the port of Umm Qasr in the largest SEAL operation ever mounted. The SBS and Royal Marine Commandos occupied the forward OPs, coordinating naval gunfire on the targets in land. After the fall of Umm Qasr, members of GROM were photographed by Reuters alongside the DEVGRU, to the embarrassment of the Polish authorities, who wanted their commitment kept secret. The GROM were withdrawn from Umm Qasr and sent to join the Royal Marine commandos attacking Basra, in the belief that the British were less likely to court publicity.

US Special Forces took up positions south of Baghdad, while Delta Force and the CIA readied the Peshmerga to attack key Iraqi positions. They were also to attack villages along the Iranian border, occupied by Ansar al-Islam, a radical Islamist group thought to be linked to al-Qaeda.

On the night of 20 March 2003, as the main force was attacking from Kuwait in the south, MH-6 Little Bird assault helicopters started attacking the Iraqi positions along the Jordanian border with electronically operated 7.62mm mini-guns and pods of air-to-ground missiles. The defences quickly crumbled. RAF Chinooks and Land Rovers streamed over the border in the dark and headed for airfields designated H-2 and H-3 after the old pumping stations on the Haifa pipeline. Saddam Hussein still had operational planes there that could have been used to deliver chemical weapons. The A-10 Warthogs made short work of anything on the ground with their nose-mounted 30mm Gatling guns, which are capable of firing 3,000 armour-piercing rounds a minute. Further backup was provided by the Harriers and the F-16s.

Once the Coalition air support had made short work of any defences the airfields could put up, the Special Forces drove straight in. With the airfields secure, Chinooks and C-130 Hercules began ferrying in ammunition, supplies, vehicles and more men. When the Royal Marines' 45 Commando and the US 75th Airborne Rangers arrived, they took over control of the airfields, while the British and Australian SAS headed out into the desert.

From the second day of Operation Iraqi Freedom onwards, the Special Forces used the two captured airfields as bases for long-range reconnaissance patrols. US Air Force Predator unmanned observation craft flew ahead, scouting for targets to be attacked. Special Forces then pushed eastwards across the desert towards Baghdad backed by air support from RAF GR7 Harriers.

Half a squadron of Australian SAS men then moved northwards towards the Syrian border. Intelligence reports indicated that Iraqi Scuds were moving across the border from Syria and setting up there. Meanwhile, the F-16 and A-10s moved up to H-3 to be on hand to provide close-air support as the SAS moved northwards and eastwards. The main highways from Baghdad to Jordan and Syria were being kept open by small groups of Iraqi commandos, leaving an escape route for Saddam Hussein and his henchmen. The British and Australian SAS moved on them, dispersing them and undertaking further area denial operations.

According to American intelligence, the Iraqis were hiding their Scud missile launchers in Syria and planning to run them over the border, fire them, then run them back before they could be hit by an airstrike. A troop of six Australian SAS were sent out in two six-wheeled Land Rovers to put a stop to this by taking out the command, control and communication headquarters of the Iraqi batteries. This operated out of five vehicles in a well-entrenched position guarded by 50 Iraqis.

As the SAS men approached, they came under heavy fire. However, the Aussies decide that, if they made a direct attack on board their vehicles, they could take the centre of the Iraqi position. They came speeding out of cover, only to find their way blocked by two vehicles manned by 20 Iraqis, who were putting up a barrage of automatic fire. It was plain they were one of the elite Iraqi units trained to take on the SAS. 'They definitely weren't conscript soldiers,' said one SAS man. 'They were very aggressive. They were very well trained. They moved towards us. We moved towards them.' The battle was on.

'They were operating in sports utility vehicles with large machine guns mounted in the rear tray,' said the troop commander. 'On observing our location, they began engaging us with heavy machine-gun fire, small-arms fire and rocket-propelled grenades.'

The SAS retaliated with their .50-calibre Browning machine gun, scattering the Iraqis.

'When you come under fire, you really don't think about it at all,' said another patrol member. 'You think about getting to the next vantage point so you can return fire. You really don't think about the rounds coming in at you. You're just making sure that you're doing your drills correctly and that you're backing up your mate in the next car.'

The truth is, he did rather more than that. Under heavy fire, he picked up a Javelin shoulder-mounted missile launcher and took out the first Iraqi vehicle. 'Both sides in this particular instance actually stopped shooting to watch this rocket cruise through the air and actually engage a moving vehicle at high speeds, moving away from us, and I think that changed the battlefield,' said the troop commander.

A second Javelin missile also found its target.

'It was a little bit daunting seeing so many enemy coming towards us,' said a third man, 'but when we saw how effective our weapons systems were in neutralising their vehicles, and you could actually physically see the shock on the enemy's faces when they did see their vehicles destroyed.'

But the battle was far from over. 'We were getting rounds splashing all around the vehicles and around the guys when they dismounted,' said the squadron commander. 'We were getting RPGs exploding over our heads, at times, and behind us.'

Under the covering fire of more .50-calibre rounds, the rest of the SAS patrol moved forward. At this stage, after seeing two of their vehicles destroyed, quite a few of the enemy started to surrender. But others were hiding in the grass, returning fire with rocket launchers and small arms.

'Several also attempted to set up an 82mm mortar tube and they were about to try to engage us with that,' said an SAS man. 'We couldn't really engage the enemy around the mortar tube because there were some surrendering, so we engaged the mortar tube with a sniper rifle and that was very effective. The round hit the tube and caused a mortar bomb that was in the tube to explode.'

That finished off the mortar crew, but other Iraqis had moved in among some Bedouin tents. As there were civilians in there, the SAS had to stop firing. 'They exploited that component of our professionalism,' said the squadron commander. 'It was a difficult time. We were also trying to effect the capture of about eight enemy who were surrendering with their arms in the air, but as soon as we had got within range [of them] they had dropped their weapons and continued firing. It was a very difficult situation.' The SAS men had no choice but to fire back. 'As soon as they are in an aggressive pose and a threat, they were neutralised,' said the commander.

Those Iraqi soldiers who surrendered were disarmed and allowed to go free. They were surprised by this and even a little hesitant to walk away in case the SAS men were not really going to let them go. They may even have been worried about being shot in the back. Even though these men might walk over the hill, pick up another gun and start shooting again, the SAS had no choice. They could not take prisoners along with them if they were going to complete their mission.

Six Aussies had killed 12 Iraqis out of a platoon of around 30. The rest surrendered. The mission was a complete success with no Australian loss of life. This unit then moved on to take the Kubaysah cement factory, one of the biggest in the Middle East. They had been ordered to clear it of all Iraqi troops and to check the site for hidden weapons. They did not want to damage the cement factory because it was part of the infrastructure of Iraq. 'If we wanted Iraq to get back on its feet quickly,' said the squadron commander, 'then we didn't want to destroy it.'

However, it proved to be guarded by scores of Iraqi soldiers who ignored the SAS's demands to surrender. It was a difficult target to assault and the Australians did not want to risk the lives of civilians inside by fighting their way in. Their commander came up with a novel solution. He called in the US Air Force.

'We requested that an aircraft, an F14, come and do a low fly, breaking the sound barrier,' said the squadron commander. 'The effect of this was a sonic boom – a massive explosion. We actually thought he had detonated ammunition inside the facility. That wasn't the case. But it broke in several windows and as result people came running out with their arms up.'

He had got the idea from one of his men, who had been in the RAAF. 'I remembered before I joined the army, with the Australian Air Force, I broke the sound barrier by mistake and broke a lot of greenhouses in South Australia,' he said. The cement works fell without a single shot being fired and netted 40 prisoners of war.

On 25 March members of the US Army's 75th Ranger Regiment captured a third strategic airfield, H-1, in a night-time parachute assault. Their immediate objective was to take complete control of the two main roads that linked Baghdad to Jordan and Syria. They were also to search for further Scud sites and close the Syrian border to prevent more missiles being brought up from there.

Over the next two weeks the Special Forces teams moved steadily towards the Euphrates valley. However, apart from these airfields and their small bases, which were guarded by UK Marines and US Rangers, the Special Forces teams were not trying to occupy ground. Instead, they aimed to keep the small Iraqi garrisons in the region off-guard. Travellers on the road from Baghdad to the Jordanian border reported few signs of Western troops apart from occasional vehicle checkpoints, suggesting they largely moved at night away from populated areas.

By the end of March, British and American Special Forces were approaching Baghdad. The Australian convoy of 15 vehicles was some 50 miles behind, having stopped off with some US Special Forces men to call in an airstrike on Al-Rutbah Prison, which was now a smoking ruin.

US Special Forces were now linking up with the Marines, and all the oil installations in southern Iraqi and the Gulf had fallen to the SBS, the SEALs and GROM. But not everything had gone the Special Forces' way. On 31 March Al Jazeera television had paraded UK equipment in the northern Iraqi city of Mosul, providing the public with a brief glimpse into the SAS role in toppling Saddam Hussein's regime. Footage showed Iraqi civilians jubilantly driving a Land Rover through the streets of the city, then a quad bike, and a collection of British weapons being displayed at an Iraqi military base. This included handheld rocket launchers, 40mm grenades, machine guns and specialist radio equipment, suggesting it did not come from a conventional British Army unit. Iraqi television said the equipment was captured after an attempted helicopter landing. The location of the incident, far from the main UK operating area around Kuwait and Basra, immediately led to media speculation that the 22nd SAS

Regiment was in some way involved. UK military spokesmen refused to comment.

In fact, the equipment belonged to the SBS, who had been patrolling the area around Mosul in northwest Iraq when they had driven right past an Iraqi patrol without a shot being fired. However, the Iraqis were a point reconnaissance unit for a much larger force armed with tanks. The SBS realised this only when they ran into the larger force face to face. Normally, this would not have caused a problem. They would simply have made a run for it, headed for the emergency rendezvous point and been airlifted out. As it was, the Iraqis had blocked off all exit points on the road. Behind them was a steep hill, cut with deep ravines.

An SOV (special operations vehicle) Land Rover is well armed, but they did not have enough weaponry to take on the large force that now confronted them. As the Iraqis opened fire, the SBS men had no alternative but to abandon their Land Rover and make a dash for it. Once in the relative safety of the hills, they decided that it would better to split into smaller groups, which would give them a better chance of survival. Most of the men got clear away, called in a helicopter and were airlifted out. But two men missed the emergency rendezvous point and had to race the 65 miles (105 km) to the Syrian border with half the Iraqi Army on their tail.

While Al Jazeera said that the Iraqis had captured the Land Rover, the Ministry of Defence dismissed this as propaganda. The Land Rover, they said, had been jettisoned from a Chinook when it had engine problems.

The Americans were furious. They said that one of the

pieces of equipment the SBS had left behind was a Stinger surface-to-air missile, later used to bring down one of their F-16 Fighting Falcons. The embarrassment of the SBS amused the SAS, though. After intense diplomatic negotiations, the two SBS men were eventually returned from Syria.

As usual, UK officials would reveal little information about the operations their Special Forces were undertaking in western Iraq. But the Coalition commander, General Tommy Franks, praised them publicly, saying, 'They have accomplished some wonderful things out there.'

The Australians have been more open about their involvement. 'In all there were around eight of us operating in the western desert, but to the Iraqis it must have seemed like 800,' said one Aussie SAS man. 'Our primary role was to stop weapons of mass destruction from being launched from the 1991 Scud Line in the western Iraqi desert, while our secondary role was to raise merry hell, "Digger style". Basically, we were an enormous itch that the Iraqis could not scratch, as we were everywhere and anywhere. One day we were in the desert, the next in a giant cement works.'

The cement works was the one at Kubaysah – dubbed 'the Temple of Doom' by the SAS – 40 miles (65 km) north of Highway One between Baghdad and Amman and 12 miles (20 km) south of al-Asad airbase, which the Australian SAS would go on to take. Along the way they had a number of running battles and captured more than 2,000 Iraqis, including Republican Guards and men from dedicated anti-Special Forces units. They largely tended the wounded, fed and watered the prisoners, then sent them home. In 42 days they found no Scuds, though they called in airstrikes that dropped more than 45 tons of bombs in the first week alone, and suffered no losses.

'The fact that the squadron suffered no casualties did not surprise me, as we minimised the risks to our own people and to the Iraqis,' said the SAS man. 'Despite the lack of casualties and the string of victories, this was no picnic as the Iraqis were well organised and well equipped. It was one on one and it was tough.'

Due to the presence of Bedouins and local Iraqis, it was impossible to move around the flat western desert in daylight. They had to go in at night. The first challenge was to negotiate a system of trenches and earth berms without being detected by the network of Iraqi border posts. Having done that successfully, they ran into an Iraqi military convoy about 20 miles (32 km) beyond the border. The ensuing firefight ended with SAS medics tending the Iraqi wounded, whom they released, as it would not have been possible to continue the mission encumbered with prisoners.

Another SAS patrol that had crossed into Iraq by night spent 96 hours in the flat, open desert without being spotted by anyone, including the local Bedouin herdsmen – an achievement in itself. After their experience in the First Gulf War, they assumed the Iraqis must have figured that the SAS would be there. As a result the patrol adopted a strategy called 'manoeuvre warfare' to put pressure on the enemy and to force them to give away their position. As a small force, their aim was always to create a disproportionate effect by using the element of surprise. Consequently, they tried to be completely unpredictable in their tactics. On the other hand, they had to deal with an unpredictable enemy, who would sometimes raise their hands in surrender, then resume firing when the SAS got closer. One of the regiment's flags bears eloquent testimony to that. It has bullet holes and powder burns from being shot at, at close range.

'Adding to our operational experience we also had the weather to contend with,' said the Aussie SAS man, 'as temperatures often ranged from minus five to 43 Celsius – and we thought Oz varied! All in all, it was a magnificent effort and a ripper achievement.'

On top of the extremes of temperature they had to endure sandstorms that reduced visibility to 30 feet (nine metres) and blew for days on end. On another occasion it rained so heavily that the group's weapons systems were clogged with wind-blown mud. The atrocious weather conditions were also a problem for the helicopters used to keep the forward team supplied. They had to fly as much as 400 miles (644 km) behind enemy lines at night, dodging Iraqi air defences and refuelling in the air along the way.

Contacts with the enemy occurred almost daily. This was partly because the Iraqis were seeking them out. However, the SAS considered that the best form of defence was attack, so they constantly hit the Iraqis to keep them on the back foot.

On their second night inside Iraq, the SAS staged a well-planned attack on a well-defended radio relay station. Achieving total surprise, a phased assault cleared the facility in what became a one-sided firefight. Then an airstrike was called in to destroy the tower. This effectively undermined Iraq's ballistic-missile capability.

The Iraqis responded the following morning. They sent five or six armed vehicles, but the SAS simply outmanoeuvred them. Fire from heavy weapons, Javelin rockets, Mk19 grenade launchers, heavy machine guns and sniper rifles forced the Iraqis to seek shelter in a number of buildings, where airstrikes finished them off.

Several days later another SAS patrol was confronted by a force of 50 Iraqis in civilian trucks and 4x4s. The Iraqis were armed with mortars, RPGs and heavy machine guns but the SAS held their own. Within the first few minutes, they knocked out one of the trucks, forcing the Iraqis to advance on foot, leaving them particularly vulnerable. However, the SAS also suffered from repeated equipment failure. One SAS man had to employ all four weapons systems on his long-range desert-patrol vehicle, one after another, as each one in turn jammed.

While some elements of the SAS were moving constantly from action to action, another team remained undetected in an OP overlooking Highway 10. At one point there was a crossroads and a truck stop defended by some 200 Iraqis. The SAS called in airstrikes over a period of 48 hours, then moved in to clear the facility. The enemy had withdrawn under cover of a sandstorm, but the team were able to confirm that the target had been neutralised.

Coalition leaders were particularly pleased because no Scuds had been fired at Israel – a development that could have massively complicated Allied war plans. Indeed, no Scuds were found. The main opposition to the Special Forces came from Iraqi commando units attempting to keep the main roads to Jordan and Syria open in case key members of the regime needed to escape if Baghdad should fall.

After the first week, action in the western desert slowed and the SAS changed strategy – they began stopping people on the highway to prevent members of the regime escaping over the border. They captured a large number of Ba'ath Party members and paramilitary Fedayeen carrying large amounts of cash as they tried to flee the country. They also stopped a convoy carrying looted communications equipment and gas masks, and made friends with local sheiks, who persuaded the enemy holding the town of Ar Ramadi, 60 miles (100 km) west of Baghdad, to surrender.

The SAS were then tasked with taking al-Asad airbase, which was held by a hundred or so armed looters. One small SAS team were hardly likely to triumph against such a force if they engaged them head to head, even though the SAS had Royal Australian Air Force F/A-18s circling above. So, while the defenders fired heavy weapons at them, the SAS responded with sniper shots, fired not to kill but close enough to their mark to scare the enemy away. 'It was a warning shot,' said the Australian squadron commander. 'If they didn't leave, then potentially we had the right to engage them and, thankfully, they took their course – the right course of action – and withdrew.'

Once the airbase was in SAS hands, they had to go through it room by room, checking for any remaining enemy, booby traps and mines. The airbase – one of Saddam's prize installations – was so massive that this took 36 hours. Once the airbase was secured, the Incident Response Regiment came in to check for WMD. Although they did not find any, they did find bunkers and abandoned buildings stuffed with arms and ammunition. The enemy had left 57 MiG jet fighters at the airbase, along with nearly 8,000 tons of ordnance. After the search was over, the Incident Response Regiment cleared and mended the runway. The first fixed-wing aircraft to land there was a C-130 Hercules transport of Australia's 36 Squadron. The base was handed over to the US 3rd Armored Cavalry Regiment in May 2003.

Some of the British Special Forces did not have nearly such an exciting time. One team complained that they found it positively boring manning an OP on a quiet road. Their job was to watch, report and target. However, there was nothing to target, as any munitions used would have been worth more than the vehicles they took out. The road was largely used by smugglers moving contraband. There was some military movement – troops, artillery, armour – but no Scuds, certainly nothing worth compromising their position for by calling in an airstrike.

As they were on the top of a high embankment, where they were unlikely to be stumbled on, the nearest they came to being discovered was when a caravan of camels came within 250 feet (76 metres) of their position, but the men with them were far too concerned with keeping the body of a Mercedes in position on the back of a camel to notice the SAS post above them.

As the war hotted up, there was more military traffic, but still no Scuds or anything that would constitute a threat – certainly no weapons of mass destruction. After a week, a mass exodus of Iraqis began. Despite the boredom of their position, the SAS men were not itching to get into action. 'I personally had no beef with the rank-and-file Iraqi Army, as they were just as much victims of Saddam's regime as anyone else,' said one of them. 'It was the Republican Guard and the Fedayeen who I despised, as they persecuted their own people.'

The only time their lives were in danger was when American ground-attack aircraft flew overhead just as a convoy was making its way down the road. The aircraft lined up to attack, but broke off. This came as some relief, as the OP was close to the side of the road and if the convoy got hit, the SAS team also risked getting 'malleted'. They could have tried to call them off with their tactical beacons, but that would have risked giving their position away.

Meanwhile, as B and D Squadrons of the SAS were operating in the western desert, G Squadron was preparing to lead the way into Basra. One team set up an OP overlooking the city. From there they could observe movements of armour and troops. They learned to predict which way they would leave the city and call in an airstrike to interdict them. They were one of several SAS teams who infiltrated the city of Basra, and between them they covered all the main roads. This meant they could judge the right time for the British to attack, or whether the regular forces closing on the city should pull back. In doing so, they saved a great many lives, both British and Iraqi.

But when deadly action was needed, they provided it. On one occasion they spotted a large enemy force of around 20 armoured personnel carriers and tanks heading for the British forces encircling the city. Alerted by the SAS OP, the British dealt with them with a force of Challenger tanks. Another time they saw an Iraqi mortar team setting up their weapon on the back of a Toyota pickup and begin bracketing a bridge held by Coalition forces. Target information was passed to the forward air controller, who in turn called in an airstrike.

Britain does not have a Special Operations Aviation Regiment like the Americans, but it does have 16 Air Assault Brigade, which led the attack on the Al Faw peninsula with its oilfields to the south of Basra. Initially the assault was going to involve landing craft as well, but when the beaches could not be cleared of mines in time, it turned into the largest helicopter assault since the Vietnam War. Eleven minutes after the first wave had set down, a US Marine Corps Sea Knight helicopter crashed over northern Kuwait, killing all four of its crew and eight passengers from 42 Commando Group (the HQ element of 3 Commando Brigade Reconnaissance Force) and, reportedly, a number of SBS men. The Americans then pulled out their air transport and it was only when the RAF stepped in with eight Chinooks that the invasion was restarted. These helicopters had to go in, in daylight, in a sandstorm, to LZs under artillery and mortar fire, but the operation was an outstanding success.

British helicopters were also used to support Special Forces operations in the desert. This often involved low-level flying at night or in a sandstorm. They flew low, increasing their angular velocity so they were not such a good target for the enemy. Nevertheless, they were frequently fired on. The British lost no helicopters during the invasion itself, but two helicopters were badly damaged in the invasion. One ran out of fuel on its way to Baghdad, and another was shot up while flying reinforcements into Al Majar Al Kabir, after a Parachute Regiment patrol was ambushed there on 24 June 2003. Later, in 2006, a Lynx was hit by a Russian-made SAM over Basra. Among the dead was 32-year-old Flight Lieutenant Sarah-Jayne Mulvihill, the first British servicewoman to be killed in overseas combat since the Second World War.

Operating alongside the Royal Marines in the invasion of Al Faw – and subsequent operations in the waterways south of Basra and around Umm Qasr – were the US Navy SEALs. They claimed to be there to 'ride shotgun' for the Marines, but in fact their role was to supply Cobra gunships, fast patrol boats and support. 'It was an arrangement that worked well for us, as the Royal Marines are fucking A1 guys who know their shit and know how to fight,' said one SEAL. 'Why they are not classed as Special Forces is beyond my comprehension as they are worth ten men … The only gripe I had working with them was that they always seemed to lack suitable equipment for their mission, a good example being a severe lack of suitable heavy weaponry for a start.'

The Royal Marines had no grenade launchers and not enough ammunition for their machines guns. The craft they were supplied with for work on Iraq's inland waterways were rigid raiders, which the Americans considered not up to the task. But the Marines never complained. Their SEAL colleague was particularly sympathetic because his uncle had fought alongside the Commandos in the Second World War. The gripe back then, too, was the lack of equipment.

While the Australian and British Special Forces, along

with the SEALs, were active in the southwest, the Delta Force led 6,000 Kurdish Peshmerga fighters into battle against Ansar al-Islam in the northeast. Between 27 and 30 March, they cleared the Beyara Valley. With an OP established on high ground and a drone overhead, they could direct Tomahawk cruise missiles and laser-guided ordnance onto targets designated by Special Forces operatives on the ground.

Special Forces teams infiltrated the Baghdad area weeks before the bombing campaign even began and guided airstrikes against the Republican Guard, while Delta Force men in the centre of the city were designating targets for British and American air raids. On the night of 2 April 2003 – just two weeks after the beginning of the war and a week before Baghdad fell – they raided two presidential palaces near Baghdad in an attempt to capture Saddam Hussein, but he eluded them.

The most famous Special Forces action of the war was the Battle of Debecka Pass, which is sometimes referred to as the Alamo of the Iraq War. On 6 April 2003, 26 Green Berets were given the task of securing a key crossroads near the town of Debecka in northern Iraq, between the cities of Irbil and Kirkuk. If they succeeded, they would cut Highway 2, preventing the Iraqi Army moving north into Kurdistan and allowing friendly forces to take the crucial Kirkuk oilfields.

The battle was fought by two 3rd Special Forces Group A-teams, who had gone through their final battle training in the pinelands of Fort Bragg, North Carolina and Fort Pickett, Virginia from October to December 2002. The two teams specialised in deep reconnaissance. Their ground mobility vehicles (GMVs) – souped-up Humvees equipped with .50-calibre heavy machine guns or Mk 19 40mm automatic grenade launchers – enabled them to travel a thousand miles in ten days without any resupply. At Fort Pickett, the teams had rehearsed how they would react if attacked by Iraqi armour. The GMVs' firepower, they knew, was not enough to see off a concerted attack by T-55 tanks. However, they were due to receive the Javelin, the Army's latest shoulder-held anti-tank missile, so the team leaders decided that, even if perilously outnumbered and faced with Iraqi tanks, they would not back down. The American Operational Detachment A (ODA) 391 came up with the motto: 'Ninety-one don't run.'

On 8 March 2003, the two teams flew from Pope Air Force Base to Romania, and on 26 March they infiltrated Iraq on an MC-130 Combat Talon, landing at As-Sulaymaniya some 60 miles (97 km) east of Kirkuk. Their first few days were spent fighting the Ansar al-Islam militant Islamic group near Halabja. Then, on 1 April, they moved to Irbil and on to a staging area, where they linked with ODA 044, a 10th Group A-team who were working with the Peshmerga militia, known to the Green Berets as 'the Pesh' or 'Peshies'.

On 4 April they were given a new mission, codenamed Northern Safari. Together with ODA 044 and their Peshmerga allies, the 3rd were to seize the Debecka intersection and hold it until they were relieved by the 173rd Airborne Brigade's artillery. The crossroads sat just to the west of a ridgeline that formed the border dividing the Kurdish-held part of Iraq from the rest of the country. The plan of attack was simple. Some 200 Peshmerga forces and a handful of ODA 044 troops would dash forward and seize the ridgeline, while ODAs 391 and 392 would support them with fire from their GMVs. There was just one problem. There was no intelligence on Iraqi forces in the area. As Captain Eric Wright, commander of ODA 391, put it, 'No one knew what was on the ridgeline or behind it.'

This was because thick haze shrouded the ridgeline and the valley beyond it, limiting visibility to less than two miles (3 km). In the absence of aerial reconnaissance, the Green Berets sought out human intelligence and quickly discovered that they were in for a fight. Farmers who grazed their livestock on the ridge told them that there were Iraqi forces on the ridge and beyond, and their positions were defended by minefields and trenches.

On 5 April, the 3rd sent two GMVs forward to reconnoitre the Iraqi positions on the ridge. From a position just behind a 12ft (3.6-metre) berm east of the ridgeline, they saw Iraqi soldiers on the ridgeline. 'They were standing on top of their bunkers like everything was OK,' said Sergeant First Class Scot Marlow, senior communications sergeant of ODA 392. That night they called in a B-52 airstrike.

In the morning, only 80 of the expected 200 Peshmerga showed up and drove straight down the road towards the 12ft (3.6-metre) dirt berm. They were stopped by a minefield and had to begin picking their way through it, which included plastic Valmira anti-tank and anti-personnel mines alongside the road.

The Green Berets decided to outflank the berm and drive straight up the ridgeline instead. CW2 Martin McKenna was keen to blast a path through the berm in case they had to make a hasty retreat, but there was no time. They heard gunfire erupting from the other side of the berm and Captain Wright ordered them forward to support the Peshmerga. But catching up with them was difficult. ODA 391 hit a trench too deep and wide for the GMVs to cross. The Green Berets had to dismount and grab a sandbag from a fighting position to fill the trench.

The next obstacle was unexploded ordnance dropped by the B-52s the night before. Again the Green Berets had to dismount and go on foot to guide the GMVs through what was essentially a minefield 2,300 feet (700 metres) deep.

South of the road, 392 had advanced up to the berm when they heard the Peshmerga's recoilless rifle firing somewhere up ahead. Then they too found themselves in a minefield. As the driver of the lead GMV tried to navigate a concertina wire barrier, WO1 Robert Parker, 392's assistant detachment commander, leaned out of the door to look underneath. 'Stop!' he yelled. The driver slammed on the brakes and the GMV stopped with its wheels just a foot (30 cm) from the prongs of an anti-personnel mine.

By now, the firing had intensified so ODA 392 had decided to reverse back to the road, down the flattened grass trail they had made on their way in. The Peshmerga had already taken the ridge. When the Green Berets caught up with them, they saw Iraqi trenches and fighting positions dug for armoured vehicles, along with two abandoned T-55 tanks. The two A-teams now linked up with the Peshmerga and engaged the Iraqis in their bunkers. After a fierce firefight, they fought their way through to the crossroads, capturing about 20 Iraqi soldiers. One of them was a major, who revealed that an Iraqi armour unit had withdrawn to the south after the bombing, leaving him and his men behind. There would be no time to prepare defensive positions if they were attacked from the south, so the 391 team leader decided it would be a good time to follow McKenna's advice and breach the berm where it crossed the road. This would allow them to withdraw quickly if necessary, and clear the way for them to be resupplied.

The intersection did not offer a commanding view of the plains, so the Green Berets sent a team up to a small ridge known as Press Hill. From there, they saw Iraqi vehicles approaching from the south. While half of 391 were busy collecting landmines to help blow the berm, the rest of the men engaged in a gunfight with Iraqi infantry. They tried to attack the vehicles with a .50-calibre machine gun, but it proved ineffective against the fast-moving trucks. The A-teams then moved forward to a position designated the 'Alamo' some 985 yards (900 metres) from the intersection. Here they were dangerously exposed. As Iraqi air-defence cannon shells burst overhead and incoming mortar and artillery rounds exploded all around, they watched transfixed as an armoured column bore down on their position.

It was then that they turned to their new Javelins. The first weapon was in the hands of Staff Sergeant Jason Brown, who had fired one only once before, in training. Sitting cross-legged on a hillside and staring through the sights of the launcher, he didn't that think he and his buddies stood a chance, but he knew that the Javelin was his team's best hope for survival. Although inexperienced, he thought that his best chance of hitting an armoured target was to use the launcher's thermal sights to see through the haze that blanketed the plain. To do that he had to wait at least 45 seconds before the launcher's cooling system would allow him to fire. Using the day sights, he could have fired immediately.

As the seconds ticked away, he saw muzzle flashes. A few seconds later, the rounds exploded on the hillside around him. The tanks were less than a mile away, but still the Javelin would not arm. Finally, Brown could loose off his first Javelin in anger. The missile streaked low above the ground, slamming into an Iraqi troop truck about 3,280 yards (3,000 metres) away. As the truck erupted in flames, the Green Berets mounted their GMVs and roared down the slope at about 70mph (112kph), shooting at the fleeing Iraqis.

But it was far from a one-way fight. The Special Forces men at the crossroads found themselves under mortar fire. USAF forward air controllers with the Green Berets identified two mortar tubes to the east, near the town of Debecka, and four GMVs set off to destroy them.

Meanwhile, seated on top of his GMV, ODA 391's junior engineer, Staff Sergeant Bobby Farmer, looked down the road and saw two white SUVs emerging from the haze to the west. They were being driven slowly down the road towards the American positions with their lights blinking on and off. Special Forces Commander Frank Antenori, 391's senior NCO, told his men not to shoot – the troops in the vehicles might be trying to surrender.

Then the grey metal form of Iraqi armoured personnel carriers emerged from the mist. The American GMVs pulled off the road to the left and to the right to take up defensive positions. Worse was to come. As soon as the Iraqis in the APCs saw the Americans, the lead vehicle began pumping out smoke. Then, through the smoke, a column of at least five T-55 tanks appeared. They were about a mile away and closing at about 40mph (65kph) with their 100mm main guns firing round after round of high explosives.

Farmer banged on the roof of his GMV to alert his comrades. 'Tanks!' he yelled.

When he heard this, Antenori jumped up on the roof of the vehicle. 'Holy shit!' he exclaimed.

Master Sergeant Kenneth Thompson and Sergeant Jeff Adamec grabbed Javelin launchers and jumped from the GMVs. Then began the maddening test of nerves as they waited for the launchers to cool down.

Meanwhile, the team attacking the mortars got the message that tanks were coming from the south and disengaged.

The Javelins were taking longer than normal to cool down, so the Green Berets pulled back some 2,950 yards (900 metres) to the Alamo ridgeline, along with the Peshmerga in one overloaded old truck.

Alerted to what was happening, Staff Sergeant Brown grabbed another Javelin and jumped on the bonnet of a GMV, and the US Air Force forward air controllers put out an urgent call for close-air support. With the combined Special Forces and Peshmerga force back on the Alamo, Brown's Javelin was ready to fire. He squeezed the trigger. The missile shot out of the tube and slowed to almost a standstill. Then its booster kicked in. It arched upwards, then came down like an arrow scoring a direct hit on the moving personnel carrier. Iraqi soldiers piled out of the burning vehicle and ran for cover in a field of tall wheat beside the road.

Sergeant Adamec and Staff Sergeant Eugene Zawojski, both armed with Javelins, joined Brown on the ridge. Together, they destroyed two trucks and two APCs within a couple of minutes. As Iraqi infantry poured out of the burning vehicles, Sergeant Farmer, Sergeant First Class Scot Marlow and Sergeant First Class Van Hines rained .50-calibre fire and Mk19 40mm grenades on them.

The T-55s had taken cover in defilade positions on the far side of the road, making it impossible for the Javelins to get a lock on their heat signatures. The Green Berets had already used up about half their ammunition, but waves of Iraqis were coming on. Then two US Navy F-14 Tomcats arrived to give close-air support, dropping 750lb ordnance and Paveway II laser-guided smart bombs. The Iraqis responded with anti-aircraft fire and airburst shells began to explode some 980 yards (300 metres) in front of the Green Berets' position. Iraqi artillery firing 152mm high-explosive shells then began to find its range and a smoke round nearly scored a direct hit. It was clear that the enemy artillery had accurately bracketed their position, so the Green Berets withdrew to Press Hill.

Despite this, about a dozen Iraqi soldiers threw down their arms and attempted to surrender under a white flag. For moment it seemed that others might join them, but two white trucks pulled up and six Arabs in white robes – the uniform of Ba'ath Party enforcers – jumped out and began shooting them. An Air Force controller called for an airstrike on the white trucks, which were destroyed.

At 07.20 hours Special Forces resupply vehicles arrived carrying ammunition and more Javelins. By then, they had only three missiles left. The Green Berets and the Peshmerga allies were then in a position to hold their own while the enemy was bombed for two hours. Eventually, Iraqi soldiers abandoned their vehicles and fled the battlefield on foot.

For the next two days Iraqi artillery and multiple rocket launchers continued to fire upon the Special Forces' positions. However, the crossroads were secured and the Green Berets crossed to Kirkuk to secure the oil facilities and prevent their destruction by Iraqi forces.

The British SAS remain a highly secretive organisation and members are rarely named, even when they are decorated, unless they are dead. The US Special Forces are not so reticent. On 14 October 2005, a trio of Green Berets – two on active service and one retired – each received the Silver Star during a ceremony at Fort Carson, Colorado. Master Sergeant Robert Collins, Sergeant First Class Danny Hall and retired First Sergeant Cornelius Clark were recognised with the military's third-highest valour award for their gallantry under enemy fire – Collins and Hall for their actions in Iraq early that year, and Clark for his heroism 40 years earlier in Vietnam.

Collins and Hall, both of the 2nd Battalion of the 10th Special Forces Group, had been deployed to Iraq earlier in 2005 in support of Operation Iraqi Freedom. During offensive operations in the Jazeera region in April, both men's aggressive actions in battle led to the defeat of attacking enemy forces and the survival of their Special Forces detachment, according to their Silver Star citations.

While searching for an anti-Iraqi forces training camp and weapons cache, Collins and Hall's joint Coalition element were engaged by a platoon-sized enemy force with mortars, rocket-propelled grenades, machine guns and grenades. After Collins personally directed close-air support from F-16 aircraft armed with 500lb (227kg) bombs, Hall led a dismounted charge into small-arms fire and RPG volleys. Collins then led his element to engage the enemy, personally eliminating at least three enemy fighters. In addition to his combat role, Hall – a Special Forces medical sergeant – managed to set up a casualty collection point and a helicopter LZ to medevac out his wounded troops. Collins and Hall then risked their lives again when, while their unit was pinned down by enemy fire, they ran through a hail of bullets to recover a critically wounded US soldier. They carried him to safety, administered first aid and saved his life.

Collins acknowledged the personal significance of his Silver Star, but said he felt that the award symbolised the heroism of his team during its battle with anti-Iraqi forces. 'It's important, but it's representative of the efforts of the team, not just my individual effort,' he said.

CHAPTER TEN
THE PACK
OF CARDS

George W. Bush may have declared 'mission accomplished' on the aircraft carrier USS *Abraham Lincoln* on 1 May 2003, but the fighting in Iraq was far from over. The 22 SAS joined the US Delta Force in Task Force 20, while the SBS joined the Green Berets in Task Force 121. During the initial hostilities, these units had operated ahead of the US Marines along the road from the south of the country to Baghdad. Other elements, particularly 'psyops' specialists and men from the CIA and MI6, infiltrated the key cities, trying to foment trouble between dissidents and the Ba'ath Party. Then, when the regime had been toppled, the units were re-formed to began searching the country for Iraq's 'most wanted'. These men were famously displayed on packs of playing cards of the 55 most wanted men.

There were other jobs for these teams to do. Even though Saddam – the ace of spades in the pack – had disappeared, his army disbanded and his country now in the hands of the Coalition, Allied troopers were regularly hit by small-arms fire, RPGs and roadside bombs. Most of this was aimed at the American sectors in Baghdad and in the Sunni-dominated north. Saddam was a Sunni Muslim and he had favoured the denomination in his administration. The Shiites in the south were less trouble initially, as they were grateful for having been released from Saddam's choke-hold. It was widely acknowledged that the British soldiers patrolling Basra and its surroundings were better trained for a peacekeeping role than the Americans due to their long experience in Northern Ireland, but even so they still got hit.

The situation was not improved by the notoriously trigger-happy attitude of Task Force 20. Named after 20 March 2003 – the day the invasion of Iraq officially began – the force originally comprised a 40-man assault team backed by a private aviation unit from the 160th Special Operations Group. It was supported by a Special Forces intelligence unit called Gray Fox – formally the US Army Intelligence Support Activity, USAISA, commonly shortened to the ISA or just 'the Activity'. It had its headquarters in Baghdad International Airport and was commanded by a US Air Force brigadier general. Task Force 20 then seconded men from the Green Berets, Delta Force and Air Force Pararescue, along with commandos from the US Navy's elite DEVGRU. As the unit expanded, operators were also brought in from Australia's and Britain's SAS counter-terrorism units, along with Poland's GROM, bringing its total manpower to 750. Its primary goal was to capture or kill high-value targets (HVTs) such as Iraqi mujahideen leaders, former Ba'ath party members and leaders of the regime.

However, in several missions in Baghdad it seems to have shot first and asked questions later. The most infamous incident occurred on 27 July 2003, when a group of westerners in civilian clothing and an expensive customised 4x4 pulled up outside the exclusive Al Sa'ah restaurant in the affluent Mansur district of Baghdad and began to observe the comings and goings from the house of Prince Rahiah Mohammed al-Habib, a prominent tribal leader, two blocks away. After a while, they got out of the car and moved slowly towards the house, believing that Saddam Hussein's son Ali was inside.

At that moment, six US Army Humvees appeared, sealing off the surrounding roads. Then there was a loud explosion and men dressed in black wearing gasmasks and body armour stormed into Prince al-Habib's house. A crowd gathered around the perimeter. While the operation was unfolding, two of Prince al-Habib's neighbours, 16-year-old student Mohammed Imad Khazalalrubai and his brother, 13-year-old Zaid, were driving home after collecting their family's monthly rations of flour, rice and cooking oil. The boys were nudging their white Chevrolet Malibu through a crowd of onlookers towards a hastily established American checkpoint when suddenly, according to witnesses, US soldiers in a Humvee 150 yards (137 metres) away opened up. They fired high-velocity rounds through the windscreen of the boys' car. The two boys dived for cover. When the firing stopped, Zaid opened the car door and stuck his head out to shake off the shattered glass. At that point, Mohammed says, a single American bullet killed him. 'My brother's blood will not go for nothing,' he screamed in anguish two days later, his wounds still swathed in bandages. 'I'll take revenge on those American sons of bitches!'

With one careless action Task Force 20 had turned an innocent student into a potential insurgent. But Zaid was not the only innocent casualty that day. A disabled man driving a Toyota Corolla containing his wife and daughter took a wrong turning near another road block. In a hail of bullets he was killed and his wife and son were wounded. On a nearby highway a man in a Mitsubishi Pajero slowed down to see what was going on and was hit by a ricochet. In all, five Iraqis lost their lives in the action. Ali Hussein was not in the house, nor had he been for months.

After the Baghdad raid, tribal leaders from around the country descended on al-Habib's home. 'My people are asking, "What action should we take?"' said al-Habib. 'I'm trying to calm them down. I'm telling them that the Americans are probably desperate. But I cannot control the feeling of my people at the moment.'

Such trigger-happy actions turned even the enemies of Saddam Hussein against the Americans. 'We have no relation whatsoever with the old regime. Most of us were imprisoned and humiliated in Saddam's time,' said Abu Bilal al-Fallujah, whose cousin launched at least two attacks on American convoys before he was killed in an explosion at Fallujah's central mosque. 'The problems started with the way the Americans ignored our ideas and customs. They humiliated us; they occupied our mosque. Of course, I will seek revenge if I am insulted.'

Many could not even see the point in tracking down Saddam Hussein. 'Saddam being caught or killed isn't good for the Americans,' said Marouf Sami Noori, brother-in-law of the then fugitive Taha Yassin Ramadan, Saddam's vice president and the ten of diamonds, who was captured on 19 August 2003 and hanged the following March. 'There are many people who would like to fight against the Americans, but if they fight now, they'll be considered Saddam's people. So the resistance will be stronger if Saddam is captured or killed.'

The Americans apologised for the behaviour of Task Force 20, but the unit continued to carry out operations in Tikrit, Saddam's home town, though they failed to find him. Meanwhile the country continued its descent into anarchy. The Jordanian Embassy was bombed on 7 August, killing 19 people. At 16.45 hours on 19 August 2003, a truck bomb went off outside the United Nations building in Baghdad, killing at least 17 people, including the UN Secretary-General's Special Representative for Iraq, Sergio Vieira de Mello, who was organising humanitarian aid for the Iraqi people. A hundred were estimated to have been injured in the blast. On 30 August, more than 124 people were killed by a car-bomb attack on the Shiite holy city of Najaf. Attacks continued throughout the summer. On 26 October, the Al-Rashid Hotel, where international administrators stayed, was hit by fire from a multi-barrelled rocket launcher while US Deputy Secretary of State for Defense Paul Wolfowitz was visiting. The following day, four suicide bombers targeted the headquarters of the International Committee of the Red Cross and Iraqi police stations across Baghdad, killing 40.

With security now a major problem, the Americans requested further assistance from the British. However, UK troops were ensconced in a relatively peaceful southern part of the country and the request was declined for fear of increased British casualties. However, the British did send members of the SAS and SBS to help guard the 'Green Zone' – the heavily defended palaces, offices and hotels where the administrators and other foreign workers now sought refuge. Around 120 Special Forces men from the SAS, SBS and 14th Intelligence Company (largely formed of ex-SBS men) were despatched, and a British lieutenant colonel was sent to the American headquarters to command them. This left just half a squadron of SAS and SBS men behind in Basra.

The British Special Forces men were integrated into the intelligence unit Gray Fox. Alongside colleagues from Delta Force and the US Navy SEALs, they collected intelligence, which was then collated and processed by the CIA, the NSA (National Security Agency) and the DIS (Defense Intelligence Service). Raw intelligence was not hard to come by. Some 3,000 men – usually ex-SAS, SBS, Delta Force, German GSG-9 or from some other Special Forces outfit – were offering their services as security experts around Baghdad. Also on hand were a number of British private military companies. These too employed ex-servicemen. With so many former colleagues working hand-in-hand with Iraqis, it was not hard to find out what was going on. Gray Fox depended on such information.

On 22 July 2003, Task Force 20 scored its first major success. An Iraqi businessman informed the headquarters of 101st Airborne Division that Saddam Hussein's two eldest sons, Qusay and Uday, were hiding out in his house in the prosperous al-Falah suburb of Mosul, some 200 miles (320 km) north of Baghdad. Both had been prominent in their father's administration and were on the pack of cards – Qusay was the ace of hearts, Uday the ace of clubs. Each had a $15 million bounty on his head.

Neither of Saddam's sons was very popular. Qusay Hussein had been a senior officer with the Republican Guard who had crushed the Shiite rising after the First Gulf War. He had also masterminded the draining of the southern marshes to punish the Marsh Arabs, who lived there and had sided with the Coalition. As Saddam Hussein's heir apparent he was in charge of security and known for his brutality. He was accused of ordering the summary execution of thousands of political prisoners to make room in the jails for more inmates.

Uday had even more enemies. As head of the Olympic Committee, he had tortured athletes who failed him. The country's soccer players were jailed after failing to qualify for the World Cup in 1994 and were forced to kick a concrete ball around. He famously abducted any women who took his fancy and raped them, sometimes murdering them afterwards. Any husband, boyfriend or family member who got in his way would also be dispatched. Even Saddam Hussein did not trust him.

As Saddam's firstborn he was to have succeeded his father, but he was dropped as heir apparent after he killed Saddam's most trusted adviser. The man had introduced Saddam to the woman who would become his second wife. For Uday this was an insult to his mother and he publicly murdered the man with an electric carving knife.

Afterwards, Saddam had Uday jailed briefly. When he was released, an attempt was made to assassinate him. So the brothers did not have many friends, but it was probably the $15 million bounties that led to their betrayal.

The information was passed via the Division's Special Forces liaison officer to Task Force 20. At the time there was a 12-man SAS team working with the Americans in Mosul. They had the advantage over the Americans in undercover operations, because they tended to speak Arabic and other local languages rather better. Their smaller teams were less conspicuous than the large units US Special Forces brought in and they made more of an effort to blend in.

The SAS men went to reconnoitre the target. It was two-storey building, and according to the reports they had received, there were just four men holed up in it. As well as Qusay and Uday, there was a bodyguard and Qusay's 14-year-old son, Mustafa. He was not in the pack of cards and there was no reason he should die.

The SAS reckoned that they could storm the house using the close-quarters battle (CQB) tactics they had practised so often at the Killing House in Herefordshire. This is the establishment where they had learned the assault tactics that had worked so well in breaking the Iranian Embassy siege in London in 1980, killing five of the six kidnappers and rescuing 19 hostages.

First, a four-man detachment was sent in on close-target reconnaissance. They were to double-check that the house was indeed occupied. It was a common in Iraq for false intelligence to be fed to the Special Forces in an attempt to lure them into a trap. They were also to ascertain what defences the house had and what sort of a fight the brothers might put up.

The team reported back that there were four individuals in the house and no sign of heavy weapons. There were two entrances to the house and they reckoned that 12 SAS men were more than enough to storm the house using explosive entry equipment and kill or capture the men inside. The SAS planned to go in that night, before the brothers got any wind that they had been betrayed.

However, the SAS were not free agents. The 101st Airborne were in charge of Mosul and the US authorities did not believe that the SAS could storm the house without taking heavy casualties. Lots of dead Coalition soldiers, they thought, would send the wrong message to the Iraqi people, who were being told that the insurgency was almost over. Lieutenant General Ricardo Sanchez, who had taken over from General Franks as commander of Coalition ground forces, authorised an altogether larger operation and the SAS were sidelined.

Shortly before 10.00 hours the following day, the 101st Airborne cordoned off the area. Then a team from the Delta Force approached the front door and knocked. When they received no reply, a megaphone was used to issue a demand: whoever was inside the house should to come out. There was no response so, ten minutes later, troops began to enter the house – even though it was broad daylight and they had warned the defenders they were coming. The assault force were immediately fired on by the occupants, who had barricaded themselves into a fortified part of the first floor of the building. Four American soldiers were wounded and the assault team were forced to withdraw.

As any element of surprise they might have had had been thrown away, so stealth was no longer an option. Instead they called in more men in the form of a quick-reaction force and brought up heavy weaponry. Meanwhile, sporadic gunfire continued from the house. At 10.45, the Americans began to 'prep the objective'. They fired on the part of the building where the four targets were holed up with Mk19 automatic 40mm grenade launchers, Humvee-mounted .50-calibre machine guns and AT4 84mm antiarmour rockets. At 11.22, more ground forces moved in, including an anti-tank platoon. Half an hour later, an OH-58D Kiowa attack helicopter joined the assault, pounding the position with 2.75in rockets, 7.62mm mini-guns and .50-calibre machine guns. By then the anti-tank platoon were in position and a psyops team moved in.

At 11.55 hours, the US commander decided to make a second attempt to enter the house. Troops went in and secured the ground floor. But again they came under fire from the first floor and the commander decided to withdraw. An hour later, the Americans fired ten larger Humvee-mounted TOW missiles into the house. Apache helicopters and A-10 Warthogs were standing by, but the US commander decided not to use them because of the risk of collateral damage.

At 13.20, troops entered the building for the third time, believing the people in the building to have been killed in the missile attack. They faced no fire as they moved upstairs, but when they reached the first floor they were again fired on. They returned fire, killing the remaining individual, who was believed to have been Qusay Hussein's 14-year-old son Mustafa. Once the building was secured, the four bodies were taken away for identification. DNA analysis confirmed that Qusay and Uday were among them.

The SAS were appalled. The siege had lasted six hours. One Iraqi bystander had been killed and five wounded. The SAS could have done the job in a fraction of the time, saved lives and prevented injuries. To add insult to injury, the SAS team were then taken on as a quick-reaction force for the 101st Airborne.

Following the debacle at Mosul, the situation in Iraq continued to deteriorate. Most civilian agencies pulled out and Task Force 20 was disbanded. The remaining British, Australian and Polish Special Forces men would join the SBS, Delta Force and DEVGRU men who now made up Task Force 121. By then the British Special Forces had taken to wearing American camouflage. This meant they could not be identified as SAS or SBS by the media and it meant that hostile forces in the Sunni triangle would not suspect they were up against hardened British troops.

On 31 October, they were tipped off that a number of Saddam loyalists – Ba'athists, Fedayeen, members of the Republican Guard and Saddam's security services – were holed up in another compound in Mosul. It was thought that they had been joined by al-Qaeda fighters who had infiltrated across the border from Saudi Arabia, Jordan and Syria, and they were armed – not just with AK-47s, but also with grenades, mortars, RPGs and shoulder-launched SAMs. Things were getting out of hand in Mosul. That morning the US headquarters at the airport had been hit by Katyushi rockets from a Soviet-made multi-barrelled rocket launcher. An American vehicle had been hit by a roadside bomb in the Qasr al-Mutran district of the city and an Iraqi police station had been peppered with rounds from a drive-by shooting.

US helicopters were sent up to fly over the city. Armed men were seen going in and out of the compound, some carrying RPGs. That afternoon, mortars were seen being loaded onto a pick-up truck parked outside. This activity was confirmed by local informants as well as Special Forces close reconnaissance. Something had to be done. The US commander on the ground decided to attack the compound that night.

The assault team would be made up of men from Delta Force, the SAS and SBS. As before, the area would be cordoned off by a large force from the 101st Airborne and Iraqi police. Again, there would be massive firepower on hand – OH-58D Kiowa attack helicopters and Humvees armed with TOW missiles, Mk19 grenade launchers and .50-calibre Brownings. The assault force would be flown into position on board MH-53 Pave Low helicopters, then driven forward in heavily armed Humvees, which would drop them some 1,650 yards (500 metres) from their objective. The six four-man teams would then approach the compound from various directions, backed up by fire support teams armed with 40mm grenade launchers. The moment they heard shooting, they were to fire grenades into the compound before the Special Forces teams went in. They were also to target the Toyota pickup outside, which was laden with ground-to-air missiles and 82mm mortars.

At around 22.00 hours, it was clear that the men inside the compound were about to make a move and the order was given to go in. Task Force 121 attacked from four different directions. The main gates were hit by a series of rifle grenades and strafed with machine-gun fire. Startled guards returned fire. The Special Forces men began pouring over the walls. SAS and SBS teams blew open the front gates and went in with their Diemacos blazing. In a heavy exchange of fire, three SAS men were wounded and one SBS man killed – the first British Special Forces man to be lost in the Second Gulf War. He was named as Corporal Ian 'Planky' Plank. He had served with the SBS in Sierra Leone, the Balkans and in Afghanistan. Eventually the compound was taken at the further cost of ten Iraqi lives, and a large number of foreign fighters were captured.

Meanwhile, the search for members of Saddam Hussein's toppled regime was still on. On 16 April at 20.03, the SAS and SBS captured Saddam's half-brother Watban Hassan al-Tikriti, the five of spades and the 37th on the most-wanted list. He was caught on the road from Mosul to Syria, trying to flee the country. As Minister of the Interior, he used to torture and murder political prisoners. He was also wanted in connection with the disappearance of 180,000 Kurds in the 1980s and the vicious repression following the Iraqi defeat in the First Gulf War. He had also arrested dozens of Baghdad market sellers for alleged profiteering in foodstuffs, and then had them hanged from lampposts after trials that lasted less than a day. He was handed over to the Iraqi Interim Government in 2004 and went on trial in 2008.

Saddam Hussein himself was captured on 13 December 2003, hiding in a spider hole in the ground at a farmhouse in ad-Dawr, 12 miles south of his birthplace, Tikrit.

Ostensibly, he was taken by the 1st Combat Team of the US 4th Infantry Division. However, along with the 600 infantrymen involved in the operation, a team from Task Force 121 were on hand. In the picture shown in the press of a bearded Saddam being manhandled from his hiding place, the man hauling him out is a 34-year-old Iraqi-American named Samir, who was an interpreter from Special Forces.

The information on Saddam's whereabouts that ultimately led to his arrest came from distant relatives and members of the PUK, the Kurdish independence party that the CIA and Special Forces had been grooming. By 10.50 on 13 December, Coalition intelligence had narrowed down his hiding place to two possible locations in ad-Dawr, which were codenamed Wolverine 1 and Wolverine 2. Operation Red Dawn was then put into operation. Only the top commanders knew that the target was the ace of spades himself, Saddam Hussein al-Tikriti, also known as HVT – High-Value Target – Number 1. For everyone else involved, it was just a regular HVT operation.

At 18.00, as darkness fell, some 600 men were helicoptered and driven into place. Among them were Special Forces operatives from Task Force 121. In command of the main force was Colonel Jim Kickey of the 4th Infantry Division, supported by Apache helicopter gunships, artillery, light armour and Humvees. The Special Forces contingent was under the personal command of General Ricardo Sanchez, at that time corps commander in Iraq. His orders were clear: 'Kill or capture HVT Number 1.'

By 20.00 hours, the main force had surrounded ad-Dawr and begun a sweep-and-clear operation. When the initial sweep yielded nothing, they sealed off a smaller area, about one square mile (1.6 km) around two farmhouses, and then began a more thorough search. Around 20.30, they were searching a hut-like outbuilding when they found the entrance to a narrow hole under a rug. It was covered with bricks and dirt and a Styrofoam insert that acted as a hatch cover. A Special Forces operative cautiously removed the Styrofoam to reveal a shaft some six to eight feet (1.8–2.4 metres) deep. They pointed their weapons inside and, by the light of their torches, took a look around. In the gloom they could see the haggard figure of Saddam Hussein, looking more like a tramp than a feared dictator. Although he was armed with a pistol, he put up no resistance.

'He was caught like a rat in a trap,' said US military spokesman Major General Ray Odierno. 'He was disoriented as he came up, then he was just very much bewildered, then he was taken away. He didn't say hardly anything at all. There was no resistance of any sort. They got him out of there very quickly once we figured out who it was. The soldiers were extremely happy and extremely excited, but very professional.'

Odierno described Saddam Hussein's bolthole as just large enough for a man to lie down in. It had a pipe and a fan for ventilation. Nearby were two small boats on the Tigris River, used to get supplies, and a battered taxi, which served as his presidential limousine. The circumstances of Saddam's capture stood in stark contrast to the opulent lifestyle he had enjoyed while in power, said General Odierno. 'You could just about see some of these palace complexes from there. I think it's rather ironic that he was in a hole in the ground across the river from these great palaces that he built where he robbed all the money from the Iraqi people.'

No communication equipment was found in the hut or farmhouse, so it was not thought that Saddam was directing insurgent attacks on the Coalition from his lair. He was whisked off in a helicopter for a medical examination and interrogation. A DNA sample was taken from the inside of his mouth and used to confirm his identity. Two other people said to be 'close allies' of Saddam Hussein were also arrested and two AK-47s and more than $750,000 cash in $100 bills were confiscated.

The capture of Saddam Hussein did not stop the insurgency in Iraq, nor did it prevent further casualties among the Special Forces. On New Year's Day 2004, two SAS men were killed in a road-traffic accident in Baghdad. Major James Stenner, seconded from the Welsh Guards, and Sergeant Norman Patterson, seconded from the Cheshire Regiment, had been out celebrating with the American Special Forces when their 4x4 hit a series of bollards at the Assassin's Gate entrance to the Green Zone. Both were killed instantly.

Saddam Hussein was held in custody at the US base, Camp Cropper, with 11 other senior Ba'athist leaders. They were handed over legally – though not physically – to the interim Iraqi government to stand trial for 'crimes against humanity' and other offences. Specifically, the Iraqi Special Tribunal charged Saddam with the crimes committed against residents of Dujail in 1982, following a failed assassination attempt. These included the murder of 148 people, torture of women and children and the illegal arrest of 399 others.

Saddam and his lawyers contested the court's authority and maintained that he was still President of Iraq, but on 5 November 2006, he was found guilty of crimes against humanity. He was sentenced to death by hanging, along with his half-brother, Barzan-Ibrahim, and Awad Hamed al-Bandar, head of Iraq's Revolutionary Court in 1982. The verdict and sentencing were both appealed but were confirmed by Iraq's Supreme Court of Appeals and, on 30 December 2006, Saddam Hussein was hanged. Other members of the regime were still on trial.

CHAPTER ELEVEN
TASK FORCE BLACK

The continuing insurgency in Iraq began to cause problems for the British Special Forces. With civilian agencies unwilling to put their personnel at risk and pulling out, more private military companies went in. With names like Control Risk, Rubicon, Global Risk Strategies, Kroll Associates and Erinys International, they employed a large number of ex-Royal Marines, Paras and Special Forces troopers. These men even ran small private armies of Gurkhas and Fijians in lieu of a proper UN peacekeeping force. They trained the Iraqi Army and Police Force, guarded buildings and oil facilities and provided security for contractors and television crews.

As the situation in Iraq deteriorated, they too got into firefights. In the autumn of 2003, two ex-SAS men in a 4x4 were ambushed by three Iraqis in a car. Plainly they did not know what they were up against. Although one ex-SAS man was hit, both returned fire. Two of the Iraqis were killed. A third was wounded. One of the ex-SAS men then strolled over to him and beat him to death. The ex-SAS man was nearly 60 at the time.

In another incident, in Tikrit, a band of Iraqis went after a CNN crew in a car, only to find the driver steering with one hand and firing a Heckler & Koch 9mm MP-5 machine pistol with the other. He was an ex-SAS man from D Squadron.

These guys were making up to £90,000 a year, three times what they could earn in the SAS. Until recently, very few men had asked to resign from the SAS – it is so difficult to get into. But the insurgency in Iraq offered action and big bucks. By the end of 2004, 40 men had asked to be released. That is the equivalent of losing two-thirds of an operational squadron in one year. At the same time, 24 men from the Boat Troops had been attached to the SBS, so an entire SAS squadron was gone.

Once the majority of Saddam Hussein's regime had been rounded up, the SAS Squadron in Iraq was assigned to the Combined Joint Special Operations Task Force, previously known as Task Force 145 but now renamed Task Force 88. Headed by the commander of Delta Force, it was composed of the cream of western Special Forces and brought together several elements. Task Force Orange gathered electronic intelligence. Task Force Green was the 1st Special Forces Operational Detachment – that is, Delta Force. (The designation 'Green' comes from its association with the army.) Task Force Blue comprises US Navy SEALs from the DEVGRU, formerly SEAL Team 6. (The 'Blue' represents the navy.) Then there was Task Force Black, made up of an SAS Sabre squadron operating initially in southern Iraq. (The 'Black' reflects the colour of the uniforms they wear in their counter-revolutionary-warfare role.) Some SBS operators are thought to be attached to Task Force Black, as are members of the SRR.

Task Force Black was supported by a company of the Joint Special Forces Support Group (SFSG), also known as Task Force Red. Another relatively new British special-operations unit, it had been formed around a core component of members of the 1st Battalion of the Parachute Regiment – 1 Para – with additional troops from the Royal Marines and the RAF Regiment. It provides infantry and specialised support to SAS and SBS special operations, and acts as a quick-reaction force for them, sealing off and guarding an area of operation. It also takes part in large-scale assaults alongside SAS and SBS forces, carrying out secondary assaults and diversionary raids, and acting as a blocking force against counterattacks. Last but not least, it provides chemical, biological, radiological and nuclear detection and protection, and supports domestic anti-terrorist operations.

Specialised air support for Task Force 88 comes from elements of the 160th Special Operations Aviation Regiment (SOAR), US 24th Special Tactics Squadron, and the UK's 7 and 47 RAF Squadrons. American military intelligence operatives working alongside the UK's Joint Support Group and the Special Reconnaissance Regiment are believed to be attached to the Task Force to provide intelligence support, while secure communications and eavesdropping capabilities are provided by 18 UK Special Forces Signals and their US equivalents in Task Force Orange.

The primary role of Task Force 88 is to hunt down senior members of al-Qaeda operating in Iraq, though elements have also been employed in Afghanistan. One of their great successes is the killing of al-Qaeda's top man in Iraq, Abu Mussab al-Zarqawi, the man who built his reputation on the internet by posting clips of himself beheading foreign captives. He was believed to have masterminded the bombing of the UN headquarters in Baghdad in August 2003, and personally beheaded the British hostage Ken Bigley in October 2004. After avoiding capture for years, he eventually headed Coalition forces' most-wanted list in Iraq, with a reward of $25 million posted for his capture – the same figure as offered for Osama bin Laden.

In June 2006, Task Force 88 tracked al-Zarqawi down to a safe house in Baquba, 30 miles (48 km) northeast of Baghdad, and called in an airstrike. An F-16C circling above dropped a GBU-12 laser-guided, 500lb (227kg) bomb. A second GPS-guided GBU-38 500lb bomb followed. Al-Zarqawi was still alive when they found him, but he died soon afterwards. Lieutenant General Stanley McChrystal, chief of the Special Operations force tracking down al-Zarqawi, was on hand to witness his death. His men then examined the corpse closely, looking for telltale green tattoos and old war wounds that confirmed the dead man was indeed al-Zarqawi. Two other men, two women and a small girl were also killed in the airstrike.

While Task Force Black's primary remit is to cover the south of Iraq, with a particular focus on Basra, they have also been used in high-profile operations in Baghdad. During Operation Marlborough in July 2005, they were employed to neutralise a suicide-bomb squad before they could reach their targets in the city. Intelligence supplied by agents run by MI6 had identified a house in Baghdad as a base for suicide bombers. It was believed that three insurgents, each with homemade explosive strapped to his chest, were planning to hit targets in the city, most likely cafés, markets or other public establishments. The SAS considered storming the building but it was decided this was too risky. If any of the insurgents detonated a bomb inside, its blast would be amplified within the structure, killing civilians in adjoining buildings. It was decided to engage the insurgents as they left.

Just before the dawn rush hour on 31 July, a 16-man SAS troop set up around the house at a range of around 300 yards (275 metres). The main element of the troop was four sniper teams, each with a shooter and a spotter. The snipers were armed with L115A sniper rifles chambered in .338 Lapua known as an AWM. The rest of the troop provided security for the sniper teams and ensured that all possible escape routes from the house were covered. Troops from Task Force Red, the Special Forces Support Group quick-reaction force, were situated close by in case things went wrong, and bomb-disposal experts were on hand.

In the rising heat of a July morning, the team lay hidden around the safe house. High above, a US Predator spy drone kept the place under video surveillance, beaming its images back to Task Force Black headquarters. Listening devices that had been hidden inside were being monitored by Arabic-speaking translators. As one intelligence officer warned, 'Targets preparing to exit,' the snipers readied themselves.

It was just past 08.00 when the insurgents stepped outside onto the street. Clad in explosive vests, the bombers represented an immediate threat to all around them, which meant the SAS had legal authority to open fire. Once they were all in clear sight, the command was given over the radio to engage. As there were civilians close by, it was essential to shoot all three bombers simultaneously to prevent any of them from detonating their explosives. If one went down first, the other two might have a chance to set their bombs off. On the word of command, three SAS snipers opened fire together – the fourth was held in reserve as a backup. Their rifles were barely heard as the bombers jerked and hit the ground. Each had been hit in the head and killed instantly. Although the .338 Lapua Magnum round sounds like an airgun, it can crack an engine block at a range of 300 yards (275 metres). On a human target at that range, it is utterly devastating. None of the explosives were detonated and many lives were saved.

In addition to hunting high-value Saddam loyalists and taking out al-Qaeda terrorists, Task Force 88 was given a new task. Following the kidnap and murder of British teacher Margaret Hassan and engineer Ken Bigley in 2004 – along with two US citizens, Jack Hensley and Eugene Armstrong – Task Force 88 was told to use its intelligence network to counter the threat from kidnappers. As a result, information from spies, informers and electronics eavesdropping operations was used to build an intelligence picture on the various hostage-taking organisations active in Iraq.

The spearhead of this operation was Task Force Black. Hostage rescue is one of the SAS's specialities and in March 2006, they demonstrated just how highly trained they were when they rescued British peace campaigner Norman Kember and two Canadians, James Loney and Harmeet Sooden, who had been kidnapped in Baghdad. The three men were part of a group of four peace activists who had been kidnapped in November 2005 by an Iraqi organisation calling itself the Swords of Righteousness Brigade. Subsequent video demands called for the release of various Iraqi prisoners in Coalition hands. Eventually, on 8 March 2006, the kidnappers killed one of the hostages, Tom Fox, a US citizen. His body was found handcuffed and bullet-riddled in a rubbish dump in Baghdad. This spurred the SAS into action.

Scotland Yard sent in trained negotiators. The Canadians flew in their kidnap experts, and FBI agents and MI6 officers in Baghdad tried to make contact with intermediaries who could put them in direct touch with the kidnappers. Meanwhile, undercover SAS men, wearing beards and dressed as Iraqis, met religious leaders and tribal elders to piece together scraps of information about the hostage-taking Swords of Righteousness Brigade. Satellite photographs, telephone intercepts and reams of other information were examined in minute detail. Intelligence officers followed up dozens of tip-offs from paid informants, community leaders and Iraqi police, but all leads had proved false until a young Iraqi who had been under surveillance for several days was captured.

The SAS had already narrowed down the likely location of the kidnappers' base to the scruffy suburbs of western Baghdad around al-Hurriyah, a stronghold of mainly Sunni insurgents and criminal gangs responsible for dozens of abductions of Iraqis. The detainee disclosed the precise address, describing the location and making sketches of the house and the nearby roads.

For weeks the SAS had been practising strategies for taking kidnappers by surprise. They used mock-ups of the types of properties where they thought the hostages were held, even though they were unsure whether the hostages were held in a basement or in a house where children lived. Now they had to act fast. Their main concern was that the hostage-takers might realise that one of their gang had been captured, kill the three Westerners and flee.

At about 03.00 on 23 March 2006, the SAS squadron commander in charge of the rescue force summoned his team at their base inside the heavily fortified Green Zone. The force consisted mainly of SAS troopers, backed by about 50 soldiers from the 1st Battalion of the Parachute Regiment and Royal Marines – all members of the Special Forces Support Group now codenamed Task Force Maroon. Australian SAS men, Canadian Joint Task Force 2 commandos, American Delta Force and DEVGRU operatives were also involved.

To avoid attracting attention, the rescue forces approached the area in a convoy of cars disguised as local taxis and pickup trucks. Predator unmanned aerial vehicles, which can monitor movements on the ground from 20,000 feet (6,100 metres), were deployed, while helicopter gunships circled high above with reconnaissance cameras, ready to swoop if required. First the SFSG troops set up a cordon several streets away from the target so that innocent civilians did not blunder into an operation that might end in a shoot-out. Then the 25-man assault group, led by the SAS, burst into the two-storey building used classic hostage-rescue techniques, storming every room simultaneously to ensure that no one escaped.

They found the three hostages sitting on the floor of a ground-floor room, bound but unguarded. There was no sign of their kidnappers. No shots were fired during the operation. In case the kidnappers were lurking nearby, the hostages were cut free, taken out of the building and bundled into the back of an army Land Rover. Less than two minutes after the rescue force had entered the building, the three Westerners were on their way to freedom. They were driven to the Green Zone, where they were handed over to waiting British officials. Professor Kember, who had always said he did not want to be rescued by military force, had been saved by exactly that and was loath to express his gratitude.

Meanwhile, the rest of Task Force Maroon moved in to search the hideout, looking for clues as to the identity of the kidnappers and evidence indicating where other Western hostages might be held. Major General Rick Lynch, a spokesman for the Coalition forces, said they suspected that the peace activists had been taken by a 'kidnapping cell' that had been behind other abductions in Baghdad. 'The key point is that it was intelligence-led and it was information gathered from a detainee that proved vital,' he said of another victory for the SAS.

However, Special Forces operations do sometimes go

wrong. On 19 September 2005, two SAS men, possibly seconded to the SRR, had to be rescued after they were arrested in Basra. Dressed as Arabs, the two had been spotted at a police checkpoint and there was a chase. After an exchange of small-arms fire, the two men gave themselves up and identified themselves as British soldiers by showing a Union flag, but they were arrested and beaten up. It has not been revealed what mission they were on. At the time it was said that they were either on a surveillance operation to observe the house of a colleague of Moqtada al-Sadr, leader of the Mahdi Army, or following an Iraqi police officer known to torture prisoners.

When the two men were arrested, the police found weapons, explosives and communications equipment in their vehicle. They were immediately accused of fomenting acts of terrorism, though an expert on Special Forces operations said that they were clearly involved in counter-terrorism as the SAS 'were in charge of hunting Iraqi extremists and neutralising them'.

As soon as he heard of the arrests, the British commander in Basra, Brigadier John Lorimer, planned a rescue mission. Less than an hour later, a convoy of Warrior armoured cars pulled up outside the police station, backed by snipers and a Lynx helicopter. As the troops tried to negotiate their way in, a crowd gathered and started throwing petrol bombs. Three soldiers were injured. One of the Warriors then knocked down the wall into the police compound, but the two captured men were no longer there.

In fact, the attack on the police compound had been a diversion. Nearby, rescuers from the same squad as the captives were blowing out the doors and windows of a smart suburban villa with plastic explosive and hurling stun grenades at the Mahdi Army militiamen guarding the two undercover soldiers. A short, intense burst of automatic gunfire was heard before the men were freed and their captors dragged away, hoods over their heads and hands tied behind their backs. The entire operation took only a couple of minutes and proceeded unhindered as attention was focused on the Army's invasion of the main police compound 100 yards (90 metres) away. Justifying the action, Brigadier Lorimer said, 'I had good reason to believe the lives of the two soldiers were at risk.'

As the British began to slim down their main force in Basra, Special Forces doubled the size of the commitment to counter Iranian-inspired attempts to make it appear as if Britain was being chased out of the country. The SAS dispatched a second squadron of 60 men to Iraq, which meant that half its total strength was in the country. This new squadron was dedicated to stopping men and munitions being infiltrated from Iran. Meanwhile, Task Force Black continued to work alongside the Americans in Baghdad.

On 5 September 2007, a 30-man SAS team assaulted a house that intelligence had pinpointed as the location of a senior al-Qaeda figure, possibly al-Zarqawi's successor. Once again, the raid was supported by paratroopers from the Special Forces Support Group, and an AWACS aircraft was overhead sending back live video to the headquarters of the joint UK-US Special Operations Task Force.

Although intelligence had accurately located the terrorist leader, it had severely underestimated the number of insurgents in the house and the scale of their likely resistance. The assault force went in front and rear. First in was Sergeant Eddie Collins, an SAS man who had joined from 3 Para. He was shot in the head and died instantly. A medical team were standing by, but there was nothing they could do. He was the seventh British Special Forces man to die in Iraq. Despite the loss of life, the insurgents were neutralised and the mission was counted a success. However, it just went to prove how tough things were getting in Iraq.

One senior SAS officer told a mess dinner that operations alongside the Americans in Baghdad were probably 'the most challenging task' the regiment had ever carried out and that the environment 'is perhaps the most hostile of current operations across the world'.

Another SAS man told the press, 'Don't be under any illusions: Baghdad is full-on, a daily diet of extreme insurgent violence combined with poverty and propaganda. We slotted [killed] a lot of insurgents, but I have to admit that we took a lot of casualties and we continue to take them.'

It was estimated that the Special Forces had killed several thousand people in Iraq. The vast majority died in airstrikes called in support of SAS operations, but a substantial number were shot dead by UK Special Forces on the ground. It is their standard practice not to keep a score card of deaths on such missions, but a source estimated that the total number killed by shooting is in the hundreds.

As the commitment of UK troops in the south of Iraq wound down, the Special Forces remaining in Baghdad found themselves drawn deeper into US operations. This caused concern in the regiment, as the US approach to special operations – particularly when to shoot to kill – is very different from that of the British.

UK Special Forces usually kept some 400 men in Baghdad. Along with a single 60-man SAS Sabre squadron, there would be a company of paratroopers, Royal Marine commandos and RAF Regiment personnel from the Special Forces Support Group, a squadron from the Special Reconnaissance Regiment and a squadron of radio-monitoring experts from 18 (UKSF) Signal Regiment. They also had specialist signallers from 264 (SAS) Signal Squadron, specially fitted-out RAF Chinook helicopters from 7 Squadron and C-130 Hercules transport aircraft from 47 Squadron. Compare that with the 47,000 US Special Forces deployed there. However, only about 1,200 of those – Delta Force and DEVGRU – were comparable to British Special Forces units.

The British Special Forces realised early in the War on Terror how differently they operated from the US counterparts. They still remembered Afghanistan in December 2001, when a four-man SBS team – 20 minutes behind the fleeing Osama bin Laden – was ordered to let the Americans take over. By the time the US special-operations troops arrived several hours later, bin Laden had escaped.

Similar tensions had arisen over an incident in Mosul in July 2003, when Coalition forces were tipped off that Saddam's sons Uday and Qusay were hiding in a villa. After reconnoitring the building, the 12-man SAS team believed they could capture the brothers so they could be brought to trial, but the US commanders had disagreed. Not only did they doubt such a small unit could capture Uday and Qusay, they were also reluctant to cede a high-profile operation to non-US forces. Although a Delta team had been used to storm the building, the operation was vastly overmanned with support troops, and stealth was abandoned in favour of high-powered weaponry. The result was mayhem. It was not the British idea of special operations. 'The problem from the start was that operational training and procedures for the top UK and US special operations forces are vastly different,' one British source said.

In Iraq, British Special Forces aimed to merge into the background, driving battered local cars and wearing cheap clothes bought in markets. They looked on aghast at their US colleagues, who drove around in new Dodge pickups. 'We used to laugh when we saw the Americans around the Green Zone,' one SAS man said. 'They would be wearing designer jeans, heavy boots and T-shirts – that was their idea of local dress. To a man they would all have pistols strapped to each leg with black plastic holster and webbing, and of course they would be wearing the latest shades. We called it "living the dream".'

But it was far from a joke. If undercover Americans were spotted for what they were, then any British forces operating alongside them would be at risk as well. Even more seriously, if US forces applied their doctrine of shooting first and asking questions later, the British risked being dragged into the same dangerous territory. When seizing an insurgent – making a 'hard arrest' – British Special Forces are not allowed to kill unless they encounter resistance. By contrast, the US Special Forces call such operations 'kill-or-capture' missions. It is no way to win hearts and minds.

But the Americans' orders came from the top. In July 2002, annoyed by their lack of progress in hunting down America's enemies, US Secretary of Defense Donald Rumsfeld issued a secret memo directing them 'to find and deal with' terrorists. The intention was to capture the terrorists for interrogation or kill them, 'not simply to arrest them in a law enforcement exercise', wrote Rumsfeld. The policy was backed by George W Bush in a secret 2004 directive authorising US special operators to 'find and finish' terrorists regardless of whether they posed an immediate threat. Many legal experts believe that this amounts to extrajudicial killing and is consequently banned under international, and therefore British, law.

Any British serviceman shooting someone who did not represent an immediate threat would be likely to face a court martial. At least one SAS soldier has already been investigated over allegations that he shot dead an Iraqi civilian. He was eventually cleared of any wrongdoing. But the British softly-softly approach to special operations does have its risks – as in the raid on 5 September 2007 that led to the death of Sergeant Eddie Collins.

The high tempo of operations also inflicted a heavy toll of injuries. By the end of September 2007, four SAS squadrons, rotating on six-month tours, had suffered 47 seriously wounded. More than 30 men had suffered critical head injuries or damage to limbs sometimes necessitating amputation. The toll of killed or seriously wounded was more than a fifth of the regiment's fighting strength. Many of the injured have been forced to leave the regiment or take desk jobs, either at the SAS base at Stirling Lines, near Hereford, or at the Directorate of Special Forces in Regent's Park, London.

'Baghdad has seen the regiment at its best, doing what we are trained for, but the cost has been high,' said one officer. 'We are suffering from a manning shortage as a result of our casualties and it will be some time before we can get back to full strength.'

Meanwhile, they continue to be hit with the high number of men dropping out to make better money in the private field. To fill the gap, members of the SAS and SBS who have finished their 22 years' service and would normally have to retire are being offered short-term contracts to stay on. These are usually senior NCOs and warrant officers, whose experience is frankly invaluable.

So far there has been little but praise for Special Forces in Iraq. Barry McCaffrey, a retired US general who went to Iraq in 2007 to compile a report for the West Point Military Academy, described Special Forces operations as 'simply magic'. Referring to Task Force 88 with its SAS element, he said, 'They are deadly in getting their target with minimal friendly losses or injuries. Some of these assault elements have done 200–300 take-down operations at platoon level.'

The question is: how long can the SAS continue operating at such a high tempo? There is concern in the regiment that it is only a matter of time before they suffer a big loss. There is also concern among senior British officers that the SAS has become so tied into US special operations in central Iraq that it will continue to fight there in an American war long after British troops had been withdrawn. Already, the remaining SAS men have been fully integrated into Task Force 88, which is commanded by the head of Delta Force. 'In the early days they were happy to join the fight and felt comfortable acting as the tip of the spear for the UK,' said one SAS man. 'But the thought now is that they have just become an extension of Delta.'

UK Special Forces are also concerned that under American control, the rules of engagement are becoming even more blurred. Ben Griffin, who left the Army in 2005, said, 'I saw a lot of things in Baghdad that were illegal or just wrong. The Americans had a well-deserved reputation for being trigger-happy.'

There was also serious concern over the way in which the US special operations forces were prepared to send Iraqis to detention facilities for what subsequently proved to be illegal interrogations. 'I knew, so others must have known, that this was not the way to conduct operations if you wanted to win the hearts and minds of the local population,' said Griffin. 'And if you don't win the hearts and minds of the people, you can't win the war.'

GLOSSARY

AAAV	advanced amphibious assault vehicle
AAV	amphibious assault vehicle
AB	ammunition bearer
ABCCC	Airborne Battlefield Command and Control Center
AC	active component
ACLC	air-cushioned landing craft
ACV	air-cushioned vehicles
AFSOC	Air Force Special Operations Command
AG	assistant gunner
AGMS	air-to-ground missile system
AGES/AD	air-to-ground engagement system/air defence
AIT	advanced individual training
AK	Avtomat Kalashnikov

AMS	acute mountain sickness
AMT	advanced military operations on urban terrain
ANDVT	advance narrowband digital voice terminal
AOD	automatic opening device
AOE	army of excellence
AP	anti-personnel
APC	armoured personnel carrier
AQT	al-Qaeda–Taliban
AR	army regulation
arty	artillery
A-S	anti-spoofing
AT	anti-tank
ATGM	anti-tank guide missiles
ATGWS	anti-tank guide weapons system
ATMP	all-terrain mobile platform
ATSC	Army Training Support Centre
ATWESS	anti-tank weapon effects signature simulator
AWACS	airborne warning-and-control system
AWM	Arctic Warfare Magnum (Accuracy International sniper rifle)
BATT	British Army training teams
BFIG	blank-firing impact grenade
BILAT	bilateral training
BMQ	basic-mission-qualified
BMT	basic-mission-trained
BNCOC	basic non-commissioned officers' course
BN	battalion
CA	civil affairs

Cal	calibration/calibre
CALFEX	combined-arms live-fire exercise
CAPEX	capabilities exercise
CAR	carbine automatic rifle
CCTS	combat crew training squadron
CENTCOM	Central Command
CG	commanding general
CIA	Central Intelligence Agency
CO	commanding officer
COMSEC	communications security
COP	close-observation platoon
CQB	close-quarters battle
CQC	close-quarters combat
CRD	chemical reconnaissance detachment
CRRC	combat rubber raiding craft
CRT	combat-readiness training
CRW	counter-revolutionary warfare
CS	close support/combat support
CSA	chief of staff of the army
CSAR	combat search-and-research
CSS	combat service support
CTC	combat training centre
CTIS	central tyre-inflation system
CTR	close-target reconnaissance
CWO	Chief Warrant Officer
DAP	defensive armoured penetration
DAV	desert attack vehicle
DCSOPS	deputy chief of staff for operations and plans
DDS	dry-deck shelter
DFC	Distinguished Flying Cross

DoD	Department of Defense
DPM	disruptive-pattern material
DPV	diver propulsion unit
DTWC	diver-through-water communication
ECCM	electronic counter-countermeasures
EDRE	emergency deployment readiness exercise
EFP	explosive formed projectile
EMP	electronic magnetic pulse
EOD	explosive ordnance disposal
EVR	emergency rendezvous point
EW	extreme weather
FARP	forward arming and refuelling point
FARRP	forward-area rearm and refuel point
FAV	fast-attack vehicle
FDC	fire-direction centre
FFAR	folding-fin aerial rocket
FIST	fire support team
FLIR	forward-looking infrared
FMB	forward-mounting base
FMQ	fully mission-capable
FM	field manual/frequency modulated
FO	forward observer
FOB	forward operating base
FOM	figure of merit
FORSCOM	US Army Forces Command
FSB	fire support base
FTX	field-training exercise
FUP	forming-up point
GL	grenade launcher
GLS	gun-laying system
GMG	grenade machine gun

GOR	general operating requirement
GPMG	general-purpose machine gun
GPS	global positioning satellite system
H&K	Heckler & Koch
HAL	helicopter attack, light
HAHO	high altitude, high opening
HALO	high altitude, low opening
HB	heavy barrel
HE	high explosive
HEPD	high explosive, point detonating
HEAT (TPT)	high-explosive anti-tank (target practice tracer)
HHC	headquarters and headquarters company
HG	hand grenade
HMG	heavy machine gun
HMMWV	high-mobility multipurpose wheeled vehicles, a Humvee or Hummer
HOES	holographic optical elements
HOPROS	head-mounted optical projection system
HQ	headquarters
HSIC	high-speed interceptor craft
HUD	head-up display
HVT	high-value target
ICRC	International Committee of the Red Cross
IDAS	interactive defensive avionics system
IED	improvised explosive device
IFF	identification friend or foe
Illum	illumination
INS	inertial guidance system
ISA	intelligence support activity

JDAM	joint direct-attack munition, a 2,000lb (907kg) GPS-guided bomb
JFACC	Joint Forces Air Component Command
JOTC	Joint Operations Training Centre
JRT	Joint Readiness Training
JRTC	Joint Readiness Training Centre
JSOC	Joint Special Operations Command
JSOTF	Joint Special Operations Task Force
JTF2	Joint Task Force 2
LAW	light anti-tank weapon
LED	light-emitting diode
LES	launch-environment simulator
LFX	live-fire exercise
LLLTV	low-light-level TV
LLRP	low-level reserve parachute
LLP	low-level parachute
LRDG	Long-Range Desert Group
LRSD	long-range surveillance detachment
LSV	light strike vehicle
LTD	laser target designator
LUNOS	lightweight universal night-observation system
LUP	laying-up point/position
LZ	landing zone
MATT	multi-mission advanced tactical terminal
MAWS(IR)	missile warning system (infrared)
M&AW	Mountain and Arctic Warfare Cadre
MBITR	multiband inter/intra-team radio
METL	mission-essential task list
MFC	mortar fire controller
MICLIC	mine-clearing line charge

MIL-STD	military standard
MILES	multiple integrated laser engagement system
ML	mountain leader
MMI	man–machine interface
MoD	Ministry of Defence
MOPP	mission-oriented protective posture
MRE	meals, ready to eat
MOS	military occupational specialty
MOUT	military operations on urban terrain
MTP	mission training plan
MUTT	military utility tactical truck
MV	merchant vessel
MWMIK	mobility weapons-mounted installation kit
NATO	North Atlantic Treaty Organisation
NAPS	nerve agent pre-treatment set
NBC	nuclear, biological and chemical
NCO	noncommissioned officer
NTC	national training centre
NVGs	night-vision goggles
OD(A)	operational detachment (A), a US Special Forces A-team
OSV	over-snow strike/support vehicle
OP	observation post
PJI	parachute-jump instructor
PLGR	precision lightweight GPS receiver
PLRF	pocket laser rangefinder
PNG	passive night goggles
PPS	precise positioning service
PTT	push to talk
QRF	quick-reaction force

RAAF	Royal Australian Air Force
RAAWS	ranger anti-armour anti-personnel weapon system
RC	reserve component
RCLR	recoilless rifle
RDX	rapid demolition explosive, royal demolition explosive or research development explosive (cyclotrimethylene-trinitramine)
RFA	Royal Fleet Auxiliary
RIB	rigid inflatable boat
RNG	range, ranger
RPG	rocket-propelled grenade
RRC	rigid raider craft
RRF	Ranger Ready Force
RSM	regimental sergeant major
RT	reconnaissance team
RTC	regimental training circular
RTU	returned to unit
RV	rendezvous
RWR	radar-warning receiver
SA	selective availability
SAS	Special Air Service
SAAD	small-arms air defence
SAM	surface-to-air missile
SATA	safety and arming test aid
SAW	squad automatic weapon
SBS	Special Boat Service
SCAMP	single-channel anti-jam man-portable
SCOBBS	School of Combined Operations, Beach and Boat Section

SCUBA	self-contained underwater breathing apparatus
SEAL	sea, air, land
SFD	Special Forces Detachment
SFSG	Special Forces Support Group
SINCGARS	single-channel ground and airborne radio system
SLR	self-loading rifle
SM	soldier's manual
SMG	sub-machine-gun
SO	Special Operations
SOAR	Special Operations Aviation Regiment
SOC	Special Operations Craft
SOCOM	Special Operations Command
SOF	Special Operations Force
SOG	Special Operations Group
SOP	standard operating procedure
SOT(A)	support operational team (A)
SOV	special operations vehicle
SOW	Special Operations Wing
SPARTAN	special proficiency at rugged training and nation-building
SPAS	special-purpose automatic shotgun
SPS	standard position service
SPW	special-purpose weapon
SR	strategic reconnaissance
SRR	Special Reconnaissance Regiment
SRTR	short-range training round
SRW	Small Raids Wing
STABO	short tactical airborne operation
STLS	Stinger training launch simulator

STOL	short take-off and landing
SWARM	stabilised weapons and reconnaissance mount
SWAT	special-weapons assault team
TACBE	tactical beacon
TACP	tactical air control party
TADSS	training aids, devices, simulators and simulations
TDFD	time-delayed firing device
TFR	terrain-following radar
TIRR	The Incident Response Regiment
TLZ	tactical landing zone
TNT	trinitrotoluene
TOW	tube-launched, optically tracked, wire-guided missile
TP	training projectile
TPT	troop proficiency trainer/target practice tracer
TRC	training readiness condition
TSC	training support centre
UAV	unmanned aerial vehicle
UMI	universal mount interface
USAF	United States Air Force
USAISA	US Army Intelligence Support Activity
USASOC	US Army Special Operations Command
USN	United States Navy
USSOCOM	United States Special Operations Command
UTM	universal transfer, Mercator
UW	unconventional warfare
VCSA	Vice Chief of Staff of the Army

WMIK	Weapons Mounted Installation Kit
WP	white phosphorus
WSP	white-star parachute

BIBLIOGRAPHY

Arden, Niall (2006), *Desert Fire: The SAS in Iraq – A Shocking True Story* (London: Hodder & Stoughton)

Care, Tom (2000), *Jihad! The Secret War in Afghanistan* (Edinburgh: Mainstream Publishing)

Collins, Tim (2005), *Rules of Engagement: A Life in Conflict* (London: Headline)

Fowler, William (2005), *SAS Behind Enemy Lines* (London: Collins)

Geddes, John (2006), *Highway to Hell* (London: Century)

Jennings, Christian (2004), *Midnight in Some Burning Town – British Special Forces Operations from Belgrade to Baghdad* (London: Weidenfeld & Nicolson)

Lee, S E (2007), *18 Hours – The True Story of an SAS Hero's Bloodiest Battle Against al-Qaeda in Afghanistan* (London: John Blake Publishing)

Lewis, Damien (2006), *Bloody Heroes – The True Story of Britain's Secret Warriors in Afghanistan* (London: Century)

McNab, Andy (1993), *Bravo Two Zero* (London: Bantam)

Micheletti, Eric (2003), *Special Forces – War on Terrorism in Afghanistan* (Paris: Histoire & Collections)

Micheletti, Eric (2006), *Special Forces – War Against Saddam Hussein* (Paris: Histoire & Collections)

Moore, Robin (2003), *Task Force Dagger* (London: Macmillan)

Naylor, Sean (2005), *Not a Good Day to Die – The Untold Story of Operation Anaconda* (New York: Penguin)

Nicol, Mark (2003), *Ultimate Risk – SAS Contact Al Qaeda* (London: Pan)

Pelton, Robert Young (2006), *Licensed to Kill – Hired Guns in the War on Terror* (New York: Crown)

Robinson, Linda (2004), *Masters of Chaos – The Secret History of the Special Forces* (New York: Public Affairs)

Rothstein, Hy S (2006), *Afghanistan and the Troubled Future of Unconventional Warfare* (Annapolis: Naval Institute Press)

Ryan, Chris (1995), *The One That Got Away* (London: Arrow)

Ryan, Mike (2003), *Secret Operations of the SAS* (Barnsley: Pen & Sword)

Ryan, Mike (2004), *Special Operations in Iraq* (Barnsley, UK: Pen & Sword Military)

Stilwell, Alexander (2007), *Special Forces Today* (Washington, DC: Potomac Books)

Tucker, Mike (2005), *Among Warriors in Iraq – True Grit, Special Ops and Raiding in Mosul and Fallujah* (Guildford, CT: Lyons Press)